TEACHING AND PARENTING

Effects of the Dual Role

JUDITH B. MACDONALD
Montclair State

UNIVERSITY
PRESS OF
AMERICA

Lanham • New York • London

Copyright © 1994 by
University Press of America®, Inc.
4720 Boston Way
Lanham, Maryland 20706

3 Henrietta Street
London WC2E 8LU England

Library of Congress Cataloging-in-Publication Data

MacDonald, Judith B.
Teaching and parenting : effects of the dual role / Judith B.
MacDonald.
p.   cm.
Includes bibliographical references and index.
1. Teachers—United States—Social conditions.   2. Parents—United
States.   3. Home and school—United States.   4. Educational
surveys—United States.   I. Title.
LB1775.2.M33   1994   371.1—dc20   93–44356 CIP

ISBN 0–8191–9389–5 (cloth : alk. paper)

 The paper used in this publication meets the minimum requirements of
American National Standard for Information Sciences—Permanence
of Paper for Printed Library Materials, ANSI Z39.48–1984.

To my son Dan and student Jim:
their similarities inspired this book.

Contents

List of Tables

Acknowledgments

My greatest thanks must go to the teachers who agreed to be interviewed. I am grateful for their efforts to talk honestly and thoughtfully about what it is like to be both a teacher and a parent. Their interest in the subject confirmed my view that the topic was worthy of exploration.

I am indebted to Montclair State for their support through a sabbatical leave and other grants of time from my teaching obligations.

My colleagues at Montclair provided another kind of support. Nancy Tumposky made helpful comments on an early version of the manuscript. Both she and John Barell were generous in their encouragement of my work. I am grateful to Muriel Becker for her help in deciding if a phrase was clear or awkward. Tina Jacobowitz and Ruth Handel were critically important in helping to find respondents for my questionnaire.

The logistics of locating teachers to interview were eased through the efforts of Adele Stern, Dr. Edward Sullivan and Dr. Abbey Bergman who, throught their leadership roles in public schools, provided me with names of teaching-parents who agreed to be interviewed.

Friends who must be thanked are Donna Gould, Judith

Ablow, Jean Bagley and Harmon Diers for their thoughtful responses to chapters of the manuscript. I especially thank Linda Steinman whose enthusiastic reaction as a teacher and mother buoyed my spirit when I needed it. I am indebted to Phyllis Tillinghast for her conviction that this research should be a book.

My daughter, Becky provided me with her invaluable insights, perceptions, and encouragement. And to my husband, David, my thanks for his humor, wisdom, and helpful perspective.

Introduction

This is a book about teachers who are also parents. It presents the teachers' views of the dual role through an analysis of their tape-recorded interviews.

At the present time I am a teacher and a mother. When I was a beginning teacher with no children of my own, I blithely but earnestly advised parents about their children. My age was somewhere between the ages of the parents and their children, and I clearly identified with my students. I wanted to tell the parents to leave their children alone, that they, the students, really knew what was best for themselves.

My perspective shifted when I became a college teacher with adolescent children of my own. Not only did I develop a healthy respect for parents which may have been long overdue, but I also viewed my students differently - as more than people to whom I teach a subject. I especially realized this after a conference with one of my freshman students. I felt that my attitude towards him was affected by my being the mother of my son. I was aware of a sense of empathy toward my student that I believe I lacked before being a parent. As I thought about other ways in which the dual role of teacher-parent affected me, I realized that my perspective towards my own two children broadened. The intensity involved in understanding them was relieved by knowing the wide range of students I teach.

Rationale

I undertook this study because I wondered how other teaching-parents felt about the dual role. Do they, like me, think that parenting has made them more empathic teachers than they had previously been? Has teaching broadened their perspective towards their own children? Do the similarities in teaching and parenting have any negative effects? Are there factors which contribute to the positive or negative nature of the dual experience? Perhaps most important, have teaching-parents derived particular knowledge which could be useful to parents who are not teachers and to educators (administrators as well as teachers) who are not parents? These are some of the questions the book addresses.

While teaching and parenting are different experiences, they share common elements. We teach and nurture in each role. We need a similar kind of energy to be a parent or a teacher. Just listening to students and children requires a special attentiveness. The settings we work in as teachers and mothers (leaving fathers aside, for the moment) also have similarities. The privacy (some have said loneliness) of the classroom is not unlike what Grumet has called the "exile of domesticity".[1]

Although there seems to be sufficient overlap in teaching and parenting to warrant exploration, few studies on this subject have been reported. The research that has been done has been confined to the effects of parenting on teaching, and most studies have only addressed the influence of mothering on teaching. These research efforts have focused on nursery and elementary school levels.[2]

In this study, I have interviewed 50 female and male teachers of high school as well as elementary and middle school for their opinions about how being a parent affects them as teachers and how teaching affects parenting.

When teaching has been compared to other kinds of work, it is described as unique because teachers unlike other workers confront "a unique set of difficulties...working with inherently changeful materials."[3] But parents, too, must contend with the changeful nature of children: "As soon as you figure out one stage, the child is well into another".[4] Should we then say that people who both live and work with the changeful nature of children are "especially unique"? While this description may be an overstatement, I argue that the perspectives of people who teach and parent are at least worthy of study.

Interviewing Approach

I deliberately chose interviewing as a method of inquiry because I thought it would best capture the teachers' percep- tions of their dual role. One of the alleged drawbacks of interviews is that informants will say what they think the interviewer wants to hear. Mindful of this possible constraint, McPherson found that teachers gave the same opinions in interviews as they did in less structured settings.[5] During the interviews I, too, had the impression that the teachers were not interested in saying what I might want to hear but rather that they wanted to express their thoughts accurately.

I share with Gilligan the view that "how people talk about their lives is of significance and the language they use and the connections they make reveal the world that they see".[6] The interviews were guided by a set of prepared questions (see Appendix A), but also included amplifications and digressions which teachers made to answer the questions as fully as they wished. I had two motives in giving the teachers the leeway to talk about aspects of the question which interested them: I thought they might be more likely to reveal the truth as they saw it; also, they might reach some realization of which they were previously unaware. Many of the teachers, in fact, said they were expressing ideas they had not realized they had and seemed to be tapping their tacit knowledge.

My approach to interviewing is in the "new tradition", if that is not an oxymoron, of research interviewing[7] in which the interviewee may discover meaning and understanding through the actual interview process. The interviews often resembled conversations. When the teachers expressed ideas that I identified with, I revealed my feelings and experiences. I share Wolcott's view that "you don't have to be neutral to be objective".[8]

My interviewing behavior was influenced by what I know about leading classroom discussions.[9] A primary goal of mine as a teacher is to stimulate the expression of students' ideas. Teaching behaviors which seem to stimulate student participation and are related to interviewing are to restate, repeat or respond minimally to what a participant has said (with a comment such as "uh huh", "I see"). These "techniques" seem to invite interviewees or students to continue to express their thoughts. These behaviors have a parallel in therapeutic settings: a therapist stimulates patient participation not only by direct questioning but also by commenting non-judgmentally on the patient's remarks.[10]

The interviews lasted approximately one hour. I recorded them on audio tape and transcribed them. I found tape recording the interviews crucial to the analysis of the teachers' responses. Since I gave the teachers the chance to respond to the rather open-ended questions as they saw fit, they produced a variety of interpretations to the questions. I have tried to capture what is distinctive in the teachers' voices as I looked for common meanings in their responses. Themes emerged from studying the data as in the "grounded theory" tradition of Glaser and Straus and the research interviewing approach of Mishler.[11]

The Setting and the Subjects

I work in the field of teacher education which includes advising student teachers in their classroom placements. This work brings me into contact with teachers, principals and administrators. Three Superintendents of Schools in New Jersey systems with which I was familiar agreed to inform their teachers of the study and directed them to contact the school secretary if they were interested in participating. I was purposely vague about the study whenever I described it to superintendents, principals, and teachers. I said only that it concerned teaching and parenting. I hoped that by saying little about its purpose I would capture the teachers' unedited views when I interviewed them.

The study took place in eight suburban schools within the three school systems in New Jersey. Fifty female and male teachers of elementary, middle and high school students volunteered to participate. Collectively, they have taught from three to 30 years on grade levels one through twelve. Most (90 percent)of the teachers taught before becoming parents and so could reflect on their teaching behavior before and after being in a parent role. They ranged in age from 35 to 55. Sixty percent of the teachers are women. Ninety percent are currently married, eight percent are divorced and two percent are widowed. They have from one to five children of their own. These numbers are similar to those reported in studies of the "typical" American teacher[12], but obviously this sort of information tells us little about the realities of teachers' lives. This book is in the tradition of studies which have described teachers' perceptions of their work and its effect on their lives.[13]

The interviews took place over a three year period. I interviewed the teachers at their schools before or after school or when they had free time during the school day. In the first year I interviewed 18 elementary and high school teachers from two school systems. In the second year of data collection I omitted interview questions whose uniformity of answers led me to realize I was not uncovering any ideas which were not common knowledge. For example, the questions, "What is most satisfying for you as a teacher?" (and "as a parent") produced very similar and predictable comments. Twenty elementary and middle-school teachers from another school system participated in this round of data collection. In the third year of the study, I interviewed 12 teachers, mainly men, to increase the population of male teachers in the study and thus try to compare male and female perceptions of the dual role.

With one or two exceptions, all of the teachers expressed great interest in the study. None had not previously thought about the effects of parenting on teaching or the reverse, but all expressed strong opinions about the influences of one role on the other. They were very eager to know what I would find out and were especially interested in comparing their views to those of other teachers.

During this third phase of the study, I developed a questionnaire based on the most pertinent and fruitful interview questions. (See Appendix B). The questionnaires were sent to 75 teaching-parents who taught on the same school levels as the interviewees. Fifty-five teachers responded to the questionnaires. Some of the respondents taught in school systems which were similar to those of the interviewees, but others taught in inner-city schools in New Jersey and New York City. Although many of the questions required teachers to use a rating scale, other questions were open-ended (i.e. "What is hardest about the dual role?"). The teachers were given the opportunity to add comments, and more than half of the teachers included additional remarks. These comments and the responses to open-ended questions were analyzed for common themes of meaning.

The book consists of six chapters. In the first chapter the similarities and differences in teaching and parenting are considered, and the teachers' reasons for entering the profession are presented. I compare the teachers' reasons with what we know about the motives of other teachers for choosing to teach.

In Chapter two I focus on themes the teachers expressed about how parenting affected them as teachers. One major effect of parenting on the teachers was an increased understanding of parents of their students. They better understood the attachment and even irrational bond that can exist between a parent and child. A male teacher with an adolescent son said: "You understand a parent's investment in their own child and how attached parents can be to their children." Also, teachers better understood the limited nature of a parent's "power". One teacher with two adolescent children said: "Prior to having my own children I wouldn't understand how a parent couldn't make a child do his homework. Now I understand you can't force Johnny to study for a test, they can't force their kids to get A's."

Being a parent helped teachers relate to parents. A middle school teacher with four children said, "I'm much more able to understand their concerns... I know the kinds of things a parent can and can't do at home".

A second effect of parenting on teaching concerned changes in teachers' attitudes toward students and in their teaching behavior. A fifth grade male teacher said: "I think my sensitivity is heightened to the busy work as homework and classwork...Before I had my own children I might not have thought about the work as clearly in terms of whether I'm just using their time or is this worthwhile, does this make a difference to their learning?"

The teachers developed a broadened perspective toward their students. A fifth grade teacher with a 12 year old son said that before being a parent: "...I only saw them as students in a classroom, respecting them, doing my job well. But I wasn't as attuned to the total life of the child. I didn't take the time. I was more concerned with the product."

Knowing the social and familial pressures on their own children enhanced the teachers' understanding of their students. A male high school teacher of teenage daughters said : "I've seen Nancy and Jenny go through stages at home-through the boyfriends, the heartbreak, the disappointment at not getting that part or that position, and I've been able to transfer that to my classroom and recognize when a child is being disappointed." A female elementary school teacher with adolescent children said, "I see the pressures children have. When they come home from school I know what they're facing with their sports programs, Brownies, Girl Scouts...I know the amounts of homework they get..."

In chapter three, "How Teaching Affects Parenting" three themes emerged from an analysis of the teachers' comments on this question: (1) The teachers developed a broader perspective toward their own children; (2) They used what they learned in teaching with their own children; (3) Patience expended in the classroom affected their reserve for their children.

An example of a broadened perspective towards his children came from a middle school teacher who said: "You see the whole variety of young people and it helps you see where your child fits in there. They (your children) do some things that somebody else might consider terrible, and you see it more in the light of what other kids do - you realize that's not really so terrible.."

When teachers used teaching knowledge "at home" they referred to specific knowledge such as "routines learned in the classroom" as well as the more abstract, such as "listening better".

Patience was a subject some teachers talked about when they reflected on how teaching affected parenting. A male high school teacher with two children said: "If I have a bad day here with the kids, I can almost see myself go home and begin to deal with my son or daughter in the way I would deal with the class, and I have to stop myself."

Chapter four, "Analysis of Related Issues in Teaching and Parenting" examines four topics which an analysis of the interview data generated. This chapter presents themes of difficulty in teaching, in parenting, and in the dual role. Also, it reveals the teachers' views about parent-teacher conferences (a) with parents who are teachers and (b) when they are in the parent role. The chapter also explores how the teachers' own parents and teachers served or failed to serve as models for them in teaching and parenting. Finally, the chapter identifies differences in how men and women teachers perceive the dual role.

Chapter five presents an analysis of the questionnaire data and a comparison of the data with the information from the interviews.

Chapter six, the conclusion, considers the uses of teaching-parents' knowledge and the roles they might play in school systems and social/educational spheres.

What the Study Is and Is Not

When I told friends or colleagues about this study, some of them would say, "But aren't you going to interview teachers who are not parents?" Obviously, to me at least, I would not because the study concerned teaching-parents' perceptions of the dual role, and teachers without children are not part of that population. Still, the persistence of the question suggests that, for some people at least, doing research means comparing groups and discovering which one is "better". This is not a book which tries to say that one needs to be a parent to be a "good" teacher. This book is not about good or effective teaching. It is in the tradition of inquiry which values what people say about their lives and their work. By revealing their thoughts about teaching and parenting the teachers have contributed to the little we know about the influences of the dual role.

The study outlined here reveals the perceptions and realizations of one group of teaching parents. I believe teaching-parents in general will want to compare their beliefs about the dual role with those reported here. As I have mentioned earlier, the teachers who were interviewed and those who answered the questionnaire were eager to know how their views compared with others in the study.

This book may be useful to teachers, administrators, and parents who have first-hand experience in only one role. Teaching-parents may be uniquely able to aid and inform such groups. They would have credibility with teachers because they are teachers, and because they are parents they may be viewed as trustworthy by other parents.

I have not tried to generalize the experience of this group of teaching-parents to other teachers who are parents. Nor do I claim that this study is a scientifically validated analysis of teaching-parents' views of their dual role. I have tried to add to what is currently known about people who both live and work with "the changeful nature of children".

NOTES

1. Grumet, 1988.
2. See Claesson, 1986; Hulsebosch, 1990; Katz, 1980; Lightfoot, 1978.
3. Lortie, 1975.
4. Sills & Henry, 1980, p. 9.
5. McPherson, 1972.
6. Gilligan, 1982.
7. Mishler, 1986.
8. Wolcott, 1990, p. 145.
9. MacDonald, 1986.
10. Lennard & Bernstein, 1960; MacKinnon & Michels; 1971.
11. Glaser & Strauss, 1967; Mishler, 1986.
12. Feistritzer, 1983.
13. See McPherson, 1972; Nias, 1989; Spencer, 1986.

Chapter One

About the People Who Teach and Parent

Differences in Teaching and Parenting

Teachers who are parents would be the first to say that hard as teaching can be, its challenges cannot compete with those in parenting. Just the vast number of books on raising children suggests that parents seem to need guidance and support.

Novelists as well as social scientists have described the potential for anguish in mothering (leaving fathers aside, for the moment, again). In *Dreams of Sleep* Josephine Humphreys wrote: "...A mother's only hope for sympathy is from other mothers... yet in spite of that sympathy *maternal despair* remains an unshared secret."[1] A character in Pamela Lively's *Passing On* says of motherhood, "What you don't know, till you're in it, is that it's a life sentence...And yet you know at the same time as you could clout them you'd actually die for them also."[2]

Men have been blamed for building a positive meaning into the word "motherhood", making it socially incorrect   for women to acknowledge the negative feelings they might have about being mothers.[3]   Thus "unhappy motherhood" was considered a contradiction in terms despite the fact that plenty of women suffer from bouts of it. "The emotional and physical pains of their children are anguishing for mothers, inducing a sense of helplessness and guilt."[4]

Grim as these descriptions may be, the good news is that women today are more able to reveal their complex feelings about mothering and get help through books, support groups, and from men who are sharing more readily in child-rearing tasks. While women still work two "shifts" - at home and at work - more men now participate actively in raising children. Even children have come to expect that their fathers be more than baby-sitters. Besides being more equitable, this trend is healthier.   More than a decade ago, Dinnerstein warned, somewhat drastically, of the negative effects of being reared by women only: "Mother-dominated infancy makes the prospect of adult sexual maturity more problematic for the girl than for the boy".[5]

When we compare teaching to parenting, the most obvious difference is in the feeling of attachment we have to a child versus a student.   Although the bond between teacher and student can be profound and meaningful, it clearly lacks the elemental and enduring connection that can develop between a parent and child.

Connections between Teaching and Parenting

While it is useful to identify the distinctions between teaching and parenting, their similar elements should also be noted.   Teachers and parents have more in common than contending with the "changeful" nature of children. When Grumet asks, "Why do teachers maintain the isolation of their kitchens in their classrooms?"[6], she identifies the loneliness of the places in which teachers and mothers work. Although it may not be commonplace to describe a classroom as lonely, many teachers, like many young mothers, feel isolated from other adults.

Being a teacher or parent requires an energetic giving of oneself; there is no "escaping" from children or students. Finally, having patience is an attribute that is important for both teachers and parents.

The commonalities in teaching and parenting should not be construed as having a negative impact on teaching-parents. Hulsebosch described how one role enriched the other: "...the mother voice within me has always been the wellspring from which my teaching has flowed, and teaching ...has, in turn, seeped back into and fed that source."[7]

Similarly, the anthropologist Catherine Bateson believed that both she as well as her mother Margaret Mead benefited as mothers from the use of their professional knowledge as anthropologists.[8]

As these teaching-parents reflect on their dual role, they describe its synergistic effects and the dialectical relation between nurturing children and educating students.

About the Teachers

Of the fifty teachers who were interviewed, thirty-two were women and 18 were men (see Table 1.1). Ranging in age from 35 to 55, 62 per cent of the teachers were in their forties. While their teaching experience spanned from three to 30 years, most were highly experienced. (Seventy-six per cent had taught for 11 to 30 years.) Forty-six per cent of the teachers taught

Table 1.1

Characteristics of the Teaching Parents

	n	%
Gender		
Women	32	64
Men	18	36
Ages of Teachers		
35-39 years	10	20
40-44 years	19	38
45-49 years	12	24
50-55 years	9	18
Teaching Experience		
3-10 years	12	24
11-20 years	29	58
21-30 years	9	18
Level of Teaching		
elementary school	23	46
middle school	17	34
high school	10	20
Number of Children		
one child	14	28
two children	27	54
three children	4	8
four children	2	4
five children	3	6

elementary school, 34 per cent taught at the middle school level and 20 per cent taught at the high school level. Most, or 82 per cent, have one or two children, 8 per cent have three children, four per cent have four children, and six per cent have five children. The ages of the children range from three to 30. As I have said earlier, most, or 90 per cent, of the teachers taught before becoming parents.

Why They Became Teachers

When I asked the teachers for their reasons for becoming teachers, I offered them five choices and also invited other responses to the question (see Appendix A). I wanted to give the teachers the structure of alternatives as well as the leeway to say whatever might be true for them, including the possibility that they chose to teach because they did not know what else to do. As it turned out, no one chose that alternative!

I did not limit the teachers' choice of reasons for becoming a teacher because I thought by not constraining their responses to a single reason I could learn more about the various aspects of their career choice (see Table 1.2). My experience in teacher education has made me aware of the circuitous ways teachers find their way into the field. Although I had once been told by a noted educator to be wary of teachers who said they always wanted to be teachers (Gilkeson, personal communication, 1972), more than 17 per cent of the teachers did, in fact, say that they "knew as a child" they wanted to be teachers.

The most frequently given reason for becoming a teacher was "being interested in children" (42 per cent), followed by "interest in subject matter" (26 per cent). Sixteen per cent chose "interested in teaching others" and twelve

Table 1.2

Reasons for Becoming Teachers

Reason	% of Teachers Who Chose Reason
Interested in Children	42
Interested in Subject Matter	26
Interested in Teaching Others	16
Wanted to Help Others	12
Parental Pressure to Teach	14
Did Not Like Other Work	8
Teaching Was a Family Tradition	8
Influenced by a Memorable Teacher	8
Other, varied reasons	12

(Note: Teachers gave multiple reasons; therefore percentages add up to more than 100 per cent.)

per cent wanted to help others". Eight per cent chose to teach because they "didn't like other work". Because "parental pressure to become a teacher" was mentioned by 7 per cent of the teachers in the first round of interviews, I included it as a choice in the second and third rounds. Again, 7 per cent of the teachers chose it as a reason for entering the field. For four of the teachers (8 per cent) teaching was a family tradition, with siblings or relatives in the profession. Another four teachers chose the teaching profession because they had a teacher whom they "loved". Four others had other first career choices: one was in industry, one in publishing, one wanted to go to law school, one to medical school. Two women said there were not many options available to them, just nursing or teaching. One female and one male teacher wanted to teach because they themselves had such mediocre teachers. Each said, "I thought I could do it better". A physical education teacher said he entered the field because "you didn't have to take a language to be a teacher". One woman became a teacher because her own child had a learning disability.

Although the teachers gave a range of reasons for becoming teachers, their principal motives were an interest in children and in subject matter. This patterns conforms to the findings from an analysis of the questionnaires.

The teachers' reasons for entering the profession differed somewhat from those reported in other studies. We have often heard that people are drawn to teaching because of the summer vacation, and the teachers Lortie interviewed did choose "the work schedule" - including summers off - as a main reason for teaching. Spencer reported that "teachers choose teaching as a career because it is respected work"[9], but none of these teachers explicitly gave that as a reason for teaching. According to the most recent research on motives for teaching, people become teachers primarily for altruistic reasons.[10] British research on primary school teachers indicates that many entered the field to help create "a more humane, socially just society."[11]   Again, except for the 12 per cent who chose "wanted to help others", the teachers were not drawn to the profession by the motive of improving society.

Although I did not specifically ask the teachers if they were satisfied with their career choice, analysis of the interviews in subsequent chapters indicates that all but three of the teachers were contented with their work. Their sense of satisfaction was tempered somewhat by the complexities in teaching itself and by the responsibilities in being both teacher and parent.

Three male teachers clearly expressed dissatisfaction. A 42 year old eighth grade teacher who, in fact, wanted to teach from the time he was a young child, said he was "burned out". He had taught for 20 years, but so did many of the other teachers. A 52 year old physical education teacher who taught for 30 years was waiting for his last child to graduate from college so he could leave the profession. A 48 year old high school teacher of communication skills was looking forward to the arrival of his early retirement date. Each teacher attributed his dissatisfaction to the change in attitudes of parents and students, especially in their lack of respect for teachers.

NOTES

1. Humphreys, 1984, p.145.
2. Lively, 1989, p.158.
3. Cameron, 1985.
4. Ruddick, 1989, p.30.
5. Dinnerstein, 1976, p.83.
6. Grumet, 1988, p.85.
7. Cited in Schubert and Ayers, eds., 1992, p.131.
8. Bateson, 1989.
9. Spencer, 1972, p.8.
10. Brookhart and Freeman, 1992.
11. Nias, 1989, p.39.

Chapter Two

How Parenting Influenced the Teachers

This was the first question in which I asked the teachers to reflect on the interaction between their personal and professional lives. Most of the teachers seemed stimulated by the question and talked with interest and conviction in response to it.

Teachers replied to the question of how parenting affects teaching with varying interpretations. Some teachers talked about very specific effects such as how their approach to homework changed. Others were more general and described how their feelings towards students changed. As I have said earlier, I purposely did not offer the teachers categories in which to fit their responses because I wanted them to reveal as much of their thinking about the question as they chose to.

The teachers' comments revealed three general themes. I have identified them as (1) parental, (2) affective/academic, and (3) social/home. I have used the teachers' words to illustrate the themes. The teachers are identified by gender, level at which they teach, and age of their children.

Parental Theme of Influence

This category identifies the ideas the teachers expressed about how being parents affected their relations with the parents of their students. In general, the teachers said when they became parents they more fully understood parents and could relate to them more easily. This theme of enhanced understanding of parents was the most commonly expressed effect of parenting on teaching.

A fifth grade teacher described how being the mother of her 14 year old son affected her as a teacher:

> "Well, there's no question in my mind that having a child is helping me be a better teacher. It's not that I wasn't a good teacher before. But this closeness to the development of a person with an emotional tie to it- that you don't have in the classroom- to see what makes him bristle, to see what, in the tone of my voice, turns him off...Now I look at the students in the class and I realize it's the same: They are somebody's main goal in life, and I'm a part of that, and I better darn well be very careful because I want to be the person in *their* life for their *parents* that I would like somebody else to be for me with my son."

For this teacher, becoming a parent made her feel more responsible about being a good teacher because she wanted that quality of care given to her son. This "golden rule" mentality is expressed elsewhere.

The teachers expressed the following ideas about how they better understood the parents of their students:

1. Attachment to children
When Katz[1] studied the differences between mothers and teachers of nursery students, she noted the greater degree of

attachment and irrationality mothers have toward their children as compared to how teachers feel towards students. A male elementary school principal with a 12 year old son alludes to these feelings of attachment and irrationality:

> "You understand a parent's investment in their own child and how attached parents can be to their children. I can't imagine a parent who does not want the best for their child in one situation or another. So when parents are ambitious for their children, if you're a non-parent, as a teacher you might say "What does she want? She wants everything for her kid." But as a parent you understand why somebody would want everything for their child."

A middle school female teacher with a 14 year old son said:

> "When I went back to teaching as a parent, I finally understood parents.... you understand that inexplicable love."

2. Limitations in Parenting

Teachers said when teachers became parents, they understood the limited nature of a parent's "power". They realized that parents could do "only so much" with children. Before they themselves became parents, the teachers expected parents to "get results" or be more effective with their children. A special education high school teacher with an adolescent learning disabled child of her own said:

> "When I talk to parents who have kids going through the same kinds of problems I've seen with my own child, I can talk to them on a different level from somebody who has never had that kind of experience with their own child and says, 'What is this parent doing wrong?' "

Teachers described how parenting can be a humbling experience. A female elementary school teacher with three children aged 9 through 18 said:

> "There's no doubt in my mind it has affected my teaching. We were without children for a long time. I was teaching and I felt that I had all the answers to what every parent was not doing correctly and now their children had all these problems. When my child arrived it was quite a learning experience. I think I became much more sensitive to children that might have learning problems. My youngest is neurologically impaired, he's a special education child. It made me aware of the fact that there are some kids in my classroom that are trying very hard and for some reason ... there's some reason why they are struggling and that I should understand that. So it's really been a good experience, I think, as far as my teaching is concerned."

Similarly, a middle school female teacher with 12 and 18 year old children said about homework:

> "Prior to having my own children I wouldn't understand how a parent couldn't make a child do his homework. Now I understand you can't force Johnny to study for a test, they can't force their kids to get A's."

A middle school male teacher with children aged 7, 9 and 12 said:

> "...You become sensitive to some of the problems that parents have when they come to you because before you might have thought, "Well, you're the parent, why don't you do something about it?"

But this teacher *also* talked about *parental responsibility*:

> "On the other hand, having been a parent you also have the sense of what it is that parents *aren't* doing that they should be doing

as well, and that you see there are children who come to school whose parents aren't in any way shape or form involved in their lives... and that makes you wonder and get angry at what they're not doing. So I think I'm more sensitive to that as well because I know what goes into parenting."

3. Using Own Parenting Experience to Relate to Parents
Being a parent helped teachers related to the parents of their students.
A fifth grade male teacher with a 19 and 13 year old:

"I've had children at this age so I know the kinds of things you're going through especially if it's your first child... All kinds of things which parents blow out of proportion which I probably did when I was younger. I can have an affinity of feeling now that I didn't have."

A middle school female teacher with children of the ages 6, 9, 13 and 16 said:

"I'm much more able to understand their concerns when, say, somebody overreacts to something- I've been there. When my kid comes home with a grade that I think is really abominable, I understand how they (the parents) feel, and I also know more of what they are really trying to ask me they say, 'How can I help?' I know the kinds of things a parent can and can't do at home".

Even *limited parenting experience* made a difference in perspective. A male elementary school principal with only a three year old son said:

"I think I tend to blame the parents less for the child's problem...Being embarrassed by my son in a restaurant brought those feelings of personal connection...it's made me much more sympathetic to the parents' role. I understood this on a certain level before, but now it's very concrete."

4. Sharing Own Experiences with Parents

Parents often feel a sense of shame when children do not perform to their expectations. "While many mothers thrive on the challenges children present, most of them are also...plagued with shame and powerlessness."[2]

When teachers share their child-rearing problems with parents, it relieves the parents' feelings of inadequacy and broadens their perspective about their problems.

A female high school teacher with two adolescent children said:

> "Just last night I called someone who was complaining about her problems. I said I understand perfectly. I have this 13 year old so I can relate to this when I'm seeing parents because they will open up...I find it kind of eases them if I say something."

One middle school teacher with 4 children who said that being a parent did *not* affect her as a teacher, but it did affect her relations with parents:

> "An 8th grader's mother was resisting referral. I called her and told her my oldest son is having difficulty. I was concerned. When she heard that she said maybe she'll send her child for referral."

A middle school female teacher with two adolescents said:

> "I can understand where they're coming from when they call me with problems. I think it's a lot easier to understand a parent's point of view when you yourself are a parent even though you're speaking as a teacher."

A sixth grade male teacher with a 14 year old son said:

> "I can very often reassure parents that it's a normal thing that one time you have a little boy and the next day you have a young man on your hands, and it flips back and forth."

5. Understanding the Working Parent

Teachers viewed the working parent differently when they became parents. A female elementary school reading teacher with a 10 year old daughter said:

> "I'm much more sympathetic to the everyday problems parents have to deal with in addition to school, and I think being a parent, particularly a working parent is a very demanding situation."

A middle school male teacher with two young children described how his perspective toward working parents changed when his wife went back to work:

> "When my wife went back to work... you get a real good appreciation of people who work. That really has an effect. You work all day and just to come home and to make the dinner and put out the garbage and keep the roof from leaking and making lunches for the next day and pretty soon it gets to be 9:00 at night."

The direct experience of being a parent helped the teachers understand the parents of their students. They empathized with the dilemmas and concerns in parenting. Before having first-hand experience as parents, the teachers' knowledge of parental problems was, in the words of one teacher, "less concrete".

Affective/Academic Theme of Influence

This category identifies how the teachers described changes both in their attitudes toward students (affective) and in their teaching behavior (academic). Teachers would begin their response with a description of affective change, "I became much more sensitive", and this heightened sensitivity resulted in a change in their classroom behavior. I have put these two kinds of changes together because the teachers often talked about them together. When the teachers described on how parenting has affected their attitudes towards students and teaching behavior, they often compared these with those they had before being parents.

1. Homework

  Homework was one of the main subjects about which teachers expressed changes in attitude and behavior. A fifth grade male teacher with four children reflected on his approach to homework (and schoolwork as well) before being a parent:

> "I think my sensitivity is heightened to the busy work as homework and as classwork. I know in my children's school they get thousands of dittos where you find the word and circle it. They hate them. *Before I had my own children* I might not have thought about the work as clearly in terms of whether I'm just using their time or whether I'm keeping them busy, and now I try to really think it out- is this worthwhile, does this make a difference to their learning?"

A sixth grade male teacher with two grown children uses his parenting experience:

"I've gone through the trial of dealing with homework with my own children. As a teacher, I now have an understanding of the value of homework and how much importance I should put on it, and realize that it has its place, but it's not the most important thing because my children have dealt with teachers that have given burdensome amounts of homework. And I've dealt with teachers who haven't given the children any homework. And I try to keep it in between."

A middle school teacher with two teenagers changed her perspective:

"I think I'm more understanding of the problems children have. Sometimes homework isn't the most important thing. I'm more understanding of the burdens children have of getting homework done on a particular night."

A middle school male math teacher with three children said:

"You see the other side. You see kids who come home with too much homework or they don't understand it- and how it affects them. If I hadn't seen that, I may not have been quite as understanding in some cases. I'm basically not strict or mean; I'm an easy going person, and I'm there to help a kid and give him a break- which has gotten me into hot water sometimes. At this level anyhow, give the kid a break, give him the extra time, and give him understanding. My daughter, especially, has a hard time so I know what they go through at home."

Being a teaching-parent can cause one to question another teacher's goals. A middle school teacher with a 10 year old son thought that *because* she was a teacher she more critically questioned the goals of her son's teacher:

"My son just got a grade of C+ back on a social studies report. He was thrilled that he got a C+, but I was concerned with what was she actually trying to teach him by giving him that grade...

Here is someone who went through the whole research process and really fulfilled the assignment yet got a C+, so what message is she actually giving him?... I don't think I would have looked at it that way if I wasn't a teacher."

2. A Broadened Perspective.

The experience of parenting caused many of the teachers to develop a broadened perspective towards their students. A female fifth grade teacher with a 12 year old son said:

"It's not that I ever disrespected students, but I might say things in a teacherish way because the teaching and the product were very important, without thinking about the total life of the child because *I didn't have one at home with "a total life"*. I only saw them as students in a classroom, respecting them, doing my job well. I was not as attuned to the total life of the child. I didn't take the time. I was more concerned with the product."

Similarly, a middle school reading teacher changed her approach in the classroom as a result of noting her daughter's development and learning process:

"I'm much more aware of the *child's point of view* and how a child learns...I think the first two, three, four years of watching a child become aware of the world and coming to conclusions about the world- it just shows they are capable of so much. *Before I parented myself, I looked at things pretty much according to the curriculum and what we needed to cover.* I've always been the kind of teacher that liked the kids to do things- like when we were studying cities we built a model city, but I think I was able to expand that- after my daughter was born, after I watched her learn on her own -to many other things, and I think what it made clearer to me was what I wanted the children to learn...I do less directing and more watching than I did as a non-parent."

A broadened perspective towards students resulted in greater flexibility in the classroom. A female elementary school teacher with three teenagers said:

> "Before I was a parent...everything was black and white . It's not that way anymore."

Another female elementary school teacher with three adult children said:

> "The child was something to work with. There were children who could learn and those who couldn't. When I came back to teaching after having my children, I realized it isn't step by step. It's more irregular."

Playing the devil's advocate, I asked the teachers if their *academic standards might be compromised* by this increase in understanding of students. A female middle school science teacher with two teen age children said:

> "What it has done is make me more realistic... The reality of life is they need a lot of time. My standards have not gotten lower, but my time line is extended. Now with that month for the research paper is the fact that date is carved in granite. And I explain that to the students: that's why you have the month. My standards are high but there is time for you to come up to my standards."

A female middle school french teacher with a 12 year old:

> "Oddly enough I think I'm tougher because I know what it means...I want a future for my child and I know it can only be done through hard work and perseverance and the best work he can do."

A female elementary school teacher with 8, 11, and 15 year old children :

> "With some children there are things you have to overlook. And with others you have to be very firm. How do you know the difference? That's a good question. Its just a matter of trying to spend as much time one to one. It's hard. You want to do for each child your very best and understand them, and it's not always easy."

3. Sensitivity, awareness and tolerance

Teachers described how being a parent made them more sensitive, aware, and tolerant in the classroom. An elementary school female teacher with children ages 9 and 12 said:

> "...I am much more aware of each child...Being aware of what will work with a child. How important it was for me as a parent to build up their egos and to make them feel special and important. I've tried to carry that over to my classroom which I don't think I was as aware of previously...If they feel good about themselves then they'll be motivated to come to school and to learn. I think that's something I realized as a parent."

A female music teacher with a 4 year old said:

> "Now that I have a child I am a little bit more aware of children's feelings. I think I used to be a little bit harsher in my attitudes as far as "we're going to do this, we're going to do that", and I feel that maybe I give a little bit more, and I think I'm much more attuned to parents' feelings."

A female middle school science teacher with a 14 and 18 year old:

> "Makes you more sensitive to an adolescent's needs. Makes me more aware of time concerns that adolescents have, more

aware of a lack of attention span, the immaturity. So I'm much more attuned to where these students are coming from having my own adolescents, and find I'm much more tolerant, much more lenient. Actually, I enjoy them (the students) more because I know what they're going through personally, having my own son at home."

A high school male teacher with two very young children:

"I think I am much more understanding. I don't know if it came with maturity or if it came with being a parent. But I think I am much more sympathetic to my students' problems than I was when I first began teaching, my first 7 or 8 years."

A middle school male teacher with a twelve year old son:

"It made me more sensitized to what this age group is going through. Seeing what these kids are going through I think maybe I should back off a little, too (at home)."

A middle school health teacher with five children said:

"It teaches you not to be judgmental, not prejudge. I don't know that I would have enjoyed teaching before I had my family. I think with my first couple of children I was a lot less patient than I was as I had more children and became more tolerant, able to cope."

The *"golden rule"* theme described earlier in which teachers *give* their students the treatment they want for their *own* children was expressed by three teachers:

A male elementary school teacher with two children said:

"I became more sensitive. I wanted to be the kind of teacher that I would want my child to have. I became kinder, nicer, more sensitive because I wanted my kids' teachers to treat my kids that way."

Another male elementary school teacher said:

> "You want people to be more understanding of the problems your kids have in school."

A female elementary teacher with an 8 and 5 year old said:

> "I'm much more aware of the emotional part of what I can give the children because I see how my son comes home emotionally affected by what has gone on in school. I try to think how I would want my child treated in school. I don't always do that. I get impatient. I do things I know are wrong."

The experience of parenting affected the teachers' perspective towards students and consequently their teaching behavior. Parenting gave the teachers a more informed view of the role of homework. It also affected the teachers' attitudes towards students by making them more aware of and sensitive to their needs. In the popular book, *Among Schoolchildren* in which a teacher's life is described, Kidder notes how being a parent affected the teacher's views of her own child's educational future:

> "Chris [the teacher] once heard a colleague say, "I'm not interested in impossible cases anymore. I'll teach the kids who want to learn." "But", Chris told herself, "some kids don't know they want to learn until you put it in their heads that they do". I'll teach the ones who want to learn. She would turn those words over in her mind and answer back that *her own son might not get taught if his teachers followed that strategy.*"[3]

Being a parent made Chris more aware of her responsibilities as a teacher.

Social/Home Theme of Influence

The teachers described the familial and social pressures children contend with. This category contains the comments the teachers made in which they revealed that knowing what they did about their own children's social and home life and pressures enhanced their understanding of their students. A high school male business education teacher described how he used the knowledge he derived from being the father of two teenage daughters:

> "I've been able to target girls in their Freshman year who have potential problems... I've seen Nancy and Jenny go through those stages at home- through the boyfriends, the heartbreak, the disappointment at not getting that part or that position, and I've been able to transfer that to my classroom and recognize when a child is being disappointed."

The teachers described the strains of social and home life:

A female elementary school teacher with 12 and 14 year old daughters said:

> "I see the pressures children have. When they come home from school I know what they're facing with their sports programs, Brownies, Girl Scouts and things like that. I know through having children and having friends some of the pressures that parents put on children. I know the amounts of homework, and also being a parent, I know what's going on with children: what's current, what's happening, what are the new fads. *Of course, there's the reverse, too. Because I know what's going on, my kids can't get away with anything.*"

A female elementary teacher with adult children describes aspects of life outside of the classroom:

"You know what's going on at home. They have dental appointments to keep... When they sit down to do their homework, it's not that they sit down to do it immediately or even all at one time. I'm aware of the distractions, the telephone, the television programs..."

A female high school teacher with two teenagers said:

"I know that kids come in with excuses that sound like they're from the moon but they really do happen in life, and sometimes I don't understand when a teacher doesn't accept that excuse because that's how family life can be."

Another female high school teacher with two adolescent daughters :

"I can understand a teen age girl who will just dissolve in tears if her hair doesn't come out right in the morning because I have one at home."

When the teachers talked about the influence of parenting on them as teachers, they told me they were expressing feelings which they had not stated in words prior to this interview. Clearly, the realm in which the teachers were most affected by their parenting experience was in relation to the parents of their students. When the teachers became parents, their understanding of their students' parents vastly increased. A second sphere of influence of parenting on teaching was the academic/affective in which the teacher's attitudes and behavior in the classroom changed due to being parents. The third category of influence, the social/home, identified themes of pressure teachers were aware students contended with and for which they made allowances when they became parents.

Some Less Clear Effects

The combination of teaching and parenting was not viewed positively by all the teachers. It was, for example, too stressful for a female middle school biology teacher:

> "Being a parent influenced me as a teacher at different stages and in different ways. When the children were little I found it made me more impatient in the classroom and that's why I stopped. At the time I felt I really couldn't do both jobs well. There was too much stress. There was just too much that was demanded of me in both situations, and I didn't feel I was going to be able to give to either of them as I wanted to."

This teacher returned to the classroom when her children entered high school and describes herself as currently very contented with her work.

Teachers differed in their beliefs about how they derived knowledge of what constitutes "normal behavior". A male principal said he had a better grasp of what normal behavior is as a result of being a teacher/principal:

> "When you teach you see a wide diversity and variety of children and you see there's a broad range. When it's your one and your only-knowing there's a range out there is very helpful because I think it allows for a little more tolerance. There are many parents who don't come into contact with other kids on a daily basis, so I don't know if they can ever have a conception of what is "normal" behavior. They might not know that their child is normal as apple pie or really way out if they don't have a basis for comparison. As a teacher you have a basis for comparison.

However, an elementary school teacher said she knew what constituted "normal" *because* she had her own children.

> "I have more feeling of normal and what's acceptable as a result of having my own children."

One middle school male art teacher responded to the question of how parenting affected his teaching by asserting that the reverse effect applied:

> "I really think it's the other way around. I find I'm a little stricter at home because I see how some of the students are behavior-wise. I wouldn't let my children get away with some of the things I see my students get away with. I really do expect more of my children. If I was in another profession, I wouldn't be aware as much."

In the next chapter we see how other teachers perceive the effects of teaching on parenting.

NOTES

1. Katz, 1980.
2. Ruddick, 1989, p.107
3. Kidder, 1982, p. 285.

Chapter Three

How Teaching Affected Their Parenting

We have seen in the previous chapter that some teachers spontaneously described how teaching affected their parenting when asked about the effects of parenting on teaching. For those teachers the connection between teaching and parenting was too intertwined to be discussed separately. My efforts to identify the influences of one role on the other stem not from indifference to their relatedness, but from the view that the analysis of each direction of influence may result in a greater understanding of the dual role.

This chapter focuses on the teachers' responses to the question of how teaching affected them as parents. Three themes emerged from an analysis of the teachers' comments: (1) their perspective towards their children broadened; (2) they used the knowledge gleaned from teaching with their own children; (3) the patience they "used" in teaching affected and sometimes depleted their reserve for their children.

Broadened Perspective Towards Own Children

Knowing a wide range of students broadened the teachers' perspectives towards their children. As teachers, they saw their children in relation to a greater number of children/students, and this perspective helped them make more rational assessments of their own children. This positive effect applied to teachers who had several children as well as those with just one child.

A middle school teacher with four children of her own said:

> "You see the whole variety of young people and it helps you see where your child fits in there. They do some things that somebody else might consider terrible and you see it more in the light of what other kids do- you realize that's not really so terrible, and if they do something that you think is great, you have a little more of a frame of reference... You've taught a lot of young people. People have confided in you. You know the kinds of things kids think, worry about, care about, and it puts your kids' concerns in a context."

A fifth grade male teacher with a 12 year old son said:

> "When you have only one [child] sometimes you don't see comparisons too well, but I have had enough experience with children in classes that I know a lot of their thinking and that helps me a great deal. "

An elementary school male principal with a 12 year old said:

> "When you teach you see a wide diversity and variety of children and you see there's a broad range. When it's your one and your only... knowing there's a range out there is very helpful because I think it allows for a little more tolerance."

Even a male high school biology teacher with five of his own children found that teaching affected his perspective as a father:

> "I think I appreciate my children because I do see a wide spectrum of students and I can appreciate the difficulty of studying, of tests, and the stresses that young people have from school, and I can relate to my own children that way and also as a teacher I know what the kids [students] are going through."

A middle school female computer teacher with an adolescent son said:

> "Just being in contact with more children...seeing children react in different ways, see all types helps."

A special education elementary level teacher with 5 children seemed to take comfort in comparing her children with students:

> "You appreciate your own...it makes you count your blessings."

Use of Teaching Knowledge with Own Children

The teachers described a variety of ways in which they applied at home what they learned in the classroom. The meaning of "teaching knowledge" ranged from the specific, such as "routines learned in the classroom" to the more abstract, such as "listening better".

Listening Experience as a Teacher

The actual practice of talking to and listening to students helped teachers better understand and relate to their children.

A middle school male teacher described how being familiar with students' behavior helped in understanding his adolescent children:

> "When I see a behavior at home I recognize it immediately: this isn't something that is aberrant or awkward or strange. I know it's something they've picked up on the street or at school...you can recognize a lot of those things, and *if you've taught long enough you know how to speak to children, and you should know how to listen and hear what they have to say.* I think those things help you a lot as a parent. I think it makes me a better parent because I think you see every variety of behavior known to man, you've had a general practice, so to speak, of parenting for a number of years and there really isn't anything new under the sun that your children will bring home to you."

A fifth grade teacher and mother of an adolescent describes the effect of experience in listening to students and contrasts it with her husband's lack of experience:

> "I really enjoy how kids think...As a parent I'm able to know my son's adolescence and all that brings along with it because I think I can listen better. If I were a parent who didn't listen for years to lots of kids and have to deal with lots of their personalities and try to help them, and yet cope with what they are... I don't get as excited as my husband. He hears something and reacts. I hear something and I want to hear more. And that gives the *child* the feeling you are listening rather than judging immediately-which I think parents do."

Use of Limits, Routines, Structure, Consistency

The organizational skills the teachers developed in the classroom were useful at home. Teachers described how they adapted their practical teaching knowledge to their own and their children's needs. A middle school male teacher with an adolescent said:

> "As a teacher, the setting of limits and the establishment of routines is the most significant thing from teaching that's been useful in the home. Maybe I would have known the importance of setting limits, but not the importance of routines - this is when we get up, this is when we have breakfast, brush teeth. I think the importance of routine became apparent as a teacher."

A female elementary school teacher with three children:

> "I'm much more structured that I used to be. Almost too much in the sense of getting my kids to get things done, checking on the homework, giving them a lot of positive reinforcement. I do a lot of subtle teaching at home that I might not have done before. I ask 'guided questions'".

A female elementary school teacher with two children said:

> "I learned the importance of consistency in teaching and that carried over to parenting."

Expectations, Strictness

In the previous chapter a few teachers said they made greater demands on their children because they were teachers. This theme recurs as teachers reflected on the effects of teaching on parenting.

A female high school special education teacher with adolescent children:

> "I think it tended to make me a little stricter in social areas at home. Because I think a lot of the kids had very lax conditions at home, and I thought maybe it was symptomatic of their problems I found especially at the high school level. I know these kids respond best to structure, and most of them don't get it at home."

A high school music teacher with two grown children said:

> "I see a lot of weaknesses that my students have, a lot of pitfalls, and I try to keep my children from falling into the same traps. Specifically- not having their homework and the effect that not having homework has on their grade."

Even a teacher (elementary, music) with only a three year old said:

> "I'm trying to prepare him so that he doesn't become one of those students that I see that's always looking around in the back of the room...I know how important school is. Once he gets to school he's going to be there a long time each day, and I think I'm trying to prepare him, not in an outward way, but just little subtleties-getting along with others, sharing, because he's an only child. I try to work on these."

Increased Understanding of child's limitations:

We have seen that the teachers' perspective was altered by the dual role. Their expectations for their children were affected by what they knew about students.

A high school special education teacher with a learning disabled daughter said:

"Instead of giving her 10 things to do, I have to give her one-with her processing problem. That's typical of teaching special ed."

An elementary school teacher with three children said:

"I better understand my child's limits. I've learned you can go only so far... The rules developed in the class I use at home."

Offering Academic Help:
A male fifth grade teacher with four children said:

"One thing I think as a teacher I can offer my children is help when they need it and don't understand what's what. I think a lot of times kids come home not really understanding what they're supposed to be doing, what the teacher wants."

Pressuring Own Children
A female elementary school teacher with adolescent children:

"I don't pressure my children. I see a lot of parents who say 'I want you to pressure her'. I said I would never pressure a 7 year old. I would never do that to my children. If I weren't a teacher I might have pressured my own children because I would have been caught up in the social aspect... mothers get together and compare notes. It's a very common practice. _____ is a very pressure oriented town."

A middle school male teacher with two children:

"I think I've come to the point now where even though I'm a teacher, I say school isn't everything, recognizing that there are so many pressures on children today, and I think just the peer pressure the kids experience is terribly powerful on them, and it's a burden."

Patience in Parenting

Patience was a subject a number of teachers spontaneously talked about when they reflected on how teaching affected them as parents. Patience expended in the classroom left an insufficient amount for parenting. Teachers felt they were obliged to be patient in the classroom and this effort in some cases depleted their "supply" of patience.

A male elementary school principal with an adolescent son said:

> "I'm paid for my patience so I must be patient at work. I exhaust my level of patience at school and am less patient with my son as a result of having had to have been patient with every child at school...I'm aware of being patient, and I think there are some people who aren't aware of being patient, they just are."

A male high school teacher with two children said:

> "If I have a bad day here with the kids, I can almost see myself go home and begin to deal with my son or daughter in the way I would deal with the class, and I have to stop myself."

A middle school male teacher with three children said:

> "Sometimes you don't have as much patience [at home], but on the other hand sometimes you understand better."

A elementary female teacher with one son:

> "Thank God he's a good student. I have less patience with him than with my students."

A female high school special education teacher with two children:

> "I have much more patience with a student than with my own daughter who has a processing problem. I have to pull myself back and try to use the techniques that I use in school with her, and I do. I think I'm more aware than a person who is not a teacher, who is not familiar with learning disabilities. I know what to do. Doing them is another matter. I don't go by my first instinct which is to holler. In school I don't know if my first instinct is to holler. I don't think so. I think it is to help which is probably why I'm so exhausted at the end of the day."

A male elementary school principal with a three year old:

> "I am probably less patient [as a parent] because I expect children to obey. My son knows I'm just Daddy so he can get to me very quickly, and a lot of that has to do with the fact that I've taken on this persona as somebody who needs to be obeyed...I think I expect kids to do stuff for me, and my son couldn't care less."

A male elementary school teacher with two children believed that his children did not benefit from his being a teacher:

> "I think being the child of a teacher hurts a child in some ways. It's difficult for me to teach my own children after having taught all day. It's very hard for me to be patient because I've been patient all day long."

Having a dual perspective of teacher and parent did not necessarily contribute to a parent's state of well-being.

An elementary school teacher with two young children said:

> "When I think of my son in the second grade, sometimes I feel I'm too hard on him at home because I'm aware of what he should be getting- what an average second grader should know. But I fluctuate. For example, I want him to be able to do it, and   I get disappointed when he's not able to do it because I think of him as the slower child in my class. On the other hand, when I'm home, I think it's only one grade. He's got his whole school career ... I know what scores are- It's just a guideline. So, on the one hand it's good I can shrug off, but on the other hand, I compare him to what the average child should be in that grade and sometimes get worried. I shift at home, comparing him, but my husband [a teacher] helps."

Barth described his frustration as an educator and parent when his daughter's learning style was at odds with the demands of her school: "Our daughter tends to work slowly and carefully and thoughtfully and gregariously, savoring and wondering about and getting lost in things along the way. Unfortunately more courses, more homework ... do not represent a very good prescription for her...As a parent I accept responsibility to help Joanna comply with more and more demanding work coming at her faster and faster. But I would like to ask the administrations and faculty to assume some responsibility as anxiety reducers in the school climate for the good of students".[1]

Concluding Thoughts

Although the question of how teaching affected parenting was meaningful to many teachers, they had more to say about the effects of parenting on teaching. For male teachers, however, the experience of teaching influenced them more as fathers than did the experience of parenting influence their teaching.

Analysis of the teachers comments about what they believed were the effects of teaching on parenting resulted in classifying the effects into three themes. The teachers believed that their teaching experience helped them develop a broadened perspective towards their own children. They described this change as a positive result of knowing a wide range of students. It was also beneficial to use the various aspects of their teaching knowledge with their own children. This knowledge included specific techniques of teaching as well as the more subtle ways of listening and responding to students. The third effect of teaching on parenting was the depletion of patience. The demanding nature of teaching left teachers with an insufficient supply of patience for their own children. In fact, two fathers thought their children were "short-changed" because they were teachers.

NOTES

1. Barth, 1990, p.175.

Chapter Four

Analysis of Related Issues in Teaching and Parenting

We have seen, so far, that except for the expenditure of patience in the classroom which left some teachers with an insufficient amount for parenting, the combination of teaching and parenting clearly had positive aspects. In this chapter I further examine what the teachers found difficult in the dual role. In the interviews I asked them what was hardest in teaching, parenting, and in being both a teacher and parent. I have focused on themes of difficulty because I believe, as others do[1], that identifying what teachers perceive of as problems is a first step towards their possible solution. Teaching-parents who both live and work with "the changeful nature of children" may grapple with problems which are unique to the dual role.

The open-ended nature of the questions I asked gave the teachers the latitude to respond in general terms or with specificity. For example, the question, "What is hard for you in teaching?" generated a specific answer such as, "the paperwork" as well as the more general response, "never being finished".

Other interview questions provided information about the relation between the professional and personal lives of the teachers. This chapter presents the teachers' ideas about parent-teacher conferences. We have seen in chapter two that one effect of being a teaching-parent is a greater understanding of parents. How the teachers felt in conferences with their children's teachers and during conferences with parents who were teachers is explored in this chapter. Another issue of focus is on models in teaching and parenting. Did the teachers raise their children as they were raised? Was their teaching behavior influenced by their own teachers? In the last portion of the chapter, I have identified how men and women differed in their perceptions of the dual role.

One question which I asked the teachers but have not included in this book concerned what they found most satisfying in teaching and in parenting. Unlike Nias[2] who found a variety of responses to the question of satisfactions in teaching, I found uniformity, and concluded that the question yielded no information which was not already common knowledge. (The most satisfying-in-teaching response was "seeing the light bulb go on"; "raising a child I am proud of" was the most satisfying-in-parenting response.)

Hard in Teaching

Analysis of the teachers' comments about what they found difficult in teaching resulted in classifying them into four categories: (1) discipline and relations with students (2) paper work, planning, and lack of time (3) curriculum and teaching decisions (4) student attitudinal changes.

1. Discipline and Relations with students
This category refers to the difficulty the teachers described in exercising authority, enforcing rules, and being consistent. A high school special education teacher said:

> "I can't decide whether I should be a pushover or hold firm, and what's really in the best interest of the child. In other words, if they have four cuts, then they're out of the class, and if they come in with the fourth cut, but they have a good story, do I let the ax fall?...I have trouble seeing that anything is that black and white -there are usually grays."

Similarly, another high school teacher found it hard to be "totally consistent":

> "Too often being able to see extenuating circumstances - I guess if I'm going to err, in any direction, I'd rather see it from the other person's point of view."

A middle school health teacher said:

> "Discipline. I tend to be very open, not as structured as some teachers, so some [students] will take advantage."

An elementary school teacher said:

> "Presenting a sense of authority because I'm very laid back and easy going...it's very hard for me to maintain the distance that's sometimes necessary..."

Another elementary teacher with adult children who has taught for 25 years said:

> "I give in a lot. I more or less give in to the ideas and thoughts, the desires of the children. I try to please everyone so in a sense that can play against you at times. There's a carry-over of wanting to be a good mother. I want this child to be happy and that one to be happy, and in a large group like this you can't do all of those things. So I have to pull back."

A middle school teacher :

> "To see a child fail, especially a child who I know has been working hard and just does not have it. And I think the same is true with my own children. When they try very hard at something and they can't achieve it, you can see the heart-break, the disappointment, and it hurts."

An elementary school teacher:

> "It's not in teaching, it's in dealing with each child: getting rapport, trust, being liked by them."

The teachers did not imply that they felt deficient in their teaching because they struggled with these concerns. Rather, they found these affective elements in teaching continued to challenge them.

2. Paperwork, Planning and Lack of Time

For many teachers paperwork and the time that preparation and planning required were perceived as the hardest aspect of teaching.

An elementary school teacher said:

"It isn't the hardest, it's the part I dislike the most- the paperwork."

A high school social studies teacher said:

"Not the classroom- that's the easiest part- all the paperwork- what comes down from the administration as far as trivial things to do. The classroom itself has never been difficult for me."

A middle school biology teacher said:

"Paperwork and planning. If you observed me in class I appear to be very relaxed. For the lesson to be as easy for the kids and cohesive and meaningful, it took a lot of planning...I don't come in and lecture."

Another middle school teacher:

"Paperwork. It requires a lot of preparation as far as knowing the material and having material prepared such as worksheets, readings, tests. I want to make sure I give enough grades in a marking period so it takes a lot of time."

A business education high school teacher:

"The preparation. The inordinate amount of time it takes to prepare and grade papers. I'm reluctant to change my courses. I use last year's lesson plans."

An elementary school teacher:

> "To do all the preparation, to spend the time, energy to get ready for the next day and be rested by the time you teach the next day."

Another elementary school teacher :

> "All the paper work - I don't go home and have a home life. I can't sit and watch TV or go out to dinner because I always have plans and things I need to do. Get through dinner, do the laundry, and do everything else. I keep thinking a 9 to 5 job where I walk out there at 5:00 and say goodbye would be easier, but I've never tried it so I don't know."

A middle school teacher:

> "Never being finished - There is always more you could do or could have done, always more things you could have looked up...If somebody would just hand me the lesson plans and say 'all right do this'." (laughs)

An elementary school teacher:

> "Time for planning - I'm very tired when I get home. I can't plan at home . I try to be here (at school) at 7:30 to plan. Juggling two worlds."

A middle school teacher:

> "The hardest I guess is getting everything done I want to get done. Just keeping up a lot of times is hardest. Doing what I should be doing or what I think I should be doing."

A middle school social studies teacher:

> "Time - I have lot of papers to correct ...It's exhausting. I don't think anybody knows who hasn't done this how tiring it is, how physically exhausting."

4. Curriculum and Teaching Issues
A middle school computer teacher:

> "Deciding what to teach them, what they really need, what's going to be expected of them."

An elementary school teacher:

> "The "how" of it. College didn't give me methods."

An elementary school principal:

> "Initially, because I was thrust into kindergarten teaching without having been really prepared... hardest for me to understand the curriculum and early child development because I didn't feel that my college courses adequately prepared me for really understanding the 5 year old."

A high school English teacher:

> "Long range planning"

A high school biology teacher:

> "To motivate kids who don't seem interested" [in his subject]

An elementary school principal:

> "When you teach somebody something and they don't get
> it...It took me a long time to realize that just because I taught
> it, it didn't necessarily mean they were learning it, and as a
> principal, just because I would like something [to happen]
> doesn't mean it's going to happen."

5. Lack of Student Respect/ Attitudinal Change

Two teachers, both men, said the hardest part of teaching was
contending with the negative attitudinal changes of students
and parents.

A middle school teacher:

> "I find it difficult to believe that kids just can't accept the fact
> they you're here to help them and after you're honest with
> them and tell them, 'I'm here because I want to be here. I could
> be doing a lot of other things, making a lot more money, maybe
> not feeling as rewarded sometimes, but I'm here for you', and
> they can't accept that. Not only will they not accept it, but
> they turn around and treat you as a rug. I had a girl say to me,
> 'Hey take it easy, I'll have my mother get you fired'... So that
> lack of respect, the lack of returning the caring attitude that
> I have for them, it's a real downer."

An elementary school teacher:

> "Lack of discipline of kids and in families...in my day, if I
> did something wrong in school, my father would give me a
> little workout...You even have to talk to parents differently,
> otherwise they walk all over you. You're just a baby sitter for
> the kids."

For one fifth grade teacher, knowing if she was "making a
difference" in students' lives was perceived as the hardest part
of teaching:

> "I guess trying to see where I made a difference in their lives...Until I gained a knowledge of what teaching and learning was all about, and what development and cognitive ability was all about and how I could make a difference in those areas, I was not satisfied with teaching."

While the loneliness of teaching has been described in studies of teachers[3], only one teacher mentioned it in the interviews. Maeroff[4] claimed professional growth is impaired by the lack of contact with colleagues. The teacher in Kidder's study said: " The worst thing about it [the isolation] is you don't even know if you're doing something wrong"[5]. Grumet asked the question: "Why do teachers maintain the isolation of their kitchens in their classrooms?"[6] The one teacher who mentioned the problem of isolation, a male high school biology teacher said, "One of the things I regret about teaching is not enough contact with other adults. You could spend your whole day just with kids." This teacher also believed that children of teachers may be at a disadvantage: "My son said there's too much pressure on him because he has a mother and father who are teachers. He realizes he can't come home and say the teacher did this-we've heard a lot of these things."

Hard in Parenting

Being a parent has been traditionally been considered a satisfying, enriching human condition. Indeed, it is only in the past fifteen years that childless couples are no longer pitied. Motherhood, as well, has only recently been viewed less sentimentally and more realistically. Ruddick offers a stark view of it: "Many mothers are cut off from other mothers because they do their mothering work in isolation or because they are driven by competition or inhibited by self doubt or simply because they are exhausted."[7]   When the teachers reflected on what was hard for them in parenting, they were undoubtedly influenced by the ages of their children. Teachers with adolescent children expressed different concerns from those whose children were very young or adults. The children of the teaching-parents ranged in age from three to thirty. Four themes of difficulty emerged from an analysis of the teachers' comments: the responsibility in parenting, insufficient time, affective concerns, and discipline decisions.

The Responsibility

A middle school single parent with two adolescents said:

> "Raising them by myself- the physical, the moral training- imparting values. I'm strict as a parent. If there's a party I call to see if the parents will be home. The same organization and planning as in teaching, but that's me."

A middle school teacher with an adolescent son:

> "Making big decisions. Worrying constantly- everything he'll be facing frightens me so much."

A middle school male teacher with five children:

> "When they go out I tell them, 'Be careful, don't drink, don't embarrass your parents, your grandparents'."

A middle school male teacher with an adolescent son:

> "Knowing that you're doing the right thing, hoping that everything you do is going to end up okay...there's so much peer pressure in the schools around here...groups that they get into..."

A high school music teacher with two adult children:

> "I guess the hardest thing is the great sense of responsibility for another life- I was totally responsible for their care."

Insufficient Time

We have seen that some teachers said not having "enough time" was the hardest aspect of teaching. Others described it as the hardest aspect of parenting. The fact that not having enough time was cited from the perspective of parent and teacher illustrates its importance to the interviewees.

An elementary school teacher with three children:

> "Just trying to keep up with everything: working a full time job and trying to juggle the three children and their activities, trying to keep track of the house. I sometimes get bogged down and get very tired and irritated. Usually I've got schoolwork to do at night. Sometimes I feel like I'm pulled in a million different directions."

A middle school teacher with five grown children:

> "Trying to keep up with the schedules and the housework."

An elementary special education teacher with two children:

> "The pressure of having a full time job-I'm exhausted-drained from the day."

A high school teacher with an adolescent daughter:

> "Being able to set aside a portion of my time- devote some stressless time to myself."

A middle school teacher with a pre-adolescent son said:

> " I think to step back and really take the time to enjoy my son, to enjoy the life we have, rather than being very caught up in it. Sometimes it all becomes overwhelming with his school, my school, my husband's work, activities, carpooling back and forth. It's a lot to juggle. Sometimes you lose sight of the fun of it and get caught up in the day to day details."

Affective Concerns

Identifying with their children, trying to understand them and give them what they need emotionally were the hardest aspect of being a parent for some teachers.

A middle school teacher with two children said:

> "When the kids are unhappy, if they're hurting, I hurt probably more than they do. I think I relate to them too much."

An elementary school teacher said of her adult daughter:

> "Letting her go and live her own life, knowing what's out there and not wanting to warn her of everything, and stepping back and saying, 'Hey, she's got a good head on her shoulders, let her use it'.

An elementary school teacher said:

> "It's the guilt-wondering if I'm not giving my children enough and being there when they need me. One of the hardest parts of this job (she now talks about teaching) is it's not a job where you leave the job. It's not an office where at 5:00 you leave your work there...I still want to spend quality time with my children."

An elementary school principal with a pre-adolescent son said:

> "My son is a pre-adolescent...he wants to be a baby one minute and the next minute he wants to be the independent teenager going off on his own and not wanting any questions asked of him, and I know this is typical of adolescence, but it's my first and only child, so the first time it hits you, it's a growth experience for the parent. So, coping with his need to be independent as well as his need to also be dependent, and having that change almost at his whim- which I know is typical of the age- is difficult for me to adjust to 'cause I have to let him go at some moments and be the nurturing daddy at others."

This comment resembles the findings of Apter in her study of mothers and adolescent daughters: "Adolescents are notoriously confusing in the way they vacillate from being much like adults to being more childish than children, infuriatingly childish as only a near-adult can be."[8]

Discipline Decisions

Knowing when and how to discipline their children was hardest for some teachers.

An elementary school teacher with a seven year old said:

> "Finding the right punishment, finding the thing that will be effective."

An elementary male school principal with a three year old:

> "There is a joke at home that my son is able to pull my chain very quickly— if he doesn't do something, if he doesn't clean up, if he's acting like a kid and I tell him not to, I'm not able to convince him, I immediately go head to head with him which he obviously enjoys tremendously."

A male middle school teacher with a seven year old said:

> "Saying   no.   Nintendo   game - now   it's   restricted   to weekends."

A male middle school teacher with adolescent children:

> "Probably saying no when you'd like to say yes...At 15, my kid still has a collar on."

An elementary school teacher with two young children said:

> "Being consistent, keeping after them to get them to do what you want them to do to develop good habits, work habits."

One elementary teacher with grown children said her teaching experience made her rigid in her mothering expectations.

> "I would try to make my first child fit into these categories in the book [she is referring to Spock's *Baby and Child Care*, 1976] because that's what I was used to in school. I felt that everything had to be so organized..."

Hardest about the Dual Role

Some of the teachers did not isolate the elements of what was hard in each role and talked about what was hard about the combination of being a teacher and parent. We have seen that a negative effect of teaching on parenting was the depletion of patience in school with the result that teachers had little left for their own children. When teachers talked about the hardest aspect of the dual role, the common theme in their comments was the feeling of exhaustion and its effects on their relations with their children.

A female high school teacher with a learning disabled child said:

> "Teaching is so exhausting that it's hard to come home and have the level of energy that your child requires."

A female elementary school teacher with two children said:

> "Being a teacher I bring home a lot of work. My evening is work, and sometimes my daughter needs a lot of help with her homework, and I have *my* homework, and it's very difficult for me to work with her...It's not that easy to work with your own child."

A female special education teacher with two children said:

> "There are those days when I don't feel like being around children- maybe I don't like the responsibility of children - either my kids or the students. There are those days that I' d like to be an editor at *Harper's Bazaar* or a telephone line girl."

An elementary school male teacher with four children:

> "Teaching is exhausting. A lot of people think it's an easy job, and I think people who think that way think back to years ago when I was in school- we were quiet and well behaved. And school isn't like that because we're teaching children to think and to question and sometimes they do that, and it's challenging... and so you come home sometimes drained, and sometimes you need to rest a while so you can deal with the problems your own kids have come home with."

A female elementary school teacher with two children:

> "There's a big emotional strain, I think, being both a parent and a teacher because you get so emotionally involved with the children you're teaching- especially when you see a child having difficulty. And then, of course, you go home and you have another emotional role to fill at home. If I were in an office, I would be dealing with adults, I wouldn't be having to give so much emotionally."

A female elementary school teacher with three children:

> "It's exhausting...I may go home and bark at my own children which really isn't fair."

A female middle school teacher with an adolescent son:

> "The hardest part is not to use up all the patience here and go home with nothing, and yell at your own kid."

A female middle school teacher with four children:

> "There were too many things day and night that were demanding. I managed to keep it in check in the classroom and did fine, but when I got home I would be more impatient. That's not right to do that... I really don't know how anybody with small children works full time like that. I couldn't do it."

A female elementary school teacher with two young children:

> "Just constantly feeling I'm on a treadmill. I enjoy teaching, and I certainly enjoy being a mother. I wouldn't give up being a teacher because I was too tired, but I find myself going to bed at 12 or 1 AM because I'm still grading papers."

A female middle school teacher with two adolescents:

> "I left teaching last year to try something else because I felt it was too emotionally, mentally, physically demanding, and I resigned and went into something else, and I was miserable- I missed the kids, the interaction with the kids. But they're both so draining and exhausting. I give essay questions- you can't test their thinking with short answers... I'm tired from both."

Research on teaching-parents confirms the hardships these teachers describe. Nias found some women teachers so conflicted between work and family life that they regretfully gave up teaching. Grumet[9] compared the isolation in teaching and mothering: "The privatization of teaching repeats the exile of domesticity". Spencer's teaching-mothers[10] believed balancing school and home added up to being responsible for three domains: teaching, caring for their homes, and their children. When Kidder described the teaching life of Mrs. Chris Zajac in *Among Schoolchildren,* he illustrated how her teaching problems were taken home and even assumed by her spouse: "Billy [the husband] said that maybe Chris [the teacher and Billy's wife] shouldn't take gym away from Clarence [her student], and Chris started scolding her husband: 'Don't tell me I shouldn't take gym away'...It wasn't a serious argument, but Chris couldn't believe she'd let this boy disrupt her home that way."[11]

Not all the teachers found the dual role sapping of time, energy and patience. A high school widower with five children said:

> "I feel better now than when I was in industry [for 1 year]. It's much more relaxing to teach. I feel sorry for people who work 9 to 5. It was refreshing to be out of the classroom for a year,

made me appreciate being here, It was refreshing mentally, helpful financially [to work in industry]. But I like summers off, getting home two hours earlier."

Teaching-parents contended with problems of having insufficient time for each role, feeling exhausted, and facing dilemmas in their relations with students and children. It could be asserted that any work combined with parenting generates challenges and fatigue. Indeed, the teaching day formally ends around 3:00, as the teacher most recently quoted pointed out. Parents who have a more conventional work schedule have even fewer hours of "free" time. What use can we make of highlighting the difficult aspects of being a teaching-parent when the working-parent works longer hours than the teaching parent? The purpose of this exploration is not to see who works harder or generate pity for teaching-parents but rather to note the particular complexities in being a teaching-parent. Although the teaching day is officially over at 3:00, in reality it does not end at that time for many teachers. The uniqueness of working and living with children is that it requires teaching-parents to give of themselves affectively and intellectually in each role without regard to how they may feel at the moment. To elicit and identify the difficulties of the dual role is not to deny its satisfactions. It many be relevant to note that with the exception of three of the 50 teachers, all expressed satisfaction with their career choice.

Teachers' Views of Parent Conferences

In chapter 2, the influences of parenting on teaching, teachers described how they became more empathic towards parents as a result of being parents themselves. In this section I further explore the relations between teachers and parents. While it would seem that teachers and parents should be natural allies, they have, in fact, been called "natural enemies."[12] Grumet asserts that "instead of being allies, mothers and teachers distrust each other."[13] Going further, novelist Josephine Humphreys wrote of mothers and teachers: "People think mothers are maniacs. No one trusts them, teachers hate them."[14]

The uneasy relationship between teachers and parents is also reported in studies on parent-teacher conferences. McPherson described the dread some teachers experienced in anticipation of conferences with parents who taught: "The most dangerous parents were those who were also teachers and thus privy to the secrets of the trade."[15] However, Claesson, Hulsebosch and Lighfoot[16] found conferences with teaching-mothers to be more productive than conferences with mothers who do not teach.

In this section I focus on parent -teacher conferences from two perspectives: (1) I look at what teachers say about having conferences with parents who are also teachers, and (2) I identify how the teachers feel when they have conferences with their children's teachers.

Conferences with Parents who are Teachers

When asked to reflect on conferences with parents who are also teachers, the teachers' comments are similar to those reported in previous studies. Some teachers found conferences were harder because teaching-parents expected more of them. Some teachers found them easier because as teachers, they understood what could be accomplished in a classroom. A few teachers thought that experience as a teacher was not a crucial element in a parent-teacher conference. The following comments illustrate the teachers' views.

An elementary school principal said:

> "Conferences are harder. I find they're more critical...the most vocal unpleasant parents I have dealt with here have been teachers, and part of it is that they know the system, and they know how to use the system, and part is that they don't have a lot of faith in teachers."

A middle school social studies teacher:

> "They're always harder. You can't BS them, you can't snow them or they usually know where you're coming from, and most expect to hear the truth...I would say that most parents that come in [for conferences] that are teachers are demanding. They demand a lot of their kids. They are not satisfied with a C student or a B student. They tell you that they want their child to do the best they can, but at the same time they have higher expectations than the average parent, and they seem to be more involved in the kid's day to day activities. They really know what's going on, they evaluate assignments, they come in with an agenda."

A high school English teacher asserted that children of teachers have more problems than other children:

> "So many of the students who have problems have mothers who are teachers. Parents known to be problems are usually teachers."

A middle school English teacher found teaching parents somewhat harder than parents in general:

> "They know the game. You have to feel them out and see if
> you can say 'Your kid is a major problem.' Sometimes I find
> it harder with those parents."

Some teachers found these conferences easier. A middle school science teacher said:

> "When I know that the parent of one of my students is a
> teacher it's different. They understand certain things that a
> parent in a different field wouldn't. Of course I have no proof
> or how much..."

A high school music teacher:

> "I think they're easier. I think they [the parents] have more
> of an understanding of the problems that their children have.
> I think they're a lot easier."

An elementary school teacher said:

> "Easier because they have a pretty good understanding of
> what's going on."

However, a middle school teacher said:

> "I think two things: I'm either their age or older. I think they
> respond to what I say. I have confidence in what I'm doing.
> I'm really interested in their child's welfare as a person. They
> are not very different from other parents."

Conferences As a Parent

In general, the teachers felt that they benefited from their role as teacher when they had conferences with their children's teachers. Because they were teachers, they believed they could communicate better with their children's teachers in parent-teacher conferences.

A middle school science teacher with two adolescents said:

> "...I can speak to a teacher as another teacher. I can explain why a time frame may be unrealistic. When my children complain, I will go into school and talk to my children's teachers...I understand the teachers, know the pressure of teaching in 1990."

A fifth grade teacher with four children:

> "I think when I have a conference with my own children's teachers that they are more prepared for the conference knowing that the parent is also a teacher and they can't sort of bluff their way through it."

A middle school teaching parent with two young children believed he knew the right questions to ask:

> "I have a better knowledge of what my son does in school because as a teacher I know what to ask...Very often when teachers talk to parents they're very tentative in saying anything - they kind of whitewash everything and make it look good or are trying not to offend the parent...I don't want that. I ask direct questions and I get the direct answer."

A middle school teacher gave the teacher helpful information about his son:

> "The teacher wanted to let me know he [the student] seemed to be real tired, and she wanted to know why he was tired, so that was a good conference. She knew I was a teacher. I detected a little edginess on her part. She appreciated the feedback I gave her about him."

A middle school teacher with two adolescents:

> "When I go for a conference for my kids, I watch for signals
> from the teachers - that they want to say that maybe my
> daughter is chatty or my son's fooling around. They don't
> want to hit you with it."

An elementary school teacher with four children felt that she
could learn more of the truth about her children's work
because she was a teacher:

> "I've always said 'Please be honest with me'. I find myself
> very relaxed with their teachers. But both boys are struggling-
> they are learning disabled. I find it hard to accept the fact that
> my children are not up to par in a particular area."

Another elementary school teacher said:

> "I know what the teachers are going through. We don't use
> jargon, we get down to the nitty gritty."

Not all the teachers found being a teacher was an advantage
in relating to their children's teachers. An elementary school
principal said:

> "My wife and I tend to stay away from school... maybe too
> much."

A middle school teacher:

> "My experience with my kids' teachers has been rather
> negative. My wife is also a teacher so between the two of us
> we usually find a lot of fault."

McPherson found that when parents became teachers they expected less from the school than before being parents. Whether this change in attitude represents cynicism or a more realistic understanding of what teachers and schools can do remains unclear.

Models of Teaching/ Teachers of Influence

"We teach the way we were taught".... a sixth grade teacher
   "We teach the way we learn"... a high school teacher

In an effort to identify the importance of their own teachers in their lives, I asked the teachers (1) if they modeled their behavior after one of their teachers, and (2) if, as students, they had a teacher who strongly influenced them.

Two teachers responded with the comments above. The first remark suggests that, consciously or not, our teaching behavior is affected by our own teachers. The second statement implies that an awareness of our own learning process is a critical factor in how we teach.

In chapter 2 I presented the teachers' reasons for becoming teachers. When asked why they became teachers, only four of the teachers said their decision was influenced by having a memorable teacher. Later in our interview when asked specifically about an influential teacher, about one half of the teachers could recall one. Only one teacher said he actually modeled his behavior after a teacher. Those who described meaningful teachers chose people from the kindergarten through college levels. Influential teachers did not necessarily teach the same subject as the interviewees. The teachers valued teachers who were challenging and dynamic, and nurturing and caring.

Intellectually Challenging/Dynamic
A middle school science teacher said:

> "The most memorable was the lady that made me switch from elementary education to biology, who was a tiny little older lady that looked like a mouse and was so dynamic and so excited by her subject that she made me run out of that classroom at the bell and run over to the registrar and change my major that very day. Her excitement did that."

Another science teacher:

> "I remember her name, everything about her. She was exciting -we never knew what to expect. I never heard of laughing in a classroom before..."

A middle school English/social studies teacher said:

> "There was an English teacher in high school. He used a book by Marshall McCluhan, *The Media Is the Message*. We analyzed the lyrics to Sgt. Pepper. He did a lot of radical stuff for back then in a Jesuit high school...He opened my mind up to a lot of things- that learning didn't have to be straight-laced and traditional."

A middle school teacher said:

> "He taught the subject well and made it come alive for us...he related to the students. He was hard but you learned from him and liked him. Hopefully that's what I do."

A french teacher:

> "An English teacher when I was a senior in high school- she was a straight-laced, unmarried lady probably in her fifties or sixties. She had such a love and a fire in her for literature,

grammar, and as I was thinking about going into teaching, I thought I want that feeling: When I'm 55, 60 years old, I want to light up like that when I teach...She had hoods reading *Macbeth*. She was a well loved teacher and was as tough as all get out."

An influential teacher did not necessarily teach a subject which the teacher currently taught.

A physical education teacher said of an English teacher:

"He taught us Shakespeare at William Paterson [a college]. I think he was the best teacher I ever had. I knew nothing about Shakespeare and he made it very interesting."

A business education teacher said of a history teacher:

"He was pretty much a role model for me. .. He was a mentor, he was that kind of parent that I was looking for but wasn't seeing in my own dad. I modeled my teaching style after him- very mobile in the classroom with a lot of changes in pace and tone."

Nurturing, Caring and Kind
A sixth grade male teacher said:

"I can remember really enjoying kindergarten. I also had a very kindhearted teacher in fifth grade, and I enjoyed both of those years. I can remember that I hated 6th, 7th, and 8th grades as did all my friends... Going to college in CUNY I had some wonderful teachers that were really good people-close to the students- and I really enjoyed that."

An elementary school teacher said:

> "There were two. One in the fifth grade who was a really giving, tender loving caring person, and a 7th grade teacher who kept encouraging me to write and responded to me as an individual."

Less Specific Characteristics

A middle school male art teacher said:

> "I really wasn't interested in art until high school and took it for four years, and this woman had a direct effect."

A fifth grade teacher said:

> "I had a mentor always. Every place I ever taught I would look at the teacher who was successful and I would want to do whatever that teacher was doing...I tended to be geared toward the   teacher who had a wonderful relationship with the students . I don't mean a "palsy" relationship or friends. I mean a relationship of respect, humor where we're not put down-where people were allowed to blossom. I always looked at those teachers and became their friends and tried to learn what they were doing."

Two teachers were influenced by the philosophy of college courses rather than by the teacher.

An elementary school teacher:

> "When I was an undergraduate, I was influenced by studies which focussed on the "whole" child."

A computer teacher:

> "I don't model my behavior after a particular teacher, but I think the Bank Street College of Education's teaching philosophy has made me very conscious of the teacher as learner."

Teachers as Models of What Not to Do

Two of the teachers rejected the way their teachers taught. An elementary school principal said:

> "They were all miserable. I was considered very bright and probably was, and I didn't do those things that laid accolades upon me. I went into teaching because I thought I be a better teacher than the teachers I had."

A middle school social studies teacher said:

> "I don't think I teach like anyone. I never liked the way I was taught. I hated it because I saw people abused. The intentions may have been good, but there was fear..."

Parent Model: Father as Model

I asked the male teachers if their parenting behavior was like their own fathers' because I hoped to get a sense of the degree to which they may have emulated or rejected their fathers' parenting behavior. Only one teacher believed his fathering behavior was similar to his own father's. The teachers said they differed from their fathers in terms of having more time to spend with their children, being more involved in their lives, and being a "different kind" of father.

Not like Father - no explicit reason

A 42 year old teacher said:

"Not at all. My siblings often say you're getting just like Dad, and I say please don't tell me that."

Another 42 year old:

"No. My mother and father were divorced and so I was raised basically by my mother. I knew my father but I didn't have him as somebody to guide me. I try to take an active role with my son."

A 51 year old:

"No. I was an only child. I have 5 kids."

A 48 year old:

"Not at all. My father is a typical first generation type. A nice person but we're not at all alike."

More time/ more involved

A 39 year old:

"I'm able to spend more time with my son, able to do more things with him. My father worked very hard."

A 38 year old:

"I'm more involved with my children. My father was 43 when I was born. By the time I was 10 he was already older. I was 23 when my first child was born."

A 45 year old:

"I'm more involved than he was. He was a very good father, very concerned about my education and general well being . I think I spend more time with my kids, enjoy my kids more than my father did."

A 40 year old:

> "No, I don't think so. We were not an affluent family, and when I was young, I remember my father working two and sometimes three jobs just to keep us well fed, well clothed."

A 45 year old:

> "Absolutely not- for a lot of different reasons. I have the time and I have the interest- in sports, for example. That's one of the reasons I stay in teaching: I have the time off when they are off. My father never even graduated from elementary school- he was an immigrant, and to him, it was always work. He worked 7 days a week- he had no time, and I look back on it, and I regret that."

More time/more involved/ "different kind" of father

A 39 year old:

> "I'm much more around than my father was and less distant. I had a much more formal upbringing."

Another 39 year old:

> "My parents were extremely strict. My father dropped out of school because of the Depression... [As a child] I had to do flashcards before I went out. I'd never do that to my kid...My parents always wanted me to do better. I don't think they understood what the best was."

A 42 year old:

> "Absolutely not...I'm a hands on father. My son at 15 won't think twice about coming up to me and putting his arm around me and kidding me... My father was a removed person."

A 50 year old:

"No, very much different- my father was in the home, but absent. He would leave at 6 AM and not get home untill 7:30 or 8:30 at night...I really didn't see an awful lot of him...I'm a very different father...I'm a very tactile person, I hug a lot whereas my dad would just go through the room..."

Somewhat Like Own Father

A 40 year old:

"Yes and no. I get to spend more time with my children because I get home a little earlier...But with my father- we went sleigh riding together. I don't work during the summer...He would have enjoyed that. He had only two weeks vacation..."

A 42 year old:

"When I was younger I was prone to be the way my father was. But as I'm getting older, as I've matured I parent more like my mother did. My father wasn't around."

Like Own Father

A 42 year old:

"Yes, I was lucky. I had a warm and sensitive father. I learned a lot about parenting from him. My father was 47 when I was born so he was mature...He led by example, he didn't preach a lot..".

Teachers differed from their own fathers partly out of inclination to be different from them but also because economic realities forced their fathers to work harder and longer than the teachers. Fathers were not as "available" as these teachers are for their children. In general, the teachers' descriptions suggest that they derive greater satisfaction in parenting than their fathers did.

Mother as Model

Not all the women teachers responded "in depth" to the question of whether their own mother served as a model for their mothering approach. Some women were noncommittal or not sure about the effects of their mothers' treatment of them. Still, compared to men teachers, women displayed more variety in their responses to the question of whether their mother's behavior was a model for them. The women described the differences between their life styles and their mothers'. Many of their mothers did not work and were more available to them than they are for their children. According to Apter, "Professional women looking back upon their childhood value the time and care their mothers bestowed on them. They see themselves as benefiting from the traditional styles of mothering."[17] The women teachers did not expressly state this view, but many seemed wistful or nostalgic about the amount of time their mothers had for them.

Despite differences in life styles, some teachers felt they nurtured their children similarly to their mothers. Others believed that they were quite different from their mothers particularly in giving their own children more responsibility than they had as children. Some teachers disapproved of their mother's mothering behavior and consciously tried (sometimes without success) to be different from them.

The following patterns were identifiable after examining the responses to the question of whether one's own mother served as a model in mothering.

Different Life Styles: Positive Recollection

A 42 year old with two children:

"She did more for us. She stayed home. I think probably in terms of nurturing, yes [she is similar to her mother]. My kids are more independent than my brothers and I were only because I'm not there and they do more for themselves."

A 44 year old with one child:

"I think I give my daughter the time and sympathy that my mother gave to me, but our life styles are different. I'm the oldest of seven children (she has only one daughter). We have very different lives. She worked for a couple of years- she was an army nurse...but I think she is an influence- very warm, loving, supportive person."

A 47 year old with four children:

"I don't know if I mothered like she mothered me, I don't think so, but I get involved in the way she did. I'm the oldest of five. She was very involved in school and in scouts and in all kinds of things that she did, so I think I use that as a model."

Not a Model, but Positive Reference

A 41 year old with one son:

"No, I don't have the patience she had. I try in certain respects to emulate her because she was a wonderful mother."

A 48 year old with two children:

"Yes, when I agree with it. When I disagree with her behavior, it was the model to avoid. She was very trusting of me and I had very few limits. She was giving, loving, she didn't work, she had more time."

A 55 year old with three children:

"She was very loving, she was non-judgmental, she never made too may rules - I'm somewhat like her that way. I remember things I didn't like."

A 42 year old with one child:

"No. In warmth and love, yes. I can see from her mistakes."

Not a Model - Neutral Reference

Two teachers refer to a difference in life styles in neutral rather than positive terms.

A 50 year old with two children:

"Only partially a role model. My mother got her MBA at 60. She was an example as a professional woman, but I got my mothering model from my grandmother. My grandmother was the old fashioned role model."

A 44 year old with two children:

"My own children say 'You sound just like BJ' [the mother]. She was 40 when she had me. So our relationship was different. I would go out and play soccer with them and play tennis and take them places like that."

Two teachers refer to life style differences. One teacher thinks her own her family life is harder than her mother's. The second teacher believed that teaching was actually beneficial for her family.

The first teacher, 35 years of age, with one child:

> "I think it's very different for this generation. My mother was available, she didn't work... my whole family has had to adjust to a working mother and that changes the complexion of the household, the family unit."

The second teacher, a 53 year old with five children:

> "I give my children more independence [than her mother did], and working was a very big plus for that. Had I not gone back to work when my children were young, I probably would have done much more smothering than I was able to do. I was too busy to be interfering in their lives, and they've all been very independent."

Negative Recollections

Life style differences.

A 35 year old with two children:

> "I never wanted to be the same as my mother, but I think I'm turning out that way. I'm different in the sense that I wouldn't say my mother didn't work because she worked inside the home- she raised 4 children, she didn't have a maid. I work outside the home and that job takes me away for about 8 hours a day, but I only have 2 children. I have to be much more organized."

Lack of Closeness.

A 47 year old with two children:

> "I didn't confide in her very much, I didn't feel terribly close to her."

A 45 year old with one child:

> "I never remember having long talks with her or sharing a lot of things with her for fear that she might disapprove r not understand."

Other Affective Differences. Teachers expressed a range of feelings about being different from their mothers.

A 45 year old with two children said:

> " When I went out, my mother would say, 'The dress looks good' whereas I would say to my daughter, 'You look good', a subtle difference. I was brought up with that kind of verbal abuse..."

A 43 year old with two children:

> "I think I'm more maternal than my mother was...I think I'm more giving than she was."

A 45 year old with three children:

> "I'm not like her although there are times I say things that I heard my mother say and I catch myself."

A 42 year old with four children:

> "I try not to be."

Another 42 year old with one child:

> "I had very little responsibility- my mother smothered me more than she mothered me."

A 40 year old with one child:

> "I tried to move away from her style."

A 40 year old with two children:

> "She had children late in life... she worked not out of necessitybut out of not wanting to be at home. My brother and I didn't have many requirements put on us so I found in reaction to that I've tried to be more strict with my children. She gave me freedoms I would never give my own children."

It probably goes without saying that a consideration of a mother's influence on a daughter's mothering behavior is limited to what is consciously remembered. The influences may be profound, elusive and even inaccessible to memory. When the teachers reflected on their mothers' influence on them as mothers, they expressed a range of feelings and recollections. Within the variety of responses is the theme that the women did not pattern their child-rearing behavior on their mothers' approach to it. In this respect they resemble their male counterparts who, with the exception of one teacher, also differed from their fathers in their parenting behavior.

Gender Differences

Comparisons between male and female teachers must be viewed as impressionistic and suggestive rather than statistically valid since this study has not utilized statistical measures. Also, because men constitute only forty per cent of the teachers, inferences about how they differ from female teachers must remain tentative. Nonetheless, there were three patterns of difference between the men and women teachers which emerged from an analysis of their responses.

Difference in Influence of the Dual Role

Male teachers said that teaching had a greater influence on their parenting than parenting had on their teaching. Although being a parent did influence on them as teachers, the experience of teaching more substantially affected their parenting behavior. While the experience of teaching affected the women in their role as mothers, being mothers more profoundly affected the women in their teaching role.

<u>Different Perceptions about Difficulty of Dual Role</u>

As I have mentioned earlier, women found the dual role "exhausting" due to affective and intellectual demands of school and home. Only one male teacher talked about the difficulties in being a teaching-parent. Like the women teachers who described what was hard about the dual role, he referred to a feeling of exhaustion due to insufficient time to do all that had to be done. While three, men said they looked forward to leaving the profession, this sentiment was not due to the combination of teaching and parenting.

<u>Gender Differences As Compared with Own Parents</u>

The societal changes which have vastly altered family life are reflected in the lives of male and female teachers. Men have more time with their children than their fathers had with them. Men work fewer hours and not as hard as their fathers, many of whom did not come home from work until late at night. While most of the male teachers worked during the summer - and some worked on a second job during the school year - they still worked less hard than their fathers and had more time for their children than their fathers did. The men's descriptions resembled Rose's allusion to the benefits men derived from the structure of family life. "Marriage and career, family and work, which so often pull a woman in different directions, are much more likely to reinforce one another for a man."[18]

The women teachers had less time with their children than their mothers had with them. They work harder than their mothers, many of whom did not work outside the home. When Grumet considered the similarities in mothering and teaching, she referred to its "boundless" nature. "In many ways the temporal structures of teaching resemble the routines of domesticity. Fluid and ubiquitous, housework and children have required women to accept patterns of work and time that have no boundaries."[19] Male teachers, for the most part, seemed to be spared this aspect of the dual role. Still, despite its complexities, it should be noted that the women teachers said that they were enriched by the dual role.

NOTES

1. See Goodlad, 1984; Maeroff, 1988; Sizer, 1984 for a variety of perspectives on the challenges in teaching.
2. Nias, 1989.
3. See Grumet, 1988; Kidder, 1989; Lortie, 1975; Maeroff, 1988.
4. Maeroff, 1988.
5. Kidder, 1989, p. 52.
6. Grumet, 1989, p. 85.
7. Ruddick, 1989, p. 103.
8. Apter, 1990, p. 119.
9. Grumet, 1988, p. 93.
10. Spencer, 1986.
11. Kidder, 1989, p. 99
12. Waller, 1932.
13. Grumet, 1988, p. 56.
14. Humphreys, 1984, p.14.
15. McPherson, 1972, p. 146.
16. See Claesson, 1986; Hulsebosch, 1990; Lightfoot, 1978.
17. Apter, 1990, p. 119.
18. Rose, 1983, p.150.
19. Grumet, 1988, p.86.

Chapter Five

Other Voices: Analysis of the Questionnaires

The actress Elaine May said about interviews: "It is the challenge of the interview form itself, the excitement of being able to create dialogue without plot, narrative without action, and intimacy without friendship that attracts me".[1] When I interviewed the teachers I, too, experienced something like "intimacy without friendship". I felt a rapport with the teachers as they revealed their thoughts in response to the questions.

I developed a questionnaire to learn how another group of teaching-parents would respond to questions posed through a more impersonal format. The questions were based on the interview questions to which the teachers responded with the most interest. Some questions required the use of a rating scale of agreement/disagreement. Others were open-ended, giving the teachers an opportunity to answer questions in their own words. At the end of the questionnaire, teachers could include additional comments. So although the questionnaire form was more impersonal than the interview, it gave the teachers the chance to include views which they did not reveal through the questionnaire items. Forty per cent of the teachers added comments at the end of the questionnaire. (See Appendix B). These comments and responses to open ended questions were analyzed for common themes of meaning.

In this chapter I present teachers' perceptions of the dual role as disclosed through their questionnaire responses. I compare these with the interviewees' descriptions.

Description of Participants

I located questionnaire participants with the help of my colleagues at Montclair State who had contacts with public school teachers. My colleagues told the teachers about the existence of the study - they knew only that much about it - and I sent teachers who were interested in participating a copy of the questionnaire. This "convenience sample" included teachers in New Jersey and New York who taught in both inner-city and suburban schools.

Seventy-five questionnaires were distributed, and fifty-five were completed and returned to me. In a letter to the participants, I told them that the questionnaires could be answered anonymously or with identification so that teachers who were interested in the results of the study could receive them. Eighty-four per cent included their names and will receive the results.

Forty-six women and nine men completed the questionnaires. (See Table 5.1). They ranged in age from 32 to 61, with 60 per cent of the teachers being in their forties. A substantial majority of the teachers - 62 per cent - had two children, 15 per cent had one child, 13 per cent three children, and two per cent each had four, five and seven children. Fifty- six per cent of the

Table 5.1

Characteristics of Questionnaire Participants

	n	%
By Gender		
Women	46	84
Men	9	16
Ages of Teachers		
32-39	9	16
40-44	19	35
45-49	14	25
50-61	10	18
(3 teachers did not respond)		
Number of Children		
one child	8	15
two children	34	62
three children	7	13
more than three children	3	6
(3 teachers did not respond)		
School Location		
Urban	24	44
Suburban	31	56
Level of Teaching		
Kindergarten	10	18
Elementary	10	18
Middle	10	18
High School	24	44
(1 teacher did not respond)		

(Note: since some teachers did not answer all questions, percentages are less than 100 per cent.)

teachers taught in suburban schools while 44 per cent taught in urban settings. A majority, or 44 per cent of the teachers, taught at the high school level, and 18 per cent, each, taught at the kindergarten, elementary, and middle school levels. One respondent did not indicate teaching level.

Compared to Interviewees

Similarities

As Table 5.2 indicates, a majority of teachers from both groups were in their forties (60 per cent of the questionnaire respondents - to be referred to as respondents- and 62 per cent of the interviewees). Most teachers of both groups were married, (i.e. 89 per cent of respondents, and 90 per cent of interviewees). The groups were similar in the number of children they had, as 77 per cent of the respondents had one or two children, compared with 82 per cent of the interviewees. Most teachers in each group taught before they became parents. Seventy three per cent of respondents taught first, and 90 per cent of interviewees also were teachers before being parents.

Differences

The groups differed in three respects. First, 44 per cent of the respondents taught in inner city schools whereas none of the interviewed teachers taught in that setting. The groups also differed with respect to teaching level. Forty-four per cent of the respondents taught high school in contrast to only 20 per cent of the interviewees. Only 18 per cent of the respondents taught at the middle school level while 34 per cent of the interviewees taught middle school. The groups are less

Table 5.2

Some Similarities and Differences between Questionnaire Respondents and Interviewees

Similarities

Dimension	Respondents	Interviewees
Percentage in 40 year age range:	60%	62%
Marital Status:	89%married	90%married
Percentage who have 2 children:	77%	82%
Percentage who Taught before Parenting:	73%	90%

Differences

Inner-city Teachers:	44%	0
Teaching Level:		
High school	44%	20%
Middle school	18%	34%
Elementary/kg.	36%	46%
Gender differences:		
Percentage of male teachers	16%	36%

different at lower levels of school, i.e., 36 per cent of the respondents and 46 per cent of the interviewees each taught at kindergarten/elementary levels. While there are fewer men than women teachers in each group, there are substantially fewer male questionnaire respondents (16 per cent compared to 36 per cent of interviewees).

Reasons for Becoming Teachers: Questionnaire Respondents

The teachers could choose among five reasons for becoming teachers. As Table 5.3 indicates, 46 per cent of the teachers entered the profession because they were interested in children. Nineteen per cent were primarily influenced by an interest in their subject. Eleven per cent wanted to help others, 13 per cent responded to parental pressure, and 11 per cent became teachers because they "did not know what else to do." One teacher gave no response to the question.

<u>Compared to Interviewees</u>

The teachers' motives for teaching are similar to those expressed by the interviewees. More than 40 per cent of each group said they became teachers because they were interested in children. Nineteen per cent and 26 per cent of the respondents and interviewees, respectively, were motivated by an interest in subject matter. Slightly more than ten per cent of the teachers in each group entered the field for altruistic reasons and due to parental pressure. Eleven per cent of the respondents "didn't know what else to do" which is somewhat like the reason, "didn't like other work" given by eight per cent of the interviewees.

Table 5.3

Comparison of Respondents' and Interviewees' Reasons for Becoming Teachers		
Reason	**Respondents**	**Interviewees**
Interest in Children	46 per cent	42 per cent
Interest in Subject	19 per cent	26 per cent
Desire to Help Others	11 per cent	12 per cent
Parental Pressure	13 per cent	14 per cent
Didn't Know What Else to Do/Didn't Like Other Work	11 per cent	8 per cent

Teaching Levels Differences among Respondents

There were some differences in the reasons the respondents gave for becoming teachers based on their teaching levels (see Table 5.4). As might be expected and as research indicates,[2] the main reason high school teachers gave for entering the profession was an interest in subject matter. Thirty three per cent cited that interest as a reason for becoming high school teachers. Twenty five per cent of high school teachers became teachers because they were interested in children. Seventeen per cent chose teaching because they wanted to help others, and another 17 per cent became teachers due to parental pressure. Eight per cent entered the field because they did not

Table 5.4

Questionnaire Respondents' Reasons for Becoming Teachers

Reason	Group		Kg.		Elem.		Middle		High School	
	n	%	n	%	n	%	n	%	n	%
Interest in Children	25	46	7	70	7	70	5	50	6	25
Interest in Subject	10	19	1	10	1	10	-	-	8	33
Desire to Help Others	6	11	1	10	1	10	-	-	4	17
Parental Pressure	7	13	1	10	-	-	2	20	4	17
Didn't Know What Else to Do	6	11	-	-	1	10	3	30	2	8

know what else to do. It should be noted that although 33 per cent of high school teachers chose an interest in subject matter as the reason for becoming a teacher, 75 per cent gave other reasons.

Fifty per cent of middle school teachers chose to teach because they were interested in children. Twenty per cent responded to parental pressure to teach, and 30 per cent entered the field because they did not know what else to do. None indicated that they chose to teach out of an interest in a subject.

Both elementary and kindergarten teachers were motivated to teach due to an interest in children. Seventy per cent of each group chose that reason for entering the profession. (Brookhart and Freeman found this to be the prevailing motive in studies of elementary level teacher candidates.) Ten percent of both elementary and kindergarten teachers were interested in the subject and wanted to help others. Ten per cent became elementary school teachers because they did not know what else to do, and ten per cent of the kindergarten teachers responded to parental pressure to teach.

Men and women differed in their reasons for teaching. Fifty-six per cent of the men became teachers due to an interest in subject matter while only 11 per cent of women teachers gave that reason. Fifty-six percent of the women became teachers because of an interest in children. No men gave that as a reason.

Teachers in urban and suburban schools had somewhat different reasons for entering the profession. Thirty per cent of the urban school teachers became teachers because they were interested in the subject as compared to only 12 per cent of teachers in suburban schools. Fifty eight per cent of suburban teachers were motivated to teach out of an interest in children while only 26 per cent of urban school teachers gave that reason. Seventeen per cent of urban school teachers entered the profession they did not know what else to do as compared to six per cent of suburban school teachers who gave that as a reason for teaching.

How Parenting Affected Teaching

The teachers used a scale from one to five to rate their level of agreement with statements pertaining to the effects of parenting on teaching. The statements were derived from ideas the interviewed teachers expressed about how parenting affected them as teachers.

Table 5.5 summarizes the teachers' beliefs about the effects of parenting on teaching. Most of the teachers agreed that the parenting experience affected them as teachers. Ninety-two per cent of the teachers expressed agreement - 56 percent strongly agreed, 36 per cent agreed - with the idea that being a parent affected them as teachers. The most notable effect of parenting on the teachers focused on their feelings toward the parents of students. Eighty-nine per cent either strongly agreed or agreed that their understanding of parents increased since they themselves became parents. Since most of the teachers taught before becoming parents, they could respond to the question of whether parenting made them more empathic toward their students than they had been before being parents. Eighty-two per cent of the teachers strongly agreed or agreed that parenting increased their feelings of empathy toward students.

Another effect of parenting on teaching was an increased understanding of the pressures students contend with. Since becoming parents themselves, the teachers better understood the social and familial pressures students confront, as 84 per cent strongly agreed or agreed that this increased understanding was a result of being a parent.

Some of the interviewees had said that one effect of parenting on teaching was an increased flexibility in the classroom. Sixty per cent of the respondents registered agreement - 35 per cent

Table 5.5

Levels of Agreement about Effects of Parenting on Teaching Reported in Percentages						
#5 = strongly agree #4 = agree #3 = do not know #2 = disagree #1 = strongly disagree 0 = not applicable						
	#5	#4	#3	#2	#1	0
Parenting Affected Teaching	56%	36%	2%	4%	2%	0
Increased Understanding of Parents	54%	35%	5%	2%	0	4%
Increased Empathy toward Students	47%	35%	5%	5%	2%	6%
Greater Understanding of Familial/Social Pressures	42%	42%	5%	4%	2%	5%
Greater Flexibility as Teacher	35%	25%	9%	20%	9%	2%
Compromised Academic Standards	11%	18%	7%	35%	24%	5%
Parenting Caused Higher Student Expectations	6%	20%	20%	27%	27%	0

strongly agreed, 25 percent agreed - that they had become more flexible in the classroom. This rate of agreement is clearly lower than the levels described in response to other statements.

I was interested in learning if the teachers thought that an increased understanding of students' perspectives and pressures might cause them to compromise or lower their academic standards. Only 29 per cent registered agreement. This low rate of agreement is similar to the position taken by the interviewees. In fact, when I asked the interviewees this question, several teachers asserted that, on the contrary, *because* they were parents, they had *higher* expectations for their students. Since a few of the interviewed teachers volunteered this viewpoint, I included the statement in the questionnaire. I asked the respondents who were parents before they were teachers if they thought that having their own children caused them to have higher expectations for their students. Only 26 per cent agreed, 54 per cent disagreed, and 20 per cent said they did not know, indicating that these teachers did not think they had higher expectations for their students as a result of being parents.

The respondents resembled the interviewees with respect to the ways they judged the influences of parenting on teaching. Both groups strongly felt that one role affected the other. Like the interviewees, these teachers believed that they better understood parents since they themselves had become parents. Both groups felt that parenting made them more empathic teachers than they had been before becoming parents. Respondents shared with interviewees the belief that parenting helped them better understand their students' familial and social pressures.

How Teaching Affected Parenting

The questionnaire contained six statements about the effects of teaching on parenting which the respondents rated according to their level of agreement/disagreement. Here, again, the statements represent ideas the teachers expressed during the interviews.

Table 5.6 summarizes the teachers' ratings of the statements. Most of the teachers, or 92 per cent, strongly agreed or agreed that teaching broadened their perspective toward their children. This was the clearest effect of teaching on parenting for the respondents, as it was for the interviewed teachers. The second most common effect of teaching on parenting was the teachers' use of their teaching knowledge with their own children. Forty-two per cent of the teachers strongly agreed and 40 per cent agreed that they used their classroom knowledge and skills at home.

More than half of the teachers, or 63 per cent expressed agreement with the idea that teaching helped them to know "what to expect" from their own children. This questionniare item was included because during the interviews some teachers described how classroom experience was useful preparation for encounters with their own children. While 63 per cent agreed with this statement, this rate of agreement is considerably less than the rates of agreement with the first two statements.

Because some of the interviewed teachers said that the patience they expended in the classroom left them with an insufficient amount for their children, I included this assertion in the questionnaire. Only about half of the respondents, or 49 per cent registered agreement with the statement. Similarly, only 45 percent of the respondents felt that a disadvantage of

Table 5.6

Levels of Agreement about Effects of Teaching on Parenting Reported in Percentages

#5 = strongly agree   #4 = agree
#3 = do not know   #2 = disagree
#1 = strongly disagree   0 = not applicable

	#5	#4	#3	#2	#1	0
Broader Perspective toward own child/ren	52%	40%	4%	4%	0	0
Use teaching knowledge at home	42%	40%	11%	5%	2%	0
Greater knowledge of what to expect of own children	13%	50%	15%	20%	2%	0
Use of patience in school leaves less for own children	16%	33%	7%	29%	15%	0
Similar energy used at home & school is a disadvantage of being a teaching/parent	16%	29%	11%	24%	16%	4%
Exert pressure on own children due to teaching	33%	22%	7%	25%	13%	0

being a teaching-parent was the use of similar energy as a parent and teacher. About half of the teachers, or 55 per cent, believed that they pressured their children about schoolwork because they were teachers. Sixty-three percent of the high school teachers, 60 per cent of middle school teachers, and 70 per cent of the elemementary school teachers agreed that they exerted pressure on their children. However, 70 per cent of the kindergarten teachers said they did not exert pressure on their children. Their forebearance does not seem to be due to having young children. The 19 children of the kindergarten teachers ranged in age from 7 to 30, with 58 per cent being 18 years of age or older.

Related Issues

Relations with Own Children's Teachers

In the interviews some teachers mentioned the fact that they found it an advantage to be a teacher when they conferred with their children's teachers. They believed they were more likely to learn the truth about their children's progress because they were viewed by the teachers as colleagues. I included an item on this topic in the questionnaire, asking teachers to rate whether they believed their relations with their children's teachers were more productive because they were teachers. Fifty three per cent agreed with the statement (31 per cent strongly agreed). However, 27 per cent disagreed, 16 percent did not know, and 4 percent rated the statement as "not applicable" indicating that the teachers did not overwhelmingly agree that being a teacher caused more productive relations with their children's teachers.

Teaching Children of Teachers

Occasionally interviewees said that they did not like teaching the children of teachers. They said sometimes these children could be difficult or the parents overly demanding. Respondents to the questionnaire item on this subject rejected this notion, as only 4 percent agreed with it, 73 percent disagreed, 16 percent indicated "did not know", and 7 percent rated it as not applicable. This response is similar to the interviewees', as only a few teachers expressed this opinion.

Models in Teaching and Parenting

The interviewees expressed a variety of views on the question about models in teaching. However, many of the questionnaire respondents seemed to reject this question, as 36 per cent did not respond to it or rated it as "not applicable". Among those who did respond, 71 per cent agreed that they were influenced by a teacher while 29 per cent indicated that they were not influenced by a former teacher. The large percentage of respondents who found the questionnaire item not applicable suggests that, in its form, it was difficult to respond to.

There was a greater response to the question on models in parenting (only two teachers did not answer it). However, the teachers seemed evenly divided in their assessment of this issue. Forty seven per cent agreed that their parenting behavior was modeled after their parent of the same gender, while 43 per cent disagreed with the statement. Ten per cent expressed no opinion. The interviewees also presented mixed feelings about whether their parents served as models for their own parenting behavior.

Best Aspect of Being a Teaching-Parent

The teachers were asked what they considered the best aspect of the dual role. This open-ended questionnaire item generated responses which seemed to fit into five categories: (1) using teaching knowledge at home (2) developing a broadened perspective (3) using child development knowledge (4) relating to children's friends (5) benefiting from schedule. The teachers' written comments illustrate the themes.

Using teaching knowledge at home
Like the interviewees, these teachers used the knowledge they had developed in the classroom for the benefit of their children. "Knowledge" includes knowing about the school system, curriculum and teaching expertise.

A female kindergarten teacher: "I can help my child deal with the system a bit better."

A female elementary school teacher: "I am more aware of the requirements of the school curriculum as well as of more resources for obtaining help."

A high school female teacher: "It helps me stay abreast of what's going on in our schools."

A middle school female teacher wrote:

> "You have a better idea of what is going on in the school. Can be helpful in dealing with your child's teachers and school, and helping your child through a time with a difficult teacher."

Several teachers wrote about using their teaching skills with their children. A male high school teacher said: "Being able to help your child in your subject matter".

A middle school teacher said: "I know different ways to help get a concept across if they didn't get it in school."

An elementary school teacher: " I know the material and what is to be taught, and I know how to teach it."

A male high school Latin teacher wrote:

> "I know what teachers can and can't, will and won't do. I know I can't rely on them to do everything (I don't want to) for my children. I can see what they [his children] do, and I spend summer and vacations supporting what they've done."

Developing a Broadened Perspective

Some of the teachers said they developed a broadened perspective, an effect the interviewed teachers also talked about. A female kindergarten teacher said:"Broadens my perspective. I am more appreciative of my own daughter's strengths and more understanding of the weaknesses."

A female middle school teacher: "I understood that my children were not unique when certain behavior occurred."

Another kindergarten teacher: "Having more insight and understanding of my children and grandchild."

A female high school teacher: "I don't take confrontations personally."

Another high school teacher: "Understanding the demands of teenagers years before my own get there."

Some teachers referred to their own affective growth: A female middle school teacher: "I've acquired very good skills in dealing patiently with children."

An elementary school teacher wrote: "Greater depth of understanding and compassion ".

A kindergarten teacher: " My profession has enabled me to be a more understanding and insightful parent."

Using Child Development Knowledge

They used what they learned about child development at home and with their students. Some teachers wrote "understanding of child development", others were more specific. A male high school teacher said: "Am well aware of developmental issues, styles, and modes of communicating at work and at home".

A female high school teacher: "Knowing basically, what they are going through at home and at school."

A female kindergarten teacher: "Knowing children develop at different rates so don't pressure them."

Relating to Children's Friends

Some teachers felt that they had better relations with their children's friends because they had taught. A male high school teacher said: "I can relate well to my kids' friends."

A middle school female teacher: "Have good rapport with my son's friends. Am more aware of problems kids encounter and the normalcy of 'stages' they go through."

A female middle school teacher: "I know most of my daughters friends/families because they have been my students."

Benefiting from Schedule

Some teachers found the best aspects of being a teaching-parent the summer vacations and having the same schedule as their children. A middle school female teacher wrote: "...summers off."

A female high school teacher: "Vacations when children are on vacation, similar hours."

When I interviewed the teachers I did not ask them what they considered the best aspect of the dual role. However, when the teachers talked about the reciprocal influences of parenting and teaching, they expressed some of the ideas the respondents identified as " the best aspect". Like the respondents, the interviewees talked about how they used their teaching knowledge "at home". Their perspective toward their own children also broadened because they taught. They, too, used what they knew about child development in each role. However, the interviewees did not talk about better relations with their children's friends nor did they discuss the positive aspects of a teacher's work schedule.

Not all the respondents answered the question about the best aspect of the dual role. Six teachers left it blank and 10 gave minimal answers. The teachers seemed to prefer responding to the question about the hardest aspects of being a teaching parent judging by the greater number of substantive answers to that question. Why the teachers more readily answered the question about the difficulty in the dual role is unclear. One speculation is that it may be easier to identify what is difficult; what is best may be more elusive or harder to define.

Hardest Aspect of the Dual Role

When the teachers were interviewed, they talked with interest and conviction about what they found hard in being a teaching-parent. Most of the respondents answered this open-ended question, suggesting that they, like the interviewees, found it of interest. Four themes emerged from an analysis of their comments: (1) insufficient time, (2) school/home tensions, (3) pressuring own children and (4) awareness of poor teaching. I have included some of the teachers' written comments.

Insufficient Time (and Energy)

The most frequently cited difficulty in the dual role was "not having enough time" (and often, energy, also). Forty- seven per cent of the teachers' comments referred to this issue. Teachers who found this a problem taught at all school levels-from kindergarten to high school.

A middle school teacher said, "No time and energy left for the routine (cooking and cleaning)."

A kindergarten teacher said,

> "Trying to balance quality time with our children and my husband while running a home and pursuing additional degrees in order to keep abreast of the current concepts in education."

Another kindergarten teacher: "Time and energy expended although I taught half days and my children were ages 12-17."

A middle school teacher: "Energy - mentally and physically exhausted by the time I get home (with more school work to do)."

An elementary school teacher: "Having enough of me left at the end of the day to nurture my own children. Needing more time alone time to recharge batteries."

A high school teacher: "Having the time to do both well."

A kindergarten teacher: "The hardest part is being female and having a full time job, a child *and* a second job at home, teaching and parenting."

A high school teacher: "Having the energy to do it all, and do it all well and fairly."

A high school teacher: "Most of my time is spent with adolescents, which is wearing on energies."

Teachers also referred to a lack of patience when they cited insufficient time and energy as a problem in the dual role. Some teachers just wrote "patience" or "having enough   patience". Others were more explicit.   One high school teacher said: "Time constraints and the loss of patience with my children when I come home from school."

Another high school teacher: "Loss of energy and patience at home due to "sameness" of interchanges."

A middle school teacher: "Most of my patience is gone, and I expect more of them (her children) also."

When the interviewees described the hardest aspect of the dual role, they, too, referred to the themes of exhaustion, insufficient time, energy and patience.

School/Home Tensions

Perhaps paradoxically, the knowledge accumulated from teaching sometimes contributed to feelings of conflict in the parental role.   Having a dual perspective - of parent and teacher-did not necessarily cause the teachers to be more objective or content.

An elementary school teacher wrote: "There's a great deal of disappointment and embarrassment on my part when my children fail to do well in school."

Another elementary school teacher: "Knowing when (or when not) to get involved in your own child's school experiences"

A high school teacher: "Continuing the teaching process at home is much more difficult when dealing with your own children. You can't be as objective."

A middle school teacher wrote: "The hardest aspect is separating myself from being the teacher at home."

Another middle school teacher: "Trying to give advice /help to my daughters when they only want to do what their teacher says."

A kindergarten teacher wrote of two tensions: the frustration a teacher feels toward indifferent parents, and the resentment one's own children feel about their mother's (a teacher) commitment to work:

> "The emotional involvement and caring one develops over a student's progress and the frustration over parents' lack of involvement. One's children can become jealous or resent one's concerns about students."

Pressuring Own Children

We have seen that 55% of the teachers said they exerted pressure on their children. Some teachers cited this as the hardest aspect of the dual role.

A middle school teacher wrote: "Pressuring my own child more because I am a teacher. I struggled with my reactions to my son's productivity or lack of it particularly since he was in the same school system."

An elementary school teacher also referred to the problem of teaching in the same school system her children attended: "My children go to school in the system I teach in and this is a disadvantage for them. I put too much pressure on them, as I know their teachers."

A high school teacher wrote: "I place too much pressure on my own children."

Awareness of Poor Teaching

Some teachers found the poor teaching practices of other teachers the hardest aspect of being a teaching-parent.

A high school teacher wrote: "Seeing some of the poor teaching and inhuman individuals that are in the teaching profession..."

Another high school teacher: "Appalled at quality of home-work given by other professionals."

And another high school teacher wrote: "Knowing how my colleagues sometimes behave (what motivates them) and keeping my mouth shut to my own children so that they can still respect them."

Many of the teachers' comments reveal the frustration they experience in being a teaching-parent. They contend with limitations of time and energy imposed by the nature of their work. Although teachers use their teaching knowledge "at home", some are unable to be as effective with their own children as they are with their students. When the interviewed teachers talked about what was hard in teaching, parenting and in the dual role, they, too, mentioned some of these problems.

Teachers' Unsolicited Comments

The teachers were given an opportunity to add comments at the end of the questionnaire. Twenty-two of the 55 teachers made additional remarks, indicating that these teachers wanted to say more than the questionnaire items allowed for. Where possible, I have tried to make connections between the comments and the ideas expressed in the questionnaire items or by the interviewees. I have also tried to note what seem to be new ideas, not previously expressed by the interviewees and respondents.

I have included information about the teachers -such as gender, age, level of teaching, ages of their children -when they provided it.

Themes of Difficulty

We have seen that teachers feel a sense of disappointment or dissatisfaction when they cannot do for their children what they can for their students. Sometimes teachers blame themselves when their child does not "measure up" to their expectations.

A 47 year old elementary school teacher with children aged 19, 17, and 11 wrote:

> "... I would like to further elaborate on the feeling that I have pertaining to the conflicts of being a teacher/parent. My oldest child, a girl, has been quite successful during her school career. However, my two sons are the opposite. No matter how hard I try, I cannot seem to successfully motivate them to aspire to greater heights. They always seem to choose to do the minimal amount of tasks required. Unfortunately I have a tendency to hold myself accountable for their failures, due to the fact that I am an educator who should be, in my opinion, more effective in motivating my own children as well as I do those that I teach."

Using teaching knowledge is not foolproof. Teachers have alluded to the problem of knowing when to intervene in a child's school situation: A 42 year old female middle school teacher with children of 13 and 11 wrote:

> "...teachers who are parents must be very careful in the way that they approach their own child's school and teachers. Over the years, I have felt uncomfortable at times having to walk that very thin line. To remember my place, and then when necessary to "go to bat" for my child. On several occasions my children have had teachers who were, in my judgment, doing a very poor job.....It is these choices that a teaching-parent is confronted with. The choice is not always an easy one."

And a 44 year old female middle school teacher with a 10 year old son refers to the issue of using her judgment as a teacher with her own child:

> "I think I *do* pressure my son more than I would if I weren't a teacher. I'm not sure, now that I think of it if 'pressure' is the correct term for me. Perhaps I show a greater concern because I think (maybe wrongly) that I really know what the teacher wants in each assignment because I know what I'd want."

Many of the teachers have talked about the complexities of being a working parent. A 32 year old female teacher refers to this problem but concludes that teaching is better than her other work:

> "It is not an easy job being both a female parent and teaching. I expend a lot of energy during the school day, then I have to go home and run errands, taxi children, cook, clean, paperwork etc. Sometimes it feels like I can't do it all and that I may be cheating my family. But I could not just sit home all day and be the parent. Coming from the food service industry into teaching has made life a little easier. Before teaching I worked 6 days 10-12 hours per day, weekends and holidays."

Positive Themes

More of the teachers who added comments identified an advantage to the dual role. Interviewed teachers have described how knowledge of children's familial and social pressures can be useful as classroom teachers. A 34 year old first grade woman teacher with adolescent children said:

> "I feel that parents who are teachers have a much better understanding of the lifestyle of children than do childless

teachers. We understand their other commitments and have a much more realistic view of the amount of time that can be spent on homework."

A former elementary school teacher, currently a principal, age 47 and mother of an 18 year old wrote: "I see a greater empathy for behavioral differences among my teachers who are parents."

Teachers referred to the theme of being able to help a parent because they had similar experience. A 43 year old kindergarten teacher with three teen aged children wrote:

> "...when a child is difficult I discuss this child with the parent and give them concrete suggestions that I think will work ...having had a bright but difficult child myself and been through a lot of worry and soul searching with each one of my children".

And a 52 year old female high school teacher: "My youngest child who is now an adult is handicapped. Being his mother helped me understand the whole constellation of problems with such students and their families."

A few teachers wrote about the positive, reciprocal effects of one role on the other. A female high school french teacher said: "I was a teacher before I became a parent, and through teaching I have developed better parenting skills."

A female kindergarten teacher with three grown sons:

> "Since my sons were older when I went back to teaching and because I taught half days, I had enough energy and time for the dual role; as a matter of fact I feel my teaching aided me as a parent and parenting greatly aided me as a teacher. I had the added advantage of parenting 3 children ..."

A 47 year old male high school teacher with two adolescent children expressed the *same* viewpoint the male interviewees on the question of how one role affected the other: "Being a parent has much more of a positive effect on teaching than being a teacher has on being a parent."

Two teachers wrote about how their own children's perspective help them as teachers. This idea was not previously mentioned by the interviewees or respondents. The 34 year old first grade teacher said:

> "We hear from our children about unfair practices of teachers and so are more aware of and able to avoid falling into them. One of these is punishing a whole class because of a few in the hope that peer pressure will improve behavior. Another is making judgments without all the facts. I could go on but I'm sure you understand that we hear both sides and so we have a better understanding of a child's point of view."

And a 41 year old first grade teacher with two adolescents:

> "My kids help me be more perceptive. They remember what it was like to be 6 and 7 and often remind me how it felt to be a first grader....I have an understanding of the expectations of their days, too; they're long and busy. School is hard work for all of us!"

Two teachers said there should be forums for teachers and parents to share ideas. A 47 elementary school teacher with three children wrote about the need of teaching-parents:

> "I wish there was a support group for parents [such] as ourselves. Such a group is truly needed in order to provide forum for us to express our concerns, frustrations and mutual support."

A kindergarten teacher with grown children said:

> "Many of the children in today's classes are from single parent homes. It would be so helpful to many teachers if the college would offer a Saturday workshop which could suggest ways to help parents and students adjust and grown positively in this situation. So many are bitter and resentful which serves to impede intellectual and social/emotional development."

Some comments of interest in this study:

A male high school teacher with two young sons: "This is very interesting - please don't wait too long to make your finds known". A 44 year old female teacher with one son: "This questionnaire is truly food for thought. Thank you for making me clarify some things in my own mind.

A 48 year old middle school English teacher with three grown children: "would love to talk to you about this!"

A 47 year old high school teacher with grown children: "I think your study is a valuable one. I look forward to learning the results."

A 43 year old female kindergarten teacher with teen age children: "It is fascinating to me the research you are doing, and I'm interested in it personally and professionally".

Concluding Thoughts

We have seen that, in general, the respondents and interviewed teachers had similar views about the effects of being a teaching parent. While they resembled each other in age, gender, marital status and number of children, they differed in other ways. Some of the respondents taught in urban schools while the interviewees taught only in suburban schools. The groups also differed in teaching levels. Some of the respondents taught at the kindergarten level, while none of the interviewed teachers did. More of the respondents taught high school while more of the interviewed teachers taught at the elementary and middle school levels.

What emerges from a comparison of the groups is that despite their differences there is a consistency in the perspectives of the teaching-parents. It might be asserted that the experience of the dual role would necessarily result in the development of common perspectives. However, the limited number of studies of teaching-parents, in turn, limits the assumption of this conclusion.

NOTES

1. <u>New York Times</u>, section 2, p. 15, April 1, 1990.
2. Brookhart and Freeman, 1992.

Chapter Six

Conclusion

If we accept Lortie's concept of teaching as unique work - because teachers, unlike others, work with the changeful nature of children - I assert that teaching-parents are especially unique. Living and working with children gives them opportunities to use what they learn from one role in the other. The teachers have given eloquent testimony about the subtle and complex effects of being a teaching-parent.

By claiming that teaching parents are in a unique position, I do not mean to imply that the dual role necessarily has uniform effects on them. Although the interviewed teachers had many characteristics in common, not the least of which was teaching in suburban settings, they also clearly differed from each other. Just in their reactions to the interview itself - some teachers relished the opportunity to be reflective and analytic. Others seemed to enjoy thinking and expressing their thoughts once the interview got underway. Still others presented factual information without interpretation or speculation. I welcomed the teachers' different approaches to the interview because it was evidence of the variations within a group which, by some of its characteristics, could be called homogeneous. It probably goes without saying that the effects of the dual role ultimately depend on whether the circumstances of a teacher's professional life and her/his personal characteristics make it possible to apply knowledge from one domain to the other. The teaching experience of a first grade teacher will not affect her parenting behavior if her children are adults. Also, an unreflective person is unlikely to abstract knowledge from one setting for use in another.

What Teaching Parents Learned

If the effects of being a teaching-parent depend on personal circumstances and perspective, can any generalizations be made about them? The patterns generated from the teachers' descriptions suggest that there were shared viewpoints about the effects of the dual role. Analysis of the content of the comments makes it possible to claim that the combination of teaching and parenting generally enlightened and enriched the teachers. What they learned is not formulaic; it is subtle and fluid. For some teachers the effects of one role on the other were so intertwined that it was difficult to describe them separately.

Not An Unequivocal Boon

The teachers' testimony also reveals that being a teaching-parent had its negative aspects. Teachers described situations which produced feelings of frustration and even sadness. It was painful for teachers who were successful with students to be unable to help their own child. Some teachers were frustrated by what they perceived to be the poor teaching their children received. A few others felt that their children were shortchanged because the patience they used as teachers left them with an insufficient amount at home.

Use of Teaching Parents in Schools

Generalizing about teaching-parents may be problematic because as a group they seem to be both unique and diverse. At the risk of overstatement, I suggest that there may be ways teaching-parents could be useful in schools. I did not ask the teachers if they thought that they might be of particular use in schools. My hunch is that question would have been off-putting. The teachers did not see themselves as special or as knowing more than other teachers. And I am not necessarily attributing these characteristics to them. Even the variety of teachers within the group of 50 interviewees defies such a formulation. Still, the testimony of the teachers reveals that many have, in fact, learned from the experience of being a teaching-parent. I think that those who have the inclination to share what they have learned could be helpful to parents and to educators without children.

With Parents

I must say that as I suggest ways in which teaching-parents may be helpful to parents, I in no way mean to imply that teachers without children are lacking in empathy, acuity or sensitivity toward students and parents.

Both the interviewed teachers and questionnaire respondents said that the clearest effect of parenting on teaching was an increased understanding of parents. When teachers became parents they understood them in new ways. They realized how powerful a parent's attachment to a child can be. They understood the limitations in parenting - that a parent could not necessarily make a child do a task. They knew first-hand how sensitive and defensive parents can be.

Being a parent has never been easy. Parents today may be more isolated and vulnerable than in previous generations. They lack the support of the extended family. In most two parent households both parents work. Women have less contact with their children than their mothers had with them. The use of "quality time" is a solution, but does it necessarily work to the satisfaction of parents and children? Parents are probably more enlightened about child-rearing than their parents were. They clearly have access to much more literature on the subject. But they have less first-hand knowledge of children. When both parents work, they not only have less time with their children, they also have less familiarity with their children's friends, and so have limited knowledge of the range of normal behavior. Teachers today are often called upon to provide support and information for bewildered parents. I suggest that teaching-parents could act as a professional and colleague to parents whose limited experience with children has made them needful of advisement. Teaching-parents could use their experience to help parents understand their children in relation to other children. Teaching-parents may have a credibility with other parents because of their parenting experience. It may be easier for parents to reveal their concerns to teachers who may have had similar problems.

Parents today may have to make more educational decisions than they were required to in the past. Yet because most parents work, they have less time than parents of previous generations to devote to school issues.

With the advent of school decentralization and possibly of school voucher plans, parents will have to make choices about their children's educational future. Teaching-parents could play a role in helping parents choose an educational program which will meet the needs of their children. Having had experience with the social and familial aspects of a student's life, teaching-parents might be able to advise parents who must make decisions with little knowledge about their educational options. The teaching-parent's perspective may be useful in the development of programs which will help parents to make educational choices about which they might feel unprepared.

With Educators

Teaching-parents may be of help to educators who do not have children. Although they have no monopoly on kindness, empathy or insight, their perspective as parents may be useful to teachers without their experience.

An elementary school principal told me that in his an affluent, suburban school, "People leave the profession because they lack the ability to relate to parents - and they can be excellent teachers".[1] He thought that the skill which some teachers lacked in communicating with parents could certainly be learned. Pre-service or in-service courses which focused on the perspective of the parent could help teachers understand them. Teaching-parents could be useful in the design of these programs.

Bridging the Gap

Parents, too, need to understand more about teachers. Some teachers described how demoralized they felt by parents' lack of respect for them. It is not news that teachers are less valued in contemporary society than in the past. Reasons for this development deserve a more through analysis than can be provided here. It must be noted though that the lack of appreciation for their work is a burden for teachers who are the targets of that sentiment.

It must also be said that not all teachers value parent involvement in school. According to John Goodlad, "most educators are comfortable when parents confine involvement [in school] to home activities that directly support their own child's education".[2]

I suggest that teaching-parents might bridge the gap that exists between parents, teachers, home and school. This idea is not new. Twenty four years ago the head of a school reported on the dissatisfaction he felt because he lacked knowledge of how his own children were doing in his own school. From this need he initiated a parent involvement program in the school.[3] I think teaching-parents could understand this perspective and could take a leadership role in developing ways to bridge the gaps of understanding between teachers and parents.

Concluding Thoughts

I do not mean to suggest that teaching-parents have all the answers to the problems of teachers and parents. In fact, some readers who are teaching-parents may wonder why they should assume new burdens when they are already overworked. My suggestions for new roles they might play would also include that they be excused from some of their conventional responsibilities. Perhaps more important than that clarification is that I reiterate my view that teaching-parents are not more able than other teachers. I suggest that we look to them for ideas because their experience might be put to a more general use.

I have looked at what teachers have said about the effects of teaching and parenting out of the conviction that we must pay attention to teachers' concerns and beliefs. There is a growing trend in education and politics which asserts that it is at our peril as a nation that we ignore teachers' needs. An initial step toward making life better for teachers is to ask them how they would want their teaching lives improved. When these teaching-parents reflected on the relation between their personal and professional lives, they identified elements of concern as well as of satisfaction.

Future Research

Occasionally I was asked if I would interview the children of teachers. I think implicit in the question was the idea that if I really wanted to learn the truth about the effects of teaching and parenting, ask the children. However, I dismissed the question as I did the one about interviewing teachers who were not parents. The merit of the question became more apparent after some teachers described the anguish they felt in being unable to help their children - although they were successful teachers. We know children can sense our feelings. What are the effects on children when they sense their parent's frustration or disappointment in being unable to help them? Future research might explore how children perceive the benefits and burdens of having a parent who is also a teacher.

NOTES

1. Personal communication, March 1990.
2. "Parents and Schools", 1988, p.1.
3. Green, 1968.

Appendix A
Teaching-Parenting Interview Questions

Date_____

Name_____

School_____

Age____   # of Children_____

Marital Status M D S W   # yrs as Teacher_____

Sex____   # yrs as Parent_____

1. Which were you first, a parent or a teacher? _____

2. For how long only a parent or only a teacher? _____

3. Why did you become a teacher?
   a. interested in children_____
   b. interested in the subject you teach_____
   c. interested in teaching others_____
   d. wanted to help others_____
   e. didn't like other work_____
   f. other_____

(Note: In the second and third rounds of interviews, I added the choice, "parental pressure to become a teacher" because it was mentioned by teachers in the first round of inquiry).

4. If first a teacher, what grade level or subjects did you teach?_____ What do you teach now?

5. Do you think your being a parent has influenced you as a teacher? In what ways?

6. Has your teaching affected your parenting? How?

7.(If not mentioned in question 5) Has your relations with parents been affected by your being a teacher?

8. What is hardest for you in teaching?

9. Hardest in parenting?

10. Hardest about the combination of the two roles?

11. What about conferences with other teaching-parents: are they easier, harder, the same as with other parents?

12. Relations with your children's teachers: are they easier or better because you're a teacher? Does it depend on your particular child, or can you describe your feelings about conferences with your children's teachers?

13. Are your concerns about your own kids heightened because you are a teacher? (are they lessened- maybe already gave answer).

14. Was your mother's mothering behavior a model for you? (or father's)

15. Was there a teacher in your life whose behavior you model your teaching approach after?

16. Is your teaching and parenting style similar or different? (i.e. permissive as a parent, strict as a teacher, etc.)

17. What is most satisfying for you as a parent?

18. What is most satisfying in teaching?
(Note: I did not ask questions 17 and 18 in the second and third rounds of interviews.)

Appendix B
Teaching/Parenting Questionnaire

Today's Date_____

Name_____(optional)

Name of School_____

School Address_____
(including zip)_____

Age_____ Marital Status: S_____ M_____ D_____ W_____
Sex: M_____ F_____

Education: BA_____BA plus 30 credits_____ plus 60_____
   MA_____MA plus 30 credits_____ Other_____

1. Why did you become a teacher? (Rank in order of importance: 1= least important, 5= most important)
a. interested in children_____ b. interested in the subject_____
c. wanted to help others_____ d. parental pressure to become
a teacher_____ e. didn't know what else to do_____
f. other_____

2. Which were you first, a parent or a teacher?
Teacher first_____ Parent first_____

Rate the following statements using the scale: 5=strongly
agree, 4=agree, 3=not sure, 2=disagree, 1=agree, 0=not applicable.
3. Teaching has broadened my perspective toward my own
children._____

4. I know what to expect from my children because I am a
teacher._____

5. I use the knowledge and skills I have developed as a teacher with my own children._____

6. The patience I expend in the classroom often leaves me with an insufficient amount for my children._____

7. The same kind of energy is used in teaching and parenting. This is a disadvantage of the dual role._____

8. Because I am a teacher I think I pressure my own children more than I might if I weren't in education._____

9. I think my relations with my children's teachers are more productive because I an a teaching-parent._____

10. I don't like teaching children whose parents are teachers_____.

11. I mother (father) my child(ren) in a similar way to that in which my mother (father) brought me up._____

12. A teacher (or teachers) I had as a student has influenced me as a teacher.   Grade level or subject the teacher taught.

_____

13. Hardest aspect of the dual role of teaching and parenting

_____

_____

14. Best aspect of the dual role_____

_____

IF YOU WERE FIRST A TEACHER, answer the following questions:

15. What grade level or subjects did you teach?_____
What do you teach now?_____

16. If you changed grade level or subject after becoming a parent did you do so: (check appropriate choice(s):
a. because you prefer this subject_____ b. because you prefer this grade level_____ c. because an opening occurred at that time_____ d. other_____

17. What are the ages and sex of you children?_____
_____

18. What age are the students you now teach?_____

Rate the following statements on a scale of: 5=strongly agree 4=agree, 3=not sure, 2=disagree, 1=strongly disagree, 0=not applicable.

19. Being a parent has affected me as a teacher._____

20. I think I am more empathic toward students now than before I was a parent._____

21. I think I have a greater understanding of parents now than before I was a parent._____

22. Before being a parent, I think I was more rigid in my expectations of students._____

23. I have a greater understanding of students' family and social obligations now than before I was a parent._____

24. Because I understand the "whole" student, I think I have somewhat compromised my academic standards._____

IF YOU WERE FIRST A PARENT BEFORE YOU WERE A TEACHER, answer the following:
25. What grade level or subject do you teach?_____

26. What are the ages and sex of you children?_____
_____

27. What age are the students you now teach?_____

Rate the following statements on a scale of 5=strongly agree, 4=agree, 3=not sure, 2= disagree, 1=strongly disagree, 0=not applicable.
28. Being a parent has affected me as a teacher._____

29. I think I'm more empathic toward students because I'm a parent._____

30. Being a parent helps me to understand the parent of my students._____

32. I understand the familial and social pressures students have because I'm a parent._____

33. I think I may compromise my academic standards because I am understanding of the "whole" student._____

34. Because I have children, I expect more of my students_____
ADD ANY COMMENTS WHICH YOU THINK MAY HELP IN UNDERSTANDING OF THE DUAL ROLE. USE BACK OF QUESTIONNAIRE. THANKS VERY MUCH!

Bibliography

Apter, Terri. *Altered loves: mothers and daughters during adolescence.* New York: St. Martin's Press, 1990.

Barth, Roland S. *Improving schools from within.* San Francisco: Jossey - Bass, 1990.

Bateson, Mary Catherine. *Composing a life.* New York: Atlantic Monthly Press, 1989.

Brookhart, Susan M. and Freeman, Donald J. "Characteristics of entering teacher candidates." *Review of Educational Research* 62 (1) 33-70, 1992.

Cameron, Deborah. *Feminism and linguistic theory.* New York: St. Martin's Press, 1985.

Claesson, Margaret A. "Teacher/Mothers: problems of a dual role." Paper presented at the Annual Meeting of the American Educational Research Association, San Francisco, 1986, April.

Dinnerstein, Dorothy. *The mermaid and the minataur: sexual arrangements and human malaise.* New York: Harper & Row, 1976.

Feistritzer, C. Emily. *The condition of teaching: a state by state analysis.* Princeton: The Carnegie Foundation for the Advancement of Teaching, 1983.

Gilligan, Carol. *In a different voice.* Cambridge: Harvard University Press, 1982.

Glaser, Barney G. and Strauss, Anselm L. *The discovery of grounded theory.* Chicago: Aldine Publishing Co., 1967.

Green, Laurence. *Parents and teachers: partners or rivals.* London: George Allen and Unwin Ltd., 1968.

Grumet, Madeline R. *Bitter milk.* Amherst: University of Massachusetts Press, 1988.

Hulsebosch, Patricia L. "Mothering and teaching: connections and collaboration." *Kappa Delta Pi Record* 26 (4) 101-05, 1990.

_____. "Significant others: teachers' perceptions on relationships with parents." In W.H. Schubert and W.C. Ayers (Eds.) *Teacher lore* (pp 107 - 132). New York: Longman, 1992.

Humphreys, Josephine. *Dreams of sleep.* New York: Viking, 1984.

Katz, Lillian G. "Mothering and teaching: some significant distinctions." In L.G.Katz (Ed.) *Current Topics in Early Childhood Education* Vol.3, (pp 47-64) Norwood NJ: Ablex, 1980.

Kidder, Tracy. *Among schoolchildren.* Boston: Houghton Mifflin, 1989.

Lennard, Henry L. and Bernstein, Arnold. *Anatomy of psychotherapy: systems of communication and exploration.* New York: Columbia University Press, 1960.

Lightfoot, Sara L. *Worlds apart.* New York: Basic Books, 1978.

Lively, Pamela. *Passing on.* New York: Grove Press, 1989.

Lortie, Dan C. *Schoolteacher.* Chicago: University of Chicago Press, 1975.

MacDonald, Judith B. "Analysis of communication patterns in social studies discussions: a strategy to promote discourse." In D.B.Strahan (Ed.) *Middle School Research* Greensboro, NC: National Middle School Association, 1986.

MacKinnon Roger and Michels, Robert. *The psychiatric interview.* Philadelphia: W.B. Saunders Co, 1971.

Maeroff, Gene I. *The empowerment of teachers.* New York: Teachers College Press, 1988.

McPherson, Gertrude H. *Small town teacher.* Cambridge: Harvard University Press, 1972.

Mishler, Elliot G. *Research interviewing.* Cambridge: Harvard University Press, 1986.

Nias, Jennifer. *Primary teachers talking.* London: Routledge, 1989.

"Parents and Schools". *Harvard Education Letter* IV (6) 1-3, Nov./Dec. 1988.

Rose, Phyllis. *Parallel lives.* New York: Knopf, 1983.

Ruddick, Sara. *Maternal thinking: towards a politics of peace.* Boston: Beacon Press, 1989.

Sills, Barbara and Henry, Jeannie. *Mother to mother baby care book.* New York: Avon, 1981.

Spencer, Dee Ann. *Contemporary women teachers.* New York: Longman, 1986.

Spock, Benjamin. *Baby and child care.* New York: Pocket Books, 1976.

Wolcott, Harry F. "On seeking -and rejecting- validity in qualitative research". In E.W.Eisner and A. Peshkin (Eds.) *Qualitative inquiry in education.* (pp. 121-152) New York: Teachers College Press, 1990.

Index

A

B

C

H

hard in parenting 61
hardest about dual role 66
    feeling of exhaustion 67
hardest aspect of the dual role 112
    awareness of poor teaching 112, 115
    insufficient time 112, 113
    pressuring own children 112, 115
    school/home tensions 112, 114
Henry 3, 11
high school 3, 5, 17
high school teachers 6
homework 26, 30, 31, 36, 37, 38
    changes in attitude 30
Hulsebosch 2, 11, 15, 71, 91
Humphreys 13, 21, 71, 91

K

Katz 2, 11, 24
Kidder 36, 61, 69, 91

L

lack of student respect 60
lack of time 56
Lennard 4, 11
Lennard and Bernstein 4, 11
Lightfoot 2, 11, 71, 91
listening 51
listening experience as a teacher 44
Lively 13, 21
Lortie 3, 11, 61, 91, 123

Q

questionnaire participants 94
questionnaire respondents
    awareness of teacching 115
    benefiting from schedule 111
    best aspect of being a teaching parent 109
    characteristics of questionnaire respondents 95
    conflicts of being a teacher/parent 117
    developing a broadened perspective 110
  flexibility 101
    hardest aspect of the dual role 112
    insufficient time and energy 21
    models in teaching and parenting 108
    pressure 118
    reasons for becoming teachers 98
    relating to children's friends 111
    relations with own children's teachers 107
    school/home tensions 114
    student's familial and social pressures 104
    teaching children of teachers 108
    understanding of parents 102
    understanding of the pressures students 102
    using child development knowledge 111
    using teaching knowledge at home 109

R

reasons for becoming teachers 17, 98
relating to children's friends 111
relations with own children's teachers 107
research on teaching-parents 69
responsibility 62
Rose 90, 91
routines learned in the classroom 43
Ruddick 14, 21, 62, 91

Autobiographical Sketch

Judith B. MacDonald is a native New Yorker who attended its public schools and began her teaching career there as an elementary school teacher. When she became a mother, she found that her perspective toward students had changed. For several years she has explored how other teaching-parents react to the dual role.

Ms. MacDonald received her B.A. from Brown University and M.A. and Ed.D. from Teachers College, Columbia University. She is currently an Associate Professor at Montclair State in the Department of Curriculum and Teaching.

Islam and Business: Cross-Cultural and Cross-National Perspectives

Kip Becker, PhD
Editor

Islam and Business: Cross-Cultural and Cross-National Perspectives has been co-published simultaneously as *Journal of Transnational Management Development*, Volume 9, Numbers 2/3 2004.

International Business Press®
An Imprint of The Haworth Press, Inc.

New York • London • Victoria (AU)
www.HaworthPress.com

Published by

International Business Press®, 10 Alice Street, Binghamton, NY 13904-1580 USA

International Business Press® is an imprint of The Haworth Press, Inc., 10 Alice Street, Binghamton, NY 13904-1580 USA.

Islam and Business: Cross-Cultural and Cross-National Perspectives has been co-published simultaneously as *Journal of Transnational Management Development*, Volume 9, Numbers 2/3 2004.

Cover design by Lora Wiggins

Library of Congress Cataloging-in-Publication Data

Islam and business : cross-cultural and cross-national perspectives / Kip Becker editor.
    p. cm.

    "Journal of transnational management development monographic "separates.""
    Includes bibliographical references and index.
    ISBN 0-7890-2516-7 (hard cover : alk. paper) – ISBN 0-7890-2517-5 (pbk. : alk. paper)
    1. Islam–Economic aspects. 2. Business–Religious aspects–Islam. 3. Economics–Religious aspects–Islam. I. Becker, Kip.

BP173.75.I766 2004
297.2'73–dc22

                                                                    2004010050

Indexing, Abstracting & Website/Internet Coverage

This section provides you with a list of major indexing & abstracting services. That is to say, each service began covering this periodical during the year noted in the right column. Most Websites which are listed below have indicated that they will either post, disseminate, compile, archive, cite or alert their own Website users with research-based content from this work. (This list is as current as the copyright date of this publication.)

Abstracting, Website/Indexing Coverage . . . . Year When Coverage Began

- *ABI/INFORM Global. Contents of this publication are indexed and abstracted in the ABI/INFORM Global database available on ProQuest Information & Learning @www.proquest.com* **2000**

- *ABI/INFORM Research. Contents of this publication are indexed and abstracted in the ABI/INFORM Research database, available on ProQuest Information & Learning @www.proquest.com* **2000**

- *Cambridge Scientific Abstracts (Risk Abstracts) <http://www.csa.com>* **1994**

- *EconLit, on CD-ROM, and e-JEL* **1994**

- *Foods Adlibra* **1994**

- *GEO Abstracts (GEO Abstracts/GEOBASE) <http://URL:www.elsevier.nl>* **2001**

- *International Development Abstracts* **1995**

- *"LABORDOC" Library-Periodicals Section "Abstracts Section" <http://www.ilo.org>* **2001**

- *Management & Marketing Abstracts <http://www.pira.co.uk/>* . . . **1994**

(continued)

* **Exact start date to come.**

Special Bibliographic Notes related to special journal issues (separates) and indexing/abstracting:

- indexing/abstracting services in this list will also cover material in any "separate" that is co-published simultaneously with Haworth's special thematic journal issue or DocuSerial. Indexing/abstracting usually covers material at the article/chapter level.
- monographic co-editions are intended for either non-subscribers or libraries which intend to purchase a second copy for their circulating collections.
- monographic co-editions are reported to all jobbers/wholesalers/approval plans. The source journal is listed as the "series" to assist the prevention of duplicate purchasing in the same manner utilized for books-in-series.
- to facilitate user/access services all indexing/abstracting services are encouraged to utilize the co-indexing entry note indicated at the bottom of the first page of each article/chapter/contribution.
- this is intended to assist a library user of any reference tool (whether print, electronic, online, or CD-ROM) to locate the monographic version if the library has purchased this version but not a subscription to the source journal.
- individual articles/chapters in any Haworth publication are also available through The Haworth Document Delivery Service (HDDS).

Islam and Business: Cross-Cultural and Cross-National Perspectives

CONTENTS

ABOUT THE EDITOR

Kip Becker, PhD, is Associate Professor and Chairman of the Department of Administrative Sciences at Boston University. Prior to entering academe, he worked with TDX systems of Cable and Wireless Ltd. in marketing, the US Department of Justice, and was a helicopter pilot for the US Army. He has published numerous articles and book chapters in national and international publications in the areas of international management, strategy, marketing, and global service sector issues. He is currently on the editorial review boards of *Marketing*, the *Journal of Yugoslav Marketing Association*, the *Journal of Marketing Channels*, and the *Journal of Teaching in International Business*, and serves on the managing board of the International Management Development Association. Dr. Becker owns a waterfront restaurant and is President of Northwind Management International which has conducted management training and consulting with governments and associations worldwide.

Introduction

This is a particularly exciting volume as it highlights Islam business issues. The volume focuses on business transactions in: Turkey, Jordan with supporting articles from Egypt and Lebanon.

Turkish Authors. The Umit Ozen and Fusun Ulengin article proposes a framework to guide corporations in their policy making and strategic planning activities. The proposed tool will help the group members to articulate their business vision and the comprehensive set of strategic objectives which will result in a clear understanding of the strategic direction of the corporation. It also underlines the basic similarities and differences of opinions among the members of a management team to see whether there are subgroups which have dominant roles in the structure of a shared map. The article by Fatih Semercioz and Burak Kocer investigates antecedents of success/failure in strategic alliances, which is implemented by airline companies as a response to globalization and liberal government policies. The relationship between Turkish Airlines and Qualiflyer Group has been taken as a case study to present the question in terms of matching the goals, partner selection, alliance management, and areas of cooperation. Suat Teker and M. Baris Akçay article concerning the Bank for International Settlements (BIS) presents an interesting discussion of bank risk and actions necessary to manage it in Turkey. The article simulates the Turkish financial crises of November 2000 and February 2001 as stress scenarios and reveals that all methods except standard method can stand the crisis in November 2000, but none of the models can stand the crisis in February 2001.

[Haworth co-indexing entry note]: "Introduction." Becker, Kip. Co-published simultaneously in *Journal of Transnational Management Development* (The International Business Press, an imprint of The Haworth Press, Inc.) Vol. 9, No. 2/3, 2004, pp. 1-2; and: *Islam and Business: Cross-Cultural and Cross-National Perspectives* (ed: Kip Becker) The International Business Press, an imprint of The Haworth Press, Inc., 2004, pp. 1-2. Single or multiple copies of this article are available for a fee from The Haworth Document Delivery Service [1-800-HAWORTH, 9:00 a.m. - 5:00 p.m. (EST). E-mail address: docdelivery@haworthpress.com].

Digital Object Identifier: 10.1300/J130v09n02_01

1

Jordanian Authors. The article by Aktham Maghyereh additionally address major financial sector liberalization. The effects of the Jordanian reform on the efficiency of the banking sector is evaluated. For the skeptics that question the lessening of government ownership/control his study purported an observable increase in efficiency and that large banks demonstrated the faster productivity growth during the liberalization. Jamal Abu-Doleh's paper provides insights into the current plans, procedures and practices of management training and development (MTD) needs assessment in the Jordanian private and public organizations. In contrast to the efficiency depicted in the prior article this article determined that the overwhelming majority of the respondents report assessing their managers training need in the absence of functional and organizational needs analysis. The article by Hala M. Sabri examines if certain dimensions of the socio-cultural values could explain certain types of organizational culture. The study first investigates employees' perceptions of the existing and preferred cultural orientations in four Jordanian organizations, and then it compares the results with other studies conducted in other cultures (American and South African).

Authors from Egypt and Lebanon. Mahmoud A. Elgamal study tests a comprehensive model of relationships between transactional and transformational leadership trust in organizations, organizational justice, intention to leave and organizational citizenship behavior. While the author is from Kuwait the study was conducted in private Egyptian organizations. The concluding article by Said M. Ladki and Mira W. Sadik examines the tourism industry in Lebanon from the devastation of the civil war to its current state. Despite the increase in the number of arrivals to Lebanon, the industry is experiencing several weaknesses that are directly affecting its advancement. Their discussion has direct relevance to other nations in the region that are seeking a share of the tourism market.

Kip Becker

SECTION I:
BUSINESS IN TURKEY

Exploring the Differences of Managers' Mental Model

Umit Ozen

Fusun Ulengin

SUMMARY. The aim of this research is to propose a framework that will guide the corporations in their policy making and strategic planning activities. The proposed tool will help the group members to articulate their business vision and the comprehensive set of strategic objectives which will result in a clear understanding of the strategic direction of the corporation. It will also be possible to satisfy agreement on strategies, good cooperation, teamwork, with an effective communication among group members. Finally, it will also be possible to underline the basic similarities and differences of opinions among the members of a management team and to see whether there are subgroups which have dominant roles in the structure of a shared map. *[Article copies available for a fee from The Haworth Document Delivery Service: 1-800-HAWORTH. E-mail address: <docdelivery@haworthpress.com> Website: <http://www.HaworthPress. com> © 2004 by The Haworth Press, Inc. All rights reserved.]*

KEYWORDS. Group decision support system, cognitive mapping, learning, strategic planning, group model building

Umit Ozen is affiliated with DupontSA, Amsterdam, The Netherlands.

Fusun Ulengin is Professor of Industrial Engineering, Istanbul Technical University Isletme Fak., Endustri Muh. Bl., 80680, Macka, Istanbul, Turkey (E-mail: ulengin@itu.edu.tr).

[Haworth co-indexing entry note]: "Exploring the Differences of Managers' Mental Model." Ozen, Umit, and Fusun Ulengin. Co-published simultaneously in *Journal of Transnational Management Development* (The International Business Press, an imprint of The Haworth Press, Inc.) Vol. 9, No. 2/3, 2004, pp. 5-27; and: *Islam and Business: Cross-Cultural and Cross-National Perspectives* (ed: Kip Becker) The International Business Press, an imprint of The Haworth Press, Inc., 2004, pp. 5-27. Single or multiple copies of this article are available for a fee from The Haworth Document Delivery Service [1-800-HAWORTH, 9:00 a.m. - 5:00 p.m. (EST). E-mail address: docdelivery@haworthpress.com].

Mintzberg (1979) notes that managers individually carry in their heads a rich dynamic map of their policy domains that they are continually updating. However, these maps are informal and largely undocumented and not communicated well to subordinates or colleagues who might be able to use the information to the organization's advantage.

On the other hand, members of an organization share to a greater or lesser extent beliefs, values, motives and orientations. The degree of sharing varies greatly between individuals in an organization, and from organization to organization (Smith 1992).

In studying organizational processes, it is useful to examine individual belief systems. It is essential, however, to examine also the extent to which these beliefs are shared by members within an organization and the subsequent strengths and weaknesses that this sharing lends to organizational functioning.

The aim of this research is, to propose a framework that will guide the corporations in their policy making and strategic planning activities. The formal modeling approach used in this study might facilitate the building of a shared map from which a requisite variety of policies could be derived in real time. The outcomes of this framework will be: (a) a clear statement of goals, key issues and strategic options, (b) an understanding of the areas where basic differences of opinions occur among the members of the management team, (c) a learning process through which the management team will finally have a common understanding and commitment to action to deliver selected policies, (d) a comprehensive decision support tool, the output of which can be used as input to the time scheduling of the realization of different strategic options and to a simulation model to analyze the viability and robustness of strategic options.

The second section gives the summary of the framework of the proposed model. The third section shows the application of the steps of the proposed model in a private corporation. The fourth section underlines the detailed analyses conducted to explore the differences between the individual and shared beliefs revealed in this real case. Finally, the conclusion and further suggestions are given.

FRAMEWORK OF THE MODEL

In the proposed methodology, the initial step is based on search conferences that will elicit the strategic thoughts about the future of the corporation. The participants of those search conferences will be composed in a way to represent the majority of the senior managers of the corporation. If the number of participants is high in this stage, it is advisable to select a creative working group of participants at the second stage, due to the impossibility of involving all the managers into all the subsequent stages. At the third step of the methodology, in order to categorize strategic ideas into groups, Textpack program (Mohler et al. 1995) will be used. At the fourth step, for each topic determined by Textpack, the working group will evaluate each idea and compare their evaluations with others. Then, the most important ones, which received high ratings from the group members, will be chosen as future strategic actions for the corporation eligible for further evaluation through cognitive map analysis. The fifth step will correspond to the structuring of ideas using cognitive mapping. After analyzing the map by Decision Explorer (Banxia Software Limited 1996), the important issues (e.g., goals, key issues, and potential options) will be determined for the corporation. Thus, senior management's understanding of strategic issues will be enhanced and a shared collective cognitive map will be generated (Ozen 2000).

CASE STUDY IN A PRIVATE CORPORATION

In this research, the corporation, which was selected to apply the proposed methodology, is the parent company of one of Turkey's largest conglomerates. Within the corporation, there are more than 70 companies active in a wide variety of manufacturing and service-related industries. In order to have a clear and shared picture of the future of the corporation, two consecutive search conferences have been held with 50 participants, who represented the majority of the corporate managers. At the beginning of those conferences, a brainstorming session was conducted to reveal the probable developments expected to affect the future of the corporation. The ideas were then classified as inside and outside developments. Inside developments were furtherly summarized under the following topics: organization, personnel and motivation, competition, marketing, control, financial situation, joint-ventures, planning and others. The outside developments, on the other hand, were summarized under economy, social life, environmental issues, technology, political issues, customers, sources, competitors and competition, new markets and businesses, organization and management. Then the participants were divided into two groups and generated a SWOT matrix. At the end of these conferences, the facilitator published conference reports.

Background of the Participants

Due to the impossibility to communicate with all of the 50 participants, a sample of 13 managers was selected as the participants of the working group. The profile of the selected working group is given in Table 1.

TABLE 1. Profile of the Working Group

PARTICIPANT	YEARS WITH THE BRIGADE	YEARS WITH CORPORATION	YEARS WITH THAT POSITION	AGE	JOB POSITION IN 1999	OCCUPATION	EXPERIENCE IN SECTOR	PART OF THE SEARCH CONFERENCES	TYPE OF BUSINESSMAN
P1	22	17	7	55	GENERAL SECRETARY	ENGINEER	ALL SECTORS	YES	PROFESSIONAL
P2	7	5	2	35	ASS. OF PLANNING DEPARTMENT	LAWYER	-	YES	PROFESSIONAL
P3	4	4	4	32	PLANNING ASSOCIATE	ENGINEER	BEVER- AGES	NO	PROFESSIONAL
P4	4	4	4	30	PLANNING ASSOCIATE	ENGINEER	FOOD	NO	PROFESSIONAL
P5	9	8	1	36	HEAD OF PLANNING DEPARTMENT	ENGINEER	TEXTILE, FINANCE	YES	PROFESSIONAL
P6	5	2	2	33	PLANNING ASSOCIATE	ENGINEER	ENERGY	NO	PROFESSIONAL
P7	7	5	4	31	ASS. OF GENERAL SECRETARY	ENGINEER	-	NO	PROFESSIONAL
P8	17	12	12	45	HEAD OF STRATEGY DEPARTMENT	BUSINESS ADMIN.	ALL SECTORS	YES	PROFESSIONAL
P9	7	4	4	35	PLANNING MANAGER	ENGINEER	FOOD	YES	PROFESSIONAL
P10	4	4	4	30	PLANNING ASSOCIATE	BUSINESS ADMIN.	TELECOM	YES	PROFESSIONAL
P11	20	20	20	45	HEAD OF HUMAN RESOURCES DEPARTMENT	BUSINESS ADMIN.	PAPER	YES	SHAREHOLDER
P12	12	12	12	41	ECONOMIST	ECONOMIST	-	NO	PROFESSIONAL
P13	7	7	7	36	IT MANAGER	BUSINESS ADMIN.	IT	NO	PROFESSIONAL
AVR.	10	8	6	37					
SD.	6	6	5	7					

As can be seen from the table, the selected members of the working group had been working in their position for an average of 6 years (Standard Deviation (SD) = 5), working for their industry for an average of 10 years (SD = 6) and had been working for their company for an average of 8 years (SD = 6). They are of middle age with an average of 37 years (SD = 7) and they are selected in a way to represent both the participants of the conferences, as well as those senior managers from the companies within the corporation who did not participate to those conferences. Therefore, the sample represents a range of senior managerial functions both from corporate management, who have already participated to the search conferences and who are responsible for formulating overall group strategy as well as from outside corporate management, who did not participate in the conferences and are not responsible of planning. However, a majority of the participants have planning experience although they are coming from different disciplines.

Categorizing the Ideas Using Textpack

In order to provide a useful guideline to the managers, and derive a comprehensive and complete cognitive map, the 99 ideas revealed from search conferences (see Appendix 1) were first categorized based on the content analysis conducted through Textpack software. According to the word frequency list developed through the software, it was possible to categorize the ideas under 46 different topics (Ozen 2000). In the next stage, the members of the group evaluated each ideas according to their importance, using a 1-7 scale (1: very low importance, 7: extremely important). Similar to the selection procedure adopted in Roberts (1976) and Ulengin et al. (1997), the most important ideas under each topic were selected using the following threshold values based on the evaluation of the working group: (a) the average value (AVR) of an idea must be higher than the average of all the 99 ideas (= 5.06), (b) the standard deviation (SD) value of an idea must be lower than the average standard deviation of the 99 ideas (= 1.54), (c) the median value (MED) of an idea must be at least 6.

As a result of this screening procedure, 35 strategic ideas from the total 99 were selected as the most relevant variables that should merit further evaluation using a cognitive map.

In fact, the sensitivity analysis conducted showed that the selected variables were robust to the changes in the threshold values. The same 35 ideas were found eligible again when the range of the threshold values were decreased by 3% and increased by 6% (see Table 2).

TABLE 2. Changing in Threshold Values

		Lower Limit	Upper Limit
Limit Ratio		3%	6%
AVR	5.06	4.91 = (5.06 * (1 − 0.03))	5.36 = (5.06 * (1 + 0.06))
SD	1.54	1.58 = (1.54 * (1 + 0.03))	1.44 = (1.54 * (1 − 0.06))

Shared Cognitive Map

In this stage, a cognitive map was created by the evaluation of each possible link in order to determine its level of agreement. Members were initially asked to fill a 35×35 matrix in which columns and rows were labelled with selected ideas. For every pair of ideas each participant was asked, "Do you think that idea A influences idea B?" According to the existence and direction of cause-effect relationship, a "+", "−" or "0" is assigned to the corresponding cell. This was the most difficult and time-consuming stage. The participants had difficulties in filling out the adjacency matrix that exhausted all the possible combinations ($35 \times 34 = 1,190$) among the variables. Consequently, it was necessary to find an alternative way. A map was generated by working with a sub-group of members. Then this map was shown to the remaining members to verify the relationships and directions between the ideas (Ozen 2000).

The aggregated map made all the participants understand the relationships and directions between the selected 35 ideas and consequently agreed on (see Figure 1).

Analysis of the Shared Map

The detailed analysis of the shared map was conducted using Decision Explorer. As a result, it was possible to identify the relative importance of the concepts in the map and determine the key issues, as well as the goals, the potent options, options and standard issues. The details of the analysis are given in Ozen et al. (2001).

Goals

Identifying goals and their interactions with one-another are a particularly important outcome of the proposed methodology. For this purpose, the Head Analysis is used to find heads of the maps that are the most superordinate.

FIGURE 1. The Aggregated Cognitive Map of the Corporation

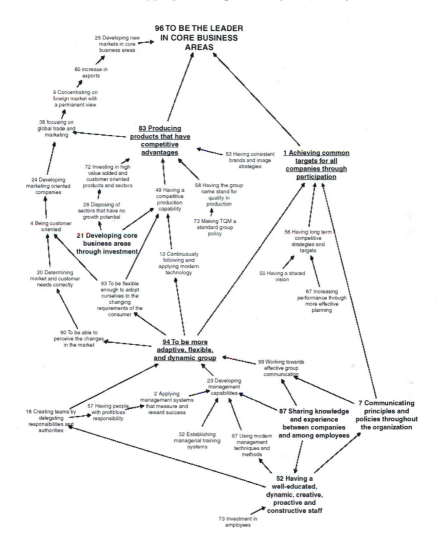

When Head Analysis is conducted to investigate the goals of the constructed map corresponding to the case study, the concept 96, "To be the leader in core business areas," was defined as the goal of the model because it has no consequential links. The goal is shown in capital letters and bold in Figure 1.

Key Issues

In the case study, the domain analysis examined each concept and calculated how many concepts were immediately related to it (i.e., directly linking in or out of the concept). Through this process, idea 94 (seven links around) and idea 83 (six links around) were identified as having a high density of links around them. They were the most densely linked concepts in the model.

The central analysis looks at concepts to the specified band level that were linked to each preceding concept, irrespective of direction. Idea 94 (15 from 26 concepts) and idea 1 (13 from 29 concepts) were observed to have the highest central scores. Therefore, they were accepted to be the potential key issues in the model.

Consequently, three issues are accepted to be the key issues of the shared map according to domain and central analysis. *Idea 1*–achieving common targets for all companies through participation, *Idea 83*–producing products which have competitive advantages, and *Idea 94*–to be a more adaptive, flexible and dynamic group (see bold and underlined ideas in Figure 1).

Linkage clustering and hierarchical set clustering analysis results validate the appropriateness of these key issues. In fact, linkage clustering which is used to split a large model into related sections, divided the model of this study into three different clusters, each cluster containing one of the key issue. On the other hand, the hierarchical set clustering analysis, which is used to produce hierarchical sets created three individual hiesets for each key issue (see Figure 2).

If the hiesets are analyzed in detail it can be seen that the first hieset is concerned with concepts related to planning, hieset 2 includes concepts related with the businesses of the corporation while the hieset 3 is composed of the human-resource related concepts.

Potent Options

Potent analysis builds on the results of hieset analysis. The potency of a concept is determined by the number of hiesets it appears in. Those constructs which support more than one of the seed set members are more potent than those supporting only one. Cotail is an analysis which searches through the model to find those "potential" options which have more than one outcome, i.e., more than one consequence leading from them. Potent

FIGURE 2. Hiesets in the Map

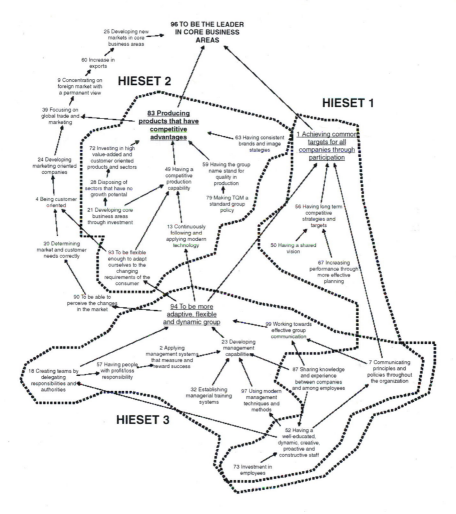

and cotail analysis conducted in this study revealed the following ideas as the potent options of the model: *Idea 7*–communication principles and policies throughout the organization, *Idea 21*–developing core business areas through investment, *Idea 52*–having a well-educated, dynamic, creative, proactive and constructive staff, *Idea 87*–sharing knowledge and experience between companies and among employees. (See bold ideas in Figure 1.)

Options

In the cognitive maps, the options are determined by the "tail" analysis. The Tail concepts are the input into the model. They enforce the logic behind the hiesets and support the other ideas.

In the case study, there are eight tails, which have no causal explanations in the model. Idea 21 and Idea 87 are also tails but they have been defined as potent issues before. Options are shown in italic in Figure 1.

The tails or options defined in the map were summarized as follows: *Idea 32*–establishing managerial training systems, *Idea 50*–having a shared vision, *Idea 53*–having consistent brands and image strategies, *Idea 67*–increasing performance through more effective planning, *Idea 73*–investment in employees, *Idea 79*–making TQM a standard group policy.

Standard Issues

After defining the goal, the key issues, the potent issues, and the options, the remaining ideas that facilitate the understanding of chains of implications are called "standard" issues on the map.

Synthesis of the Shared Map

Collapsing the map is the most useful analysis when a model is very large. The model can be reduced to contain only those concepts which are important in the map. Those concepts are defined in a set by the user before collapsing the model. It is possible to hide all ideas which are not members of the specified set, while maintaining links (whether direct or going through other ideas) between ideas in the set. Only ideas in all such sets are displayed.

In the case study, the goal (Idea 96), the key issues (Idea 1, Idea 83 and Idea 94), and the potent options (Idea 7, Idea 21, Idea 52, and Idea 87) were defined in a set. Then, the map was collapsed to contain only those ideas. The collapsed model is given in Figure 3. Thus, it is easy to summarize the whole model by only showing important concepts and the relationship between them.

According to the collapsed map, the group members strongly prefer to grow in core business areas rather than entering new business areas. The corporation should be active mainly in eight business areas, namely finance, textiles, chemicals, automotive, cement, food, retailing and tires. The corporation aspires to be the leader in every core business areas in which it invested. Competitive production advantages are expected to be obtained by investing in technology, developing process improvement and cost reduction techniques and satisfying the best production with low cost and high quality. To meet these challenges, the management should attempt to position the firms to become more competitive in the future.

Group communication is also found to be essential for a successful competitive environment. Group communication is useful in understanding the visions and the mission of the corporation, gathering the right participants, evaluating information, making timely decisions, providing information about progress to the other organizations, completing projects on schedule and tracking and learning from customer reactions. Effective communication is expected to create flexible organizations. The experience and knowledge which have been accumulated in the companies should be shared with employees and other companies.

Finally, according to the participants, unless dynamic, proactive and well-educated people are employed, the group will not become flexible and dynamic. Therefore, the quality of employees is very important for the corporation. Over the years, the influence of professional managers has increased in decision making. Therefore, without the support of the

FIGURE 3. The Collapsed Map

talented management team, the current growth momentum cannot be sustained.

INDIVIDUAL VERSUS SHARED BELIEFS

In this section, the differences and similarities in the perceptions of the group members are analyzed in detail. The aim was to determine the relative power of group members in determining the nature of the shared map and specify whether the analysis conducted was cohesive enough to have developed shared understandings, shared language and a collective map that could be used as a general perspective of the organization.

Measuring Differences Between Participants

In order to get an overall indicator of differences for each member of the working group, the matrix distance score, similar to that used by Smith and Wirth (1992), is used. The matrix distance score (MD) is calculated as the sum of the absolute differences as well as the square root of the sum of the squared differences between each identically positioned cell of the relative evaluation matrix. Table 3 shows the group members who have the most similar and dissimilar ideas with respect to each other in terms of the future of the organization. On the other hand, Table 4 examines the harmony of each group member with the whole working group average.

As can be seen from Table 4, the first four working members (P11, P13, P12 and P7) seem to have totally different thoughts with respect to the group. When the profile of these members is analyzed from Table 1, it can be seen that none of these four members, expect P11, have participated in the search conferences. In fact, P11, who has actually one of the

TABLE 3. Participant's Ranking of Difference and Matrix Distance Scores

	Group members' ranking in order of difference	The sum of absolute differences	The square root of the sum of the squared differences
Most different	P6 and P11 P5 and P11 P9 and P11	221 220 220	28.20 28.53 27.20
Most similar	P2 and P4 P4 and P9 P2 and P9	104 107 109	14.14 15.59 14.14

TABLE 4. Group Member's Ranking of Difference with Respect to the Group

	P1	P2	P3	P4	P5	P6	P7	P8	P9	P10	P11	P12	P13	Total
P11	25.06	24.56	27.68	26.25	28.53	28.20	26.57	24.90	27.20	26.32	-	22.49	26.48	314.24
P13	26.96	22.67	24.72	23.83	27.29	24.21	24.52	23.30	23.94	24.86	26.48	25.24	-	298.02
P12	25.06	23.35	26.68	23.85	24.58	26.06	24.54	22.85	25.38	24.84	22.49	-	25.24	294.92
P7	25.50	21.38	22.67	23.17	24.86	23.90	-	26.38	23.71	22.20	26.57	24.54	24.52	289.40
P8	19.65	20.47	22.93	21.75	21.02	21.28	26.38	-	21.02	23.13	24.90	22.85	23.30	268.68
P1	-	20.37	18.44	18.47	21.31	21.28	25.50	19.65	20.93	21.93	25.06	25.06	26.96	264.96
P5	21.31	19.42	20.69	16.16	-	20.76	24.86	20.02	18.71	20.81	28.53	24.58	27.29	264.14
P6	21.28	16.61	18.36	16.91	20.76	-	23.90	21.28	19.77	20.69	28.20	26.06	24.21	258.03
P10	21.93	16.91	18.08	17.78	20.81	20.69	22.20	23.13	18.84	-	26.32	24.84	24.86	256.39
P3	18.44	17.18	-	17.00	20.69	18.36	22.67	22.93	18.92	18.08	27.68	26.68	24.72	253.35
P9	20.93	14.73	18.92	15.59	18.71	19.77	23.71	21.02	-	18.84	27.20	25.38	23.94	248.74
P4	18.47	14.14	17.00	-	16.16	16.91	23.17	21.75	15.59	17.78	26.25	23.85	23.83	234.90
P2	20.37	-	17.18	14.14	19.42	16.61	21.38	20.47	14.73	16.91	24.56	23.35	22.67	231.79
Total	264.96	231.79	253.35	234.90	264.14	258.03	289.40	268.68	248.74	256.39	314.24	294.92	298.02	-

conference members, shows the highest dissimilarity with the rest of the group and seems to be detached. The reason is that P11 is not a professional but a family member. He is in charge of human resources in the corporation and although he is a member of the family, he is not a member of the board. He is not related to the general strategic planning studies of the corporation either. On the other hand, Table 3 shows that P11 has most dissimilar thoughts with respect to P6, P5 and P9, and P2-P4, P4-P9 and P2-P9 share the most similar thought with each other. In fact, Table 1 shows that the last remaining nine members of Table 4 have all been working for the planning activities of the corporation and they have been working in the same department. This results with a harmony in their thoughts about the future of the corporation.

Cluster Analysis

Cluster analysis is a multivariate data analysis technique used in grouping objects according to the characteristics they possess. If the classification is successful, the objects within clusters will have similar characteristics and there will be important differences between clusters. There are two basic types of algorithms: hierarchical and nonhierarchical (Ketchen et al. 1996; Hair et al. 1995).

In this research, both hierarchical and nonhierarchical clustering are used subsequently. In the first stage, a hierarchical technique is used to establish the number of cluster. In the next stage, K-means clustering is used taking the number of cluster revealed from the hierarchical clustering and ANOVA test is conducted to interpret the clusters.

Hierarchical Clustering Results

In this research, Ward's method is selected as the agglomeration procedure because this clustering procedure minimizes the within-cluster sum of square at each stage. Ward's method attempts to combine clusters with a small number of observations and form clusters, which tends to have the same number of objects. The distances between objects are measured through squared Euclidean Distance measure.

One of the ways of visually representing the steps in a hierarchical clustering solution is with a display called a dendrogram. The dendrogram identifies the clusters being combined and the values of the coefficients at each step. The dendrogram produced by the SPSS program does not plot actual distances but rescales them to numbers between zero to 25 (Axelrod 1976).

Figure 4 contains the dendrogram for the complete 13 participants (P1, P2, . . . , P13). Since many of the distances at the beginning stages are similar in magnitude, it is not possible to tell the sequence in which some of the early clusters are formed. Looking at the dendrogram, it appears that a two-cluster solution may be appropriate, since it is easily interpretable and occurs before the distance at which clusters combine becomes too large. The first cluster contains nine people. It is interesting that each of them either has worked before or is still working at the planning department of the headquarters. It is seen that the corporate strategies have been communicated very well within the department. These corporate employees are familiar with the corporate planning activities. They participate in such kind of planning activities and work together. Therefore, they show similar decision patterns. The second cluster contains four people. These people are either new employees or shareholders or employees working in different companies of the corporation. As they are not involved in corporate planning activities, people in this group see the world quite differently from the planners at the headquarters. A similar result was also found by examining the harmony of each group member with the whole working group average in Table 4.

FIGURE 4. The Dendrogram for 13 Group Members

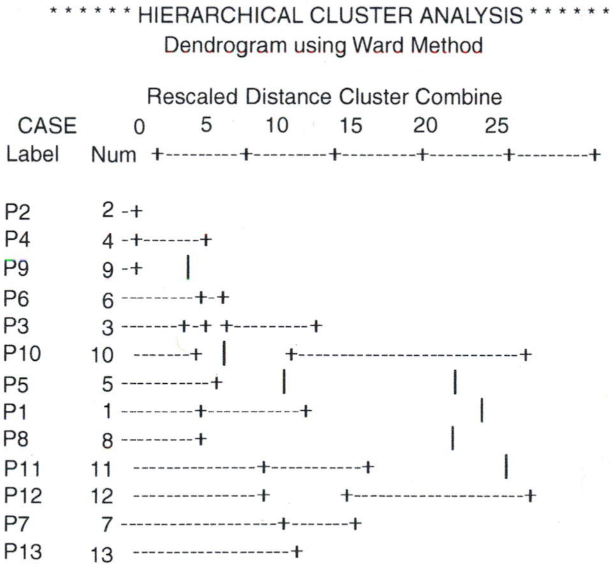

```
* * * * * * HIERARCHICAL CLUSTER ANALYSIS * * * * * *
               Dendrogram using Ward Method


                 Rescaled Distance Cluster Combine
    CASE      0     5     10    15    20    25
    Label   Num  +---------+---------+---------+---------+---------+

    P2       2 -+
    P4       4 -+-------+
    P9       9 -+       |
    P6       6 ---------+-+
    P3       3 -------+-+ +---------+
    P10     10 -------+ |        +--------------------------+
    P5       5 ----------+       |                          |
    P1       1 ---------+--------+  |                          |
    P8       8 ---------+              |                    |
    P11     11 ---------------+-----------+            |
    P12     12 ---------------+        +--------------------+
    P7       7 ------------------+-------+
    P13     13 ------------------+
```

The dendogram shows that cluster 1 is composed of 9 managers (P1, P2, P3, P4, P5, P6, P8, P9, P10) while cluster 2 is composed of 4 managers (P7, P11, P12, P13). Based on the common characteristics of the members of each cluster, cluster 1 and cluster 2 will be initially called as "Group 1" and "Group 2." They will be given appropriate labels in section 4.3, based on the different test results.

General Characteristics of the Shared and Unshared Ideas

The ideas given in Figure 5 represent all the ideas shared/unshared by the members of each grouped revealed through cluster analysis. In fact, these ideas include all the ideas that are not yet screened according to the threshold parameters defined before. Among those ideas, the bold ones are those selected to be the inputs of the shared cognitive map.

The characteristics of the individuals assigned to each group through cluster analysis show that groups of individuals who work closely together share a set of common beliefs. In fact, all the members of Group 1 are planners working at the headquarters and their shared beliefs are an integral part of their group's cultural identity. The others, which are grouped as Group 2, are senior managers of the leading companies of the corporation or they have no experiences in planning or production activities.

The same screening procedure was used separately for Group 1 and Group 2, by using the evaluation of ideas. Group 1 consists of nine people. If the working group is generated by these nine people, the selection

FIGURE 5. Ideas Shared Between Group 1 and Group 2

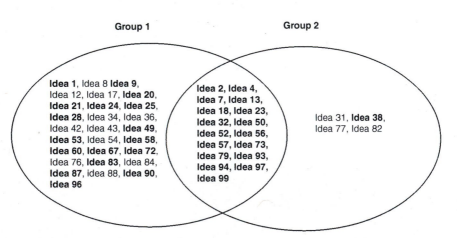

criteria or threshold values will be different. Similarly, if the working group is generated only by the four members of Group 2, the general average and standard deviation of 99 ideas of these four people will be different too. The threshold values for each Group 1 and Group 2 are shown in Table 5.

When the threshold values were used to select the important ideas for each group, Group 1 proposed 45 ideas. Among them, 34 were elected as inputs of the shared map, while members of Group 2 proposed only 21, among the ideas 18 were selected as inputs of the shared map. The members of Group 2, who are in fact not related with planning, seem to be more conservative and uncomfortable in proposing ideas (see Figure 5).

There were 17 ideas in the intersection of Group 1 and Group 2, these shared ideas were more related to human-resource related concepts, as shown in hieset 3 in Figure 2.

The relative emphasis given to different strategic dimensions by different participants is highlighted by connecting points on each vector. The "star" that results, as shown in Figure 6, illustrates by its deformation the strategic emphasis of different informants.

In fact, in the "star" map, the ideas are placed in the clockwise manner according to their differences in terms of the differences of the group averages. For example, the group averages show the greatest differences in ideas 60, 21, 24, etc., while approximately a consensus in the importance of ideas 18, 23, 13, 52, 96, and 97.

The greatest differences between the groups are coming from the business related ideas. However, the most consensus is achieved on especially human-resource related ideas and the goal of the model (Idea 96).

The number of clusters found from the hierarchical clustering phase are used as input for the K-means clustering and ANOVA test is conducted to interpret the information. By this way, for each cluster, the mean value on each of the 99 rating variables is obtained and the univariate F ratios and levels of significance comparing the differences between the group means are analyzed (see Table 6). Table 6 only shows 18 of the 99 variables which exhibit significantly different patterns (5% confidence interval). The other variables were not found dif-

TABLE 5. Threshold Values of Group 1 and Group 2

	AVR	ST	MED
GROUP 1	5.33	1.29	6
GROUP2	4.45	1.64	6

FIGURE 6. Star Map

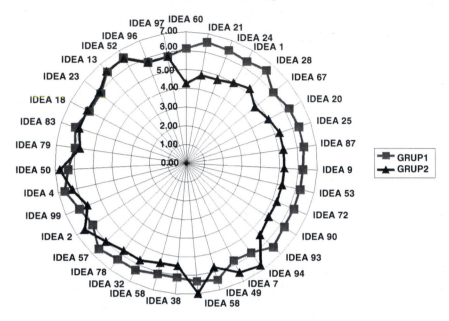

ferent between the two groups. Thus, in interpreting and ultimately labelling the cluster, it is focused on these significant variables and their respective group means.

Group 1 members especially give importance to focusing on technology-intensive areas but strongly believe in being a leader especially in Turkey. Therefore, they believe that the company's mission should be a national market leader using its own capabilities rather than relying on joint ventures. They can be called "nationals."

Group 2, however, has a much global perspective. They believe that the future of the company is in globalization and not only being a national leader. For this purpose, instead of relying on national resources, they want the company to grow through joint ventures, to diffuse all over the world and be a worldwide company.

CONCLUSION AND FURTHER SUGGESTIONS

This paper proposes a framework to guide the managers in building a shared belief of the goals, key issues and options for the future of a com-

TABLE 6. Group Means and Significance Levels for Two-Group Nonhierarchical Cluster Solution*

#	IDEA	Group 1 Average	Group 2 Average	F	Sign
5	Building on and improving the present image.	4.9	5.3	5.296	0.042
10	Concentrating on technology intensive business areas.	4.1	3.0	16.277	0.002
12	Continuing our growth internationally.	6.1	4.8	14.127	0.003
21	Developing core business areas through investment.	6.6	4.8	6.217	0.030
26	Developing our own technology through collaboration with our university.	3.6	3.0	6.144	0.031
27	Developing own technology through R&D activities.	4.9	3.0	23.608	0.001
55	Having JV with production facilities overseas.	3.4	3.3	6.092	0.031
60	Increase in exports.	6.1	4.3	5.272	0.042
66	Increasing overseas investment to strengthen our current markets and create new market areas.	5.8	4.5	16.263	0.002
67	Increasing performance through more effective planning.	6.0	4.8	11.497	0.006
68	Invest in R&D.	5.7	4.8	58.761	0.000
70	Investing in areas where we do not need JVs.	4.2	1.5	6.175	0.030
78	Making the development of technology in our core business areas a priority.	5.7	3.5	15.343	0.002
83	Producing products that have competitive advantages.	6.2	6.0	6.044	0.032
84	Production on a global scale.	6.2	3.5	5.357	0.041
86	Realizing vertical integration in companies.	3.1	2.8	4.735	0.052
92	To be an important player in the world.	4.0	3.3	10.917	0.007
93	To be flexible enough to adopt ourselves to the changing requirements of the consumer.	6.4	5.5	7.447	0.020

* Only those significant at 5% confidence level are represented.

pany. Managers can use this framework repeatedly to reassess the organization's direction, thereby cultivating both their own competencies in strategic thinking and their understanding of how strategic decisions connect to the market. When the results of the study is beneficial for the firm, all the decision-makers will want to participate in such activities more than before.

The framework also permits to describe and measure the similarities and differences among between managers' beliefs, and to examine how they can be grouped together in order to underline the basic beliefs that constitute the basis of their similarities. In fact, the case study conducted in a private company in order to test the validity and usefulness of the proposed framework resulted with findings which are consistent with the work of many researchers who have emphasized that coordinated action is often achieved without a high degree of common beliefs (Smith 1992). The research revealed that the members of a team having a relatively longer history of shared experiences show similar beliefs. Therefore, the case study also underlined that the validity and usefulness of a cognitive map depend solely on the appropriate configuration of the expert group who contributes to the preparation of the shared map. For example, in order to avoid the criticism of building models that represent only the concerns of the most powerful elite, less powerful stakeholders should also be added to the list of the management team. The selection of the appropriate members having different perspectives is, thus, crucial in obtaining appropriate cognitive maps.

As a further suggestion, it is also necessary to underline that strategic thinking needs to be continuously renewed if it is to remain socially efficient. This requires a flexible and dynamic conceptual framework of underlying assumptions being used in the organization. Therefore, the changes that will occur in the perspective of the corporation should be continuously revealed. If those changes necessitate a considerable revision in the map, a strategic meeting bringing together decision-makers should be organized to revise the map using the proposed framework.

REFERENCES

Axelrod, R. (1976). *Structure of Decision*. Princeton University Press, 91.

Daniels K., Chernatory L. and Johnson G. (1995). Validating a Method for Mapping Managers' Mental Models of Competitive Industry Structures. *Human Relations*, 48(9), 975-991.

Decision Explorer 3 Reference Manual (1996). Banxia Software Limited, University of Strathclyde, Scotland.

Fiol, C. M. (1992). Maps for Managers: Where Are We? Where Do We Go from Here?. *Journal of Management Studies*. 29(3), 267-285.

Hair, J. F., Anderson, R. E., Tatham, R. L., Black, W. C. (1995). *Multivariate Data Analysis with Reading*, Fourth Ed., Prentice-Hall International, Inc., London.

Ketchen, D. J. and Shook, C. L. (1996). The Application of Cluster Analysis in Strategic Management Research: An Analysis and Critique. *Strategic Management Journal*, 17, 441-458.

Langan-Fox, J., Wirth, A., Code S., Langfield-Smith, K. and Wirth A. (2001). Analyzing Shared and Team Mental Models. *International Journal of Industrial Ergonomics*, 28, 99-112.

Langfield-Smith, K. (1992). Exploring the Need for a Shared Cognitive Map. *Journal of Management Studies*. 29(3), 349-367.

Langfield-Smith, K. and Wirth, A. (1992). Measuring Differences Between Cognitive Maps. *Journal of Operational Research Society Ltd.* 43(12), 1135-1150.

Lee, S., Courtney Jr. JF, O'Keefe, RM. (1992). A System for Organizational Learning Using Cognitive Maps. *OMEGA*, 20(1), pp. 23-36.

Mintzberg, H. (1979). *The Structuring of Organizations.* Englewood Cliffs, N.J., Prentice-Hall International, Inc., London

Mohler, P. P. and Züll, C. (1995). *Textpack PC, ZUMA (Zentrum für Umfragen, Methoden und Analysen).* Mannheim, Germany.

Ozen, U. (2000). Modeling and Analyzing Strategic Thoughts Using Cognitive Mapping, Unpublished Ph.D. Thesis. Istanbul Technical University.

Ozen, U. and Ulengin, F. (2001). *Analyzing Strategic Thoughts of Corporations: A Case Study in a Private Firm.* Paper presented at the 19th International Conference of the System Dynamics Society, Emory Conference Center, Atlanta, USA.

Ozen, U. and Ulengin, F. (2001). *A Methodology to Develop Efficient Future Horizons in Corporations.* Paper presented at EURO 2001: The European Operational Research Conference, Erasmus University, Rotterdam, Holland.

Phillips, L. D. and Phillips, M. C. (1993). Facilitated Work Groups: Theory and Practice. *Journal of the Operational Research Society.* 44, 533-549.

Roberts, F. S. (1976). Strategy for the Energy Crisis: The Case of Commuter Transportation Policy, In: R. Axelrod (ed.), *Structure of Decision* (142-179). Princeton University Press, New Jersey.

Rose, R. A. (1988). Organizations as Multiple Cultures: A Rules Theory Analysis. *Human Relations.* 41(2), 139-170.

Smith, L. K. (1992). Exploring the Need for a Shared Cognitive Map. *Journal of Management Studies.* 29, 349-367.

Ulengin, F. and Topcu, I. (1997). Cognitive Map: KBDSS Integration in Transportation Planning. *Journal of Operational Research Society*, 48, 1065-1075.

APPENDIX 1

Strategic Future Ideas for Corporation

Idea 1	Achieving common targets for all companies through participation.	Idea 34	Establishing production facilities everywhere in the world.
Idea 2	Applying management systems that measure and reward success.	Idea 35	Evaluate further possible investment opportunities with all JV partners.
Idea 3	Become the largest company in Turkey.	Idea 36	Executing cost cutting programs.
Idea 4	Being customer oriented.	Idea 37	Find equilibrium between growth, profit, and risk.
Idea 5	Building on and improving the present our image.	Idea 38	Focusing on global trade and marketing.
Idea 6	Choosing the best investments to give the quickest production and the highest sales.	Idea 39	Foreseeing and affecting government decisions.
Idea 7	Communicating principles and policies throughout the organization.	Idea 40	Foreseeing investment in potential future industries.
Idea 8	Concentrate on a small number of big businesses.	Idea 41	Giving more importance to company identity.
Idea 9	Concentrating on foreign market with a permanent view.	Idea 42	Growing via merger and acquisition.
Idea 10	Concentrating on technology intensive business areas.	Idea 43	Growth based on business capabilities suited to market needs.
Idea 11	Conducting strategic planning studies with foreign advisors.	Idea 44	Growth in core business areas with new products.
Idea 12	Continuing our growth internationally.	Idea 45	Growth of our group without JVs.
Idea 13	Continuously following and applying modern technology.	Idea 46	Growth through acquiring privatized companies.
Idea 14	Controlling competitors through partnerships.	Idea 47	Growth through JVs.
Idea 15	Cooperation with companies well known for their brands and technology.	Idea 48	Growth via greenfield.
Idea 16	Cooperation with foreign countries who are studying the possibility of investment in Turkey.	Idea 49	Having a competitive production capability.
		Idea 50	Having a shared vision.
		Idea 51	Having a structure that follows, creates, and evaluates opportunities.
		Idea 52	Having a well-educated, dynamic, creative, proactive and constructive staff

Idea 71	Investing in developed technologies.
Idea 72	Investing in high value-added and customer oriented products and sectors.
Idea 73	Investment in employees.
Idea 74	Making integration, trouble-shooting, and modernization investments.
Idea 75	Making investments in growing industries.
Idea 76	Making investments to minimize cost and improve quality.
Idea 77	Making our group more institutionalized.
Idea 78	Making the development of technology in our core business areas a priority.
Idea 79	Making TQM a standard group policy.
Idea 80	Market control through strategic cooperation.
Idea 81	Moving from industrial and financial identities to a commercial identity.
Idea 82	Preserving our culture and creating a team spirit.
Idea 83	Producing products that have competitive advantages.
Idea 84	Production on a global scale.
Idea 85	Providing education to improve quality of employees.
Idea 86	Realizing vertical integration in companies.
Idea 87	Sharing knowledge and experience between companies and among employees.

Idea 17	Create and improve global brands.	Idea 53	Having consistent brands and image strategies.	Idea 88	Strengthening employee-employer dialog to improve working relations.

Idea 17 Create and improve global brands.
Idea 18 Creating teams by delegating responsibilities and authorities.
Idea 19 Decreasing hierarchies.
Idea 20 Determining market and customer needs correctly.
Idea 21 Developing core business areas through investment.
Idea 22 Developing growth in potential new business areas.
Idea 23 Developing management capabilities.
Idea 24 Developing marketing oriented companies.
Idea 25 Developing new markets in core business areas.
Idea 26 Developing our own technology through collaboration with our university.
Idea 27 Developing own technology through R&D activities.
Idea 28 Disposing of sectors that have no growth potential.
Idea 29 Diversification into markets and products to get premium returns.
Idea 30 Establishing close contacts with major universities.
Idea 31 Establishing equal participation of professionals in management.
Idea 32 Establishing managerial training systems.
Idea 33 Establishing new JVs for new markets.

Idea 53 Having consistent brands and image strategies.
Idea 54 Having decision conferences and follow-up meetings to create a common understanding.
Idea 55 Having JV with production facilities overseas.
Idea 56 Having long term competitive strategies and targets.
Idea 57 Having people with profit/loss responsibility.
Idea 58 Having the group name stand for quality in production.
Idea 59 Importing and selling JV partners' products.
Idea 60 Increase in exports.
Idea 61 Increase product diversification through investments.
Idea 62 Increased growth in markets already led by the group.
Idea 63 Increased supply through new JVs to become self-sufficient.
Idea 64 Increasing employee loyalty to the group.
Idea 65 Increasing investments based on knowledge and capital.
Idea 66 Increasing overseas investment to strengthen our current markets and create new market areas.
Idea 67 Increasing performance through more effective planning.
Idea 68 Invest in R&D.
Idea 69 Investing heavily in Turkey.
Idea 70 Investing in areas where we do not need JVs.

Idea 88 Strengthening employee-employer dialog to improve working relations.
Idea 89 Strive for economies of scale.
Idea 90 To be able to perceive the changes in the market.
Idea 91 To be able to sell our technology.
Idea 92 To be an important player in the world.
Idea 93 To be flexible enough to adopt ourselves to the changing requirements of the consumer.
Idea 94 To be more adaptive, flexible, and dynamic group.
Idea 95 To be the leader in new business sectors in Turkey.
Idea 96 To be the leader in core business areas.
Idea 97 Using modern management techniques and methods.
Idea 98 Using Turkey's closest neighbors as a market and production base.
Idea 99 Working towards effective group communication.

Strategic Alliances in the Aviation Industry: An Analysis of Turkish Airlines Experience

Fatih Semercioz
Burak Kocer

SUMMARY. This paper investigates antecedents of success/failure in strategic alliances, which is implemented by airline companies as a response to globalization and liberal government policies. The relationship between Turkish Airlines and Qualiflyer Group, the largest airline alliance in Europe until its collapse in 2001, has been taken as a case study to present the question in terms of matching the goals, partner selection, alliance management, and areas of cooperation. Two factors at the macro-level and four factors at the micro-level are found to be important to succeed in strategic airline alliances. *[Article copies available for a fee from The Haworth Document Delivery Service: 1-800-HAWORTH. E-mail address: <docdelivery@haworthpress.com> Website: <http://www.HaworthPress. com> © 2004 by The Haworth Press, Inc. All rights reserved.]*

KEYWORDS. Strategic alliances, alliance performance, aviation industry, qualiflyer group, Turkish airlines

Fatih Semercioz is Assistant Professor, Faculty of Business Administration, Istanbul University, Avcilar, Istanbul, Turkey (E-mail: fsemerci@istanbul.edu.tr).

Burak Kocer is Research Assistant, Faculty of Economics and Administrative Sciences, Istanbul Bilgi University, Kustepe, Istanbul, Turkey (E-mail: bkocer@bilgi.edu.tr).

[Haworth co-indexing entry note]: "Strategic Alliances in the Aviation Industry: An Analysis of Turkish Airlines Experience." Semercioz, Fatih, and Burak Kocer. Co-published simultaneously in *Journal of Transnational Management Development* (The International Business Press, an imprint of The Haworth Press, Inc.) Vol. 9, No. 2/3, 2004, pp. 29-45; and: *Islam and Business: Cross-Cultural and Cross-National Perspectives* (ed: Kip Becker) The International Business Press, an imprint of The Haworth Press, Inc., 2004, pp. 29-45. Single or multiple copies of this article are available for a fee from The Haworth Document Delivery Service [1-800-HAWORTH, 9:00 a.m. - 5:00 p.m. (EST). E-mail address: docdelivery@haworthpress.com].

During the last decade "strategic alliances" dominated both the corporate world and the international management literature, as a "business model." Strategic alliances, which are becoming an increasingly important management strategy for the future, represent a cooperative and complementary approach to achieving market reach; drive customer loyalty, supplement operational capability and help drive down costs (Stickler, 2001).

Alliance activities reshaped competitive strategies in the aviation industry through globalization, where state-control was the dominant factor that influenced operational decisions. Soon, just about every airline will most likely become a member of a network to have global presence. Yet, building strategic alliances involving exchange, sharing or co-development of technologies and services become the competitive edge of air carriers seeking cooperation to provide cost reduction and economies of scale. Cooperation strategies such as code sharing, sub-contracting, franchising, and global marketing links allow airline companies to focus on core business activities.

To reduce the economic impact of deregulation and liberalization of commercial aviation, which started during the early 1980s, airlines throughout the world have concluded a wide range of alliance and partnership agreements, globally around 375 by mid-1997, covering many areas of airline activities, services and operations (Groenewege, 1999). Building international alliances is particularly important for carriers in developing countries (i) to increase their competitiveness against developed countries' large carriers and (ii) to enhance their bargaining power in operational matters such as airport charges, fuel prices, and aircraft maintenance. The success of the collaboration, however, primarily depends on a clear understanding of the expectations of each party, and aligning with the right partner with compatible goals.

DEVELOPMENT OF AIRLINE ALLIANCES

The aviation industry, one of the fastest growing sectors of world economy, experienced a large shift over last decades in the sense of moving from regulation and state ownership to global consolidation. The Airline Deregulation Act passed by the US Congress in November 1978 with its main objective that the marketplace should determine the airlines' business decisions in the future (Groenewege, 1999) was a major influence shaping the aviation industry. Thereafter, other industrialized countries such as Canada, EU countries, and Japan adopted policies to liberalize the aviation industry and bring about a more competitive environment. Air transport has been liberalized within the fifteen states of the European Union since January 1993, and among the seventeen states of the European Economic Area (EEA) since January

1994 (Esperou, 2001) with a package of measures giving some flexibility to increase capacity or adjust fares on cross-border routes without the need for a process of negotiation between the two countries concerned (AEA, 1997). Whilst deregulation allowed carriers to drop unprofitable routes and concentrate on core, lucrative slots (Dana, 2000), this regulatory reform was limited essentially to commercial matters such as pricing, capacity, and market entry (Groenewege, 1999). Indeed, bilateral government agreements still support flag carriers, a nation's preferred air carrier operating international scheduled services, in the following sense: In order to reach beyond one's borders, the governments of any two countries have to establish bilateral agreements that will ultimately lead to a vast web of bilateral agreements on a worldwide scale (Agusdinata & De Klein, 2001).

If a designated airline company is to represent a country, then the nationals of the country in question must have majority ownership and dominant managerial control over the airline (Agusdinata & De Klein, 2001). For example, American laws restrict foreign ownership to a quarter of an airline's voting shares; on the other hand, the limit in Europe is 49% (Economist, 1998). Such barriers against mergers and acquisitions encourage carriers to cooperate through network alliance agreements. Networks have generally been defined to include the multiplicity of ways in which at least two firms or subunits within the firms may be organized as hybrids to cooperate for mutual benefit (Koza & Lewin, 1999). Increasingly, airlines have become involved in horizontal relationships with the aim of developing a mutually advantageous agreement that strengthens market share (Dana, 2000). For most internationally operating airlines, the question is no longer whether or not to join an alliance group, but rather with whom, and to what extent (Kleymann & Seristö, 2001). In practical terms, airline alliances and partnerships have become a way for airlines to bypass bilateral conventions that prevent them from flying to certain countries or from owning foreign airlines (Groenewege, 1999). In addition to legal constraints, the current situation of the market is another important factor that encourages airlines to cooperate through alliances that have flexibility advantage over mergers. Indeed, flexibility is what is required within a turbulent and uncertain market. Collaborating with a number of global partners can balance turbulence by diminishing dependency on one particular region (Agusdinata & De Klein, 2001).

Code sharing and integrated computer reservation systems (CRSs) are milestones of airline cooperation. Code sharing is an example of airline cooperation, where one carrier allows another to share its codes and so appear to have more flights (Dana, 2000). In essence, this is an agreement between two airlines by which an aircraft from one airline operating a given flight carries its own flight number as well as that of the other airline. This allows the non-operating airline to sell the flight as its own (Groenewege, 1999). On the other hand, an integrated CRS allows the carriers to display and sell each other's seats and provide customers with a wide range of service.

Fan et al. (2001) identified three possible levels of cooperation in the aviation industry: ordinary, tactical, and strategic. At the ordinary level, carriers serving an airport infrequently may choose to outsource the handling of general sales or airport functions to another carrier or handling agency. Tactical cooperation usually takes the form of two carriers cross-selling each other's capacity on selected routes, or one carrier marketing its code on another's flights. Cooperation at this level is generally limited to specific routes or regions, and the carriers involved are still marketed as independent entities. Finally, strategic airline alliances are characterized by joint, dedicated marketing entities for network-wide cooperation (Fan et al., 2001), which provides partners with mutual benefit that is generated through voluntary agreements involving exchange, sharing, or co-development of products, technologies, or services (Gulati, 1998). Reciprocal frequent flyer program (FFP) recognition, extensive code sharing, shared lounges, integrated reservation systems, joint ground handling, and catering (Dana, 2000; Groenewege, 1999; Fan et al., 2001; AEA, 1999) are typical means of delivering a superior customer service in the aviation industry. In this study, we believe it is useful to include other forms of airline cooperation (e.g., operations support), resulting in more complex integration of partners, to the strategic level, given the *long-term* nature of the "strategy" term. Cooperation for operations support involves aircraft maintenance, joint fleet planning, and joint purchasing of spare parts (Groenewege, 1999).

By the end of 1999, global airlines formed 4 major alliances (see Table 1).

THE QUALIFLYER GROUP

The Qualiflyer Group, largest airline alliance in Europe, was founded by Swissair (SR) with Austrian Airlines, Sabena, AOM France, Crossair, Lauda Air, TAP Portugal, and Turkish Airlines (TK) in March 1998. Air Europe and LOT Polish joined in 1999, and Air Littoral,

TABLE 1. Global Airline Alliances as of 1999

Star Alliance	United Airlines, Lufthansa, Air Canada, Thai Airways, SAS, Varig
Oneworld	American Airlines, British Airways, Qantas, Cathay Pacific, Iberia, Finnair
The Qualiflyer Group	Swissair, Sabena, TAP, Turkish Airlines, AOM, Crossair, Air Europe
KLM/Northwest	KLM, Northwest

Portugalia and Volare Air in 2000. By the end of the year 2000, the Qualiflyer Group was serving more than 200 destinations in Europe and over 330 destinations worldwide. The fleet utilized over 450 aircraft and maintained hubs in Brussels, Istanbul, Lisbon, Milan, Nice, Paris, Warsaw, and Zurich, among others (PR Newswire, 2001).

Qualiflyer used to have three characteristics that distinguished it from other alliances: (i) all of its partners were Europe-based companies, whereas other airlines preferred to build intercontinental alliances; (ii) though the partnership looked like the alliance of equals, in terms of the governance structure Swissair was the dominant party to influence strategic decisions with its so called "equity-based" alliance strategy; (iii) partners did not engage in strong business relations with each other, cooperation was rather based on individual relations between Swissair and other members.

Swissair was the heart of the Qualiflyer Group with its equity stakes in most of the member airlines. This was in sharp contrast to the other global airline alliances such as the Star Alliance and Oneworld (Suen, 2002). Specifically, 70.52% of Crossair, 49.79% of Volare Air (including Air Europe) 49.5% of Sabena, 49.5% of Air Liberte (including AOM), 49% of Air Littoral, 37.6% of LOT, and 10% of the Austrian Airlines, parent company of Lauda Air were owned by the Swiss carrier (AEA, 2001). Group philosophy that bound members together was "One Voice–One Face–One Spirit" toward their customers (PR Newswire, 2000). This philosophy required standardization of the quality of customer services and highly integrated operational activities. The alliance level goals were set as codeshare where possible and cooperate on IT, baggage handling, sales, training, cargo, and maintenance and to establish a common Qualiflyer FFP (Suen, 2002), in order to realize the group's vision.

TURKISH AIRLINES

Turkish Airlines, the national flag carrier of Turkey, is a mid-sized airline company whose majority stake (98.17%) is owned by the Turkish Privatization Administration (TPA). The remaining shares are traded on the Istanbul Stock Exchange. Turkey's national carrier, ranked among "The Largest 200 Companies in the Developing World" by *Business Week* (Travel Agent, 2001), experienced a phenomenal growth since its creation in 1933 and increased its route network to 66 scheduled cross-border destinations with 66 aircraft in fleet, as of 1998. Today, the company employs almost 12,300 people. Turkey's location at the periphery of Europe was a significant strength, which made TK an attractive company that provides its partners with the opportunity of having a hub centered in Eastern Europe.

The alliance concept fell into TK's strategic agenda in a critical period, when the government decided to privatize the company. In accordance with the consolidation trend in the industry Turkish carrier believed that it was not possible to compete individually. For General Manager Mr. Bolayirli it was clear that a successful alliance strategy became a matter of survival for airline companies in today's turbulent environment (IMKB Bulten, 1999). Alliances allow the opportunity for airlines to combine their networks into entities which have some of the characteristics of global brands, operating in a much larger range of markets than a single carrier could serve (AEA, 1998). Achieving economies of scale through cooperation was an important motive for the carrier to consider alliance strategy. A fleet of 66 aircraft was not providing them with competitiveness in the global arena against large European carriers, such as Lufthansa with 280, British Airways 271, and Air France 205 aircraft in fleet as of 1998. For example, TK used to have two flights to the US: Chicago (5 days/week) and New York (7 days/week), whereas Lufthansa flew to both Chicago and New York from Frankfurt twice a day. It would require TK an investment of millions of Euros and many years to reach such a large size through expanding the fleet, recruiting the necessary human capital, and so on.

The company's attractiveness during the privatization process was expected to increase through becoming a company that provides customers with a wider service portfolio and partnership with a well-positioned brand in the aviation industry. TK's board of directors declared that the Japanese carrier JAL, South Korean Asiana, and Swissair were considered as potential partners to cooperate in passengers and ticketing activities. The board further reported that cooperation would be limited to commercial matters; equity-based cooperation was definitely out of question (IMKB Bulten, 1998).

Research Question

Our research interrogates the underlying factors in Turkish Airlines' (TK) success/failure in its partnership with the Qualiflyer group.

Purpose

Given the above mentioned research question, we explored: (i) the factors that encouraged TK to enter a Europe-based international alliance; (ii) partner selection process; (iii) methods applied by TK to manage the relationships with the group; and (iv) strategic alliance performance from TK's perspective.

Data Collection

Both primary and secondary data were collected to evaluate the research question. Semi-structured interview method was used to collect primary data. We prepared a questionnaire that includes open-ended statements related to four main categories: characteristics of TK, characteristics of the Qualiflyer Group, TK and Qualiflyer relationship, and alliance performance appraisal. Secondary data was collected from Association of European Airlines Yearbooks (fleet compositions, scheduled destinations), Istanbul Stock Exchange Bulletins (announcements of TK's board of directors).

Sample

Our sample consisted of informants from Agreements Department and Revenue Management Department, since market share increase and customer service expansion were primary objectives of the company and mostly these departments worked in alliance related activities. We also contacted the Association of European Airlines and made an interview on quality rating studies.

Data Analysis

We combined our primary and secondary data with earlier studies on strategic alliances to interpret our findings.

Limitations

We obtained most of the information from Turkish Airlines and constructed our analysis from Turkish Airlines' perspective. In order to come up with a better explanation of relationships among partners, informants from other major partners of the Qualiflyer Group should also be included to the research.

Factors Affecting Alliance Performance

In this research we investigate factors that affect alliance success at two different levels: micro and macro. Management literature cites many factors at the micro level affecting the overall performance of strategic alliances such as analyzing prospective partners from different aspects, flexibility in management of the alliance, building trust with partners, constructive management of conflict, uncertainty of partners' behaviors, continuity of boundary personnel responsible for the interface between the firm and the alliance, managing partner expectations, adaptability to change, implementation of mechanisms to periodically monitor alliance success, the minimization of power imbalances, level of cooperation and the opportunistic behavior (Gulati, 1998; Kleymann & Seristö, 2001; Dyer et al., 2001; Das & Teng, 1998), changes in partners' objectives over time, and so on. We summarize the above-mentioned micro level factors into four dimensions: compatible objectives, analyzing prospective partners, managing the alliance activities, and level of cooperation. In addition to those factors, we believe macro-level factors also influence alliance success, especially when parties involved are from different nations. Macro-level factors include differences in political and economic cultures and international regulations on competition.

Macro-Level Factors

Economic and Political Differences

The Turkish economy has been experiencing an important structural change over the last two decades. This change is centered at economic liberalization through privatization for decreasing the state role in commercial activities. However, Turkey has not been able to accomplish the privatization program as planned, mainly because of political, legal and labor constraints on the implementation of the program (Ertuna, 1998). TK's privatization, which was planned to be completed in December 1998 (Borsa Market, 1999), has always been a priority in Turkey's economic program. Fifty-one percent of the shares owned by the TPA has been offered to real persons, legal entities, and joint ventures (TPA, 2002). Delay of the privatization process affected TK's relationships with the Qualiflyer Group dramatically for two reasons.

Firstly, commercial agreements would be binding for the company's future; therefore, the company was not willing to enhance cooperation. Thus, General Manager Bolayirli declared that they were still a Qualiflyer member, but they put joint project development on hold until the privatization is completed (Para, 2000). This makes sense, when one thinks that binding agreements with the Qualiflyer partners would make the company less attractive to the potential investors that were not Qualiflyer members.

Secondly, most business-related decisions are subject to be approved by the TPA, and even by the State Planning Organization (SPO) sometimes. This inflexible nature of the state was decreasing TK's ability to participate in group projects. CEO Bolayirli explained that privatization, which was expected to be completed in December of 1998, was an important basis for the company plans concerning the Qualiflyer Group and complained about not being able to cooperate with the group members in any activity, besides code sharing and coordinated FFP (Borsa Market, 1999).

International Regulations

Competition is much more apparent between global alliances on long-haul routes than inside the European area (Esperou, 2001). This requires the European countries to develop a common strategy and governance regulations. However, fragmentation of the European aviation market is preventing European airlines from improving their competitiveness at a global level (European Parliament, 2000). For example, strategic alliances involving European Commissions (EC) and non-EC carriers fall outside the scope of European regulations and this legal gap is opening the door to complex controversies (Sparaco, 1997). These controversies made integration difficult for Qualiflyer Group that was established by EC and non-EC member countries' carriers. Unlike

Swissair, the other global alliances all had members who were allowed to operate in the EU without restrictions (Suen, 2002).

Micro-Level Factors

Compatible Objectives

It is important to determine the strategic goals of a potential partner and to ensure that they do not conflict with the organization's goals (Keuning, 1998). The Turkish carrier expected Asia Pacific and Latin America to be the fastest growing markets in the coming 5-year period (Bolayirli, 2001). Therefore, global expansion of the market presence was an important motive for the company to enter an alliance relationship. The primary objectives that encouraged TK to consider the alliance strategy were: (i) enlarging the route network; (ii) enhancing the customer potential; (iii) strengthening competitiveness; and (iv) increasing revenues with no additional cost.

Scholars often cite market access among the primary motives to enter an alliance relationship (Bleeke & Ernst, 1993; Ellis, 1996; Suen, 2002; Stickler, 2001). A major motivation for establishing relationships among the companies in a network is that each offers a core competency that the other ones do not have (Cravens et al., 1994). In case of the aviation industry this core competency appears to be the access to a specific market. Alliances strengthen airline networks by serving markets otherwise unavailable to them, either for regulatory reasons or through economic necessity (AEA, 1997). Considering, especially, Swissair's wide destination network in Europe, TK has achieved a larger presence in this market. However, the particular size of the regions served in terms of revenues is also an important fact to evaluate, along with the number of additional destinations provided by the partners. TK was already flying to major hubs and most-demanded destinations in Europe (i.e., 9 airports in Germany). The additional destinations reached through code sharing (i.e., Malta through Zurich) were mostly small regions in Europe, which have a limited demand from and to Istanbul. Beyond Europe destinations were more valuable for becoming a global alliance, the ultimate goal of TK; however, only Swissair flew to more intercontinental destinations than TK did (24 v. 66), Sabena and Austrian Airlines' used to have almost the same intercontinental presence with the Turkish carrier. Swissair, indeed, concentrated on regional markets more than the global market. All additional partners were strong in domestic routes within the Europe. Air Europe and AOM France gave

Swissair access to the French domestic market, and in AOM's case, access to France's overseas territories, Volare brought the Italian regional market, while TAP provided access to the Portuguese market, and connections to South America. Truly global airline alliances with European, North American and Asian partners provide a better value proposition to customers than does the Qualiflyer's regional focus (Suen, 2002). The group was planning to increase its global competitiveness with the possible entrance of Delta Airlines into Qualiflyer; however, the long-established link between the first group and Delta has not progressed in terms of reaching the same level of integration as KL/NW or Lufthansa/SAS/United (AEA, 1999).

Analysis of Prospective Partners

Synergy potential from complementary route networks was the main criterion for TK to evaluate prospective partners. By the end of 1997, Swissair (SR) used to have 93 scheduled destinations within Europe and 66 beyond Europe. Other two established groups in 1998 were Star Alliance and KLM/Northwest partnership. The number of scheduled destinations of Star member Lufthansa, and KLM were 127 within Europe and 150 beyond Europe, 63 within Europe and 85 beyond Europe, respectively (AEA, 1997). Increasing the number of alliance partners in the early stages of the alliance increase the potential benefits for three main reasons: Firstly, the network of the alliance will cover a larger part of the world and the partners will have access to more new markets. Secondly, the alliance will move towards achieving the ideal of offering global seamless service, and, thirdly, there will be more advantages to be achieved from economies of scope, scale and learning (Agusdinata & De Klein, 2001). This makes the Star a more desirable alliance with its 6 members to join for TK. On the other hand, the large route network of Star also makes the alliance a more difficult one to enter. Within the alliance, the increased size will be accompanied by diminishing additional value with each new partner because of increasing overlap in partners' networks and city duplication (Agusdinata & De Klein, 2001). Cooperation with Swissair was actually started in 1997 on joint flight basis: the establishment of Istanbul-Geneva-Istanbul and Izmir-Zurich-Izmir routes was an early sign of the potential enhancement of cooperation between the two parties. On January, 1998 the board of directors declared that THY signed a letter of strategic purpose with the Swissair Group to establish a basis for cooperation that involves commercial and technical issues, information technologies, ground handling, cargo, duty-free, and catering (IMKB Bulten, 1998).

It is also important to evaluate how a potential partner behaved in its earlier cooperation experiences for effective partner selection (Esener, 1997). A comprehensive financial analysis of the potential partner was not considered as being necessary by TK, since an equity-based partnership such as merger or acquisition was not in question. However, each of Swissair's earlier alliances, European Quality, Global Excellence and Atlantic Excellence, collapsed after a series of mergers, each of which reduced the value of the group to the remaining members, thereby making the alliance increasingly unattractive (Suen, 2002). In November 2001, Swissair resumed operations and filed for bankruptcy status after serious financial difficulties caused by both mismanagement and environmental difficulties.

Management of Relationships with the Alliance

Being a state-owned enterprise was an important factor affecting TK's relationship with the Qualiflyer Group. Building a network of interorganizational relationships may require changes in the corporate cultures. Organizations that are less formal and more flexible will be more successful in alliance strategy (Cravens et al., 1994). Being bound by the budget constraints set by the government limited the company's ability to develop crucial projects with regards to the group, timely and effectively. Decisions on critical issues such as aircraft purchasing, recruitment and starting new routes would be made faster, if the company were a private one.

Dyer et al. (2001) suggest that establishing a dedicated strategic alliance function help companies to manage relationship with partners more effectively, through improving knowledge management efforts, increasing external visibility, providing internal coordination, and eliminating both accountability and intervention problems. Turkish Airlines did not organize a single department to manage relationships with the Qualiflyer Group. They established a small unit reporting to the Agreements Department that was responsible for Qualiflyer relationships; however, this unit ceased after a short period of time. Each department was responsible for different aspects of alliance relationships.

Four projects constituted the basis for operational integration: (i) joint ground handling, (ii) integration of IT systems, (iii) establishment of a single front office and back office, (iv) cooperation on technical operations.

The issue of alliance cost versus benefit is important as the groups begin creating formal management structures for functions such as IT and marketing. Estimated costs just for bilateral links in reservations/marketing vary widely, from $1.5 million to $13 million (Feldman, 2000). The main cost of the alliance partnership was adaptation of IT systems between the group and TK. Another Qualiflyer related investment was the 16.6% stake in Qualiflyer Ground Handling Ltd. On the other hand, a minor cost for TK was related to listing the airfares. In order to make airfare information available for almost every travel agency around the world, carriers have to pay a fee per route to Airline Tariff Publishing Corporation (ATPCO) that collects this information and distributes it to global distribution systems and computer reservation systems. Code sharing brings an additional cost to listing the airfares for the same destinations twice, once for the flights the carrier operates by itself, and once for the flights the carrier operates through its partners.

Level of Cooperation

Considering their market-related objectives, code sharing was an important tool for Turkish carrier to maximize membership benefit. Airline code sharing may have advantages for developing countries insofar as it can offer the possibility of serving very thin routes at minimal cost and using the rights unused so far. It can thus be an instrument to facilitate the participation of developing nations' airlines in international air transport (Groenewege, 1999). However, TK was able to establish code share agreements with only three of the members of the Qualiflyer Group: Swissair, Sabena, Austrian Airlines.

Two of the operational integration projects were accomplished. First, the group started a Zurich-based joint venture for ground handling activities in August, 1998. Qualiflyer Ground Handling Ltd. was financed equally by founding members and the employees were assigned by all of those participating members (IMKB Bulten, 1998). TK participated in this investment with a 16.6% equity stake. Second, TK revised its IT systems for effective coordination.

The other two projects to complete operational integration remained unrealized. The group was not able to start a single front office and merge back offices. This project was planned to provide partners with significant cost reduction through joint marketing synergy.

The next unrealized project, cooperation on technical operations, would increase partners' bargaining power in purchasing aircraft, accessing to airport services with lower charges; and reduce cost of aircraft maintenance. Swissair planned to operate with an all-Airbus fleet by 2006. They expected to cooperate with other airlines in the Qualiflyer

Group to provide economies of scale in aircraft maintenance (Reed, 1999). Austrian and Sabena started the integration process with the Swiss carrier. Various Boeing models were dominant aircraft types in TK's and Sabena's fleet, whereas the major part of Austrian Airlines and Swissair fleet consisted of Airbus models. Therefore, joint aircraft maintenance would be constrained by the mismatch between the aircraft types of partners, even they intended to cooperate. In order to overcome this constraint in the long-term, partners should cooperate in fleet planning. It appears to be that TK did not initiate joint fleet planning process within the 3-year life of the alliance, since their aircraft orders involved Boeing models, whereas all other members started to switch to Airbus, which were compatible with the Swissair fleet (see Table 2). TK ordered only 1 Airbus model in year 2000.

Standardization of customer service qualities of the member airlines was an important consideration to realize alliance philosophy "one voice–one face–one spirit." We intended to compare Qualiflyer carriers' quality ratings to display to what extent the group achieved a standard level of service quality. "However, no official institution in Europe is currently rating European carriers' service quality. EU is preparing a rating system "Quality Indicators" that evaluates the carriers with similar criteria (i.e., delays, lost baggage, passengers denied boarding) to those of the US Department of Transportation. In addition to that, most of the Association of European Airlines (AEA) members signed "Airline Passenger Service Commitment." Standards mentioned in this contract (i.e., offer lowest fare available, notify passengers of known delays, deliver baggage as quickly as possible, take measures to speed-up check-in) can be used as a basis for effective evaluation" (In-

TABLE 2. Qualiflyer Fleet Composition and Orders (1998)

	Aircraft in fleet		Aircraft on order	
	Airbus	**Boeing**	**Airbus**	**Boeing**
TK	19	33	0	26
SR	41	5	27	0
SN	7	31	38	0
OS	10	0	15	0
TAP	17	14	20	0

AEA (1998). Association of European Airlines Yearbook.

terview). In this study we evaluated standardization of customer services using Airline Quality Rating performed by Skytrax, a private company based in Oxford, since this was the only data available on airline quality rating including European carriers, at the time of writing. Skytrax evaluated 9 Qualiflyer carriers, 5 of which were rated with 3 stars and 4 of which with 4 stars, 5 stars representing the premier quality status. This rating indicates that partners were not able to standardize their customer service activities to accomplish the "one face" vision.

CONCLUSIONS

Liberalization of the airline market allowed carriers to reach a wider area of the world. Especially, airlines with a larger fleet and financial resources are more likely to benefit from this trend in the industry. This makes alliance strategy an important source of synergy for developing country airlines to increase their competitiveness against large carriers. As the research conducted displays, alliance success is not a result of micro factors only, but also a consequence of the interdependencies between macro and micro factors. Macro factors limited TK's ability of cooperation with the Qualiflyer Group, mainly because of economic and political differences. Incomplete privatization as a macro factor affected alliance success through its influence on micro-level factors: (i) it was a source of uncertainty for TK's strategic behaviors and alliances do not appreciate partners with uncertain futures; (ii) it was a barrier against the managerial flexibility required for complete integration; (iii) it caused lack of cooperation since binding commercial agreements would decrease TK's attractiveness to non-Qualiflyer carriers.

Our research also displayed that in order to receive maximum benefit in alliance strategy, prospective partners have to evaluate each other's strategic objectives in partner selection process and monitor whether there is a change in those objectives after they establish the alliance relationship. Swissair expanded the Qualiflyer Group with the involvement of regional European carriers (i.e., Volare, Air Liberte, Air Littoral); however, global competition was the main challenge for European carriers, as well as for TK. Cost is another consideration in the partner selection process, since integration with partners may require large investments in systems such as information technologies. These investments increase switching costs when companies decide to leave the existing partnership and join into a new group.

Because of macro and micro factors mentioned in this paper, Turkish Airlines did not achieve its objectives with the Qualiflyer Group, though the company obtained some positive results. Qualiflyer did not help TK to increase their global competitiveness as much as they expected, because of the regional focus of the group. However, the Turkish carrier enhanced its brand value through association with a well-known European brand name. Integration with Europe does not solely depend on bilateral agreements between Turkish and European governments. Turkish companies may globalize their operations and marketing capabilities through international strategic alliances (Esener, 1997). Another important gain for TK is that it was an experience for them on alliance strategy, which is the most significant concept in the future of the aviation industry.

European carriers should develop common strategies and long-term objectives for effective cooperation, which will help European states to achieve their vision: "Single European Sky."

REFERENCES

AEA (1997). Association of European Airlines Yearbook.

AEA (1998). Association of European Airlines Yearbook.

AEA (1999). Association of European Airlines Yearbook.

AEA (2001). Association of European Airlines Yearbook.

Agusdinata, B., & De Klein, W. (2001). The dynamics of airline alliances. *Journal of Air Transport Management*. [On-line], available. www.sciencedirect.com.

Bleeke, J., & Ernst, D. (1993). The way to win in cross-border alliances. Collaborating to Compete. Edited by: Bleeke & Ernst, New York: John Wiles & Sons Publishing.

Bolayirli, Y. (2001). Current issues in air transport sector. Civil Aviation Department Meeting. March, [On-line], available: www.ubak.gov.tr.

Cravens, D.W., Shipp, S.H., & Cravens, K.S. (1994). Reforming the traditional organization: the mandate for developing networks. *Business Horizons*. July-August, 19-28.

Dana, L.P. (1999). Expanding services at British Airways. *Strategic Direction*, 16:1, pp. 6-8.

Das, T.K. & Teng, B.S. (1998). Between trust and control: Developing confidence in partner cooperation in alliances. *Academy of Management Review*, 23:3, [On-line], available: www.ebscohost.com.

Diger ozel durum aciklamalari (1999). *IMKB Bulten*, November 4.

Dyer, J.H., Kale, P., & Singh, H. (2001). How to make strategic alliances work. *MIT Sloan Management Review*, summer, 37-43.

Ellis, C. (1996). Making strategic alliances succeed. *Harvard Business Review*, 74:4, [On-line], available: www.ebscohost.com.

Ertuna, O. (1998). Constraints of privatization: The Turkish case. Mediterranean Development Forum, September 3-6.

Esener, O. (1997). Stratejik Ortakliklar, Istanbul: IMKB Yayinlari.

Esperou, R. (2001). The main challenges for European air transport. *ECAC News*, 20, 19-22.

European Parliament (2001). *Official Journal of the European Communities*. February 7, [On-line], available: www.knoweurope.net.

Fan, T., Vigeant-Langlois L., Geissler, C., Bosler, B. & Wilmking, J. (2001). Evolution of global airline strategic alliance and consolidation in the 21st century. *Journal of Air Transport Management*, [On-line], available: www.sciencedirect.com.

Feldman, J.M. (2000). Alliance costs start building. *Air Transport World*, 37:6, 41-48.

Groenewege, A.D. (1999). Compendium of International Civil Aviation, 2nd edition, Quebec: IATA.

Gulati, R. (1998). Alliances and networks. *Strategic Management Journal*, 19, 293-317.

Keuning, D. (1998). Management. London: Pitman Publishing.

Kleymann, B., & Seristö, H. (2001). Levels of airline alliance membership: Balancing risks & benefits. *Journal of Air Transport Management*, 7:5, [On-line], available: www.sciencedirect.com.

Koza, M.P., & Lewin, A.Y. (1999). The coevolution of network alliances: A longitudinal analysis of an international professional service network. *Organization Science*, 10:5, 638-653.

One world few airlines (1998). *The Economist*. 349:8087, [On-line], available: www.ebscohost.com.

Reed, A. (1999). SR technics shows off. *Airtransport World*, May, 86-89.

Sirket haberleri (1998). *IMKB Bulten*, July 20.

Sirket haberleri. *Borsa Market*. May 24, 1999.

Sirket haberleri (2000). *Para*, December 11.

Skytrax (2002). Airline Quality Rating, [On-line], available: www.airlinequality.com.

Sparaco, P. (1997). New carrier relationships create legal complexities in Europe. *Aviation Week & Space Technology*, 147:20, [On-line], available: www.proquest.com.

Stickler, J. (2001). Building successful strategic alliances. *Strategic Direction*, 17:8, 3-4.

Suen, W.W. (2002). Alliance strategy and the fall of Swissair. *Journal of Air Transport Management*, uncorrected proof, [On-line], available: www.sciencedirect.com.

The Qualiflyer Group implements Sabre alliance manager partner displays (2000). *PR Newswire*, May 10, [On-line], available: www.findarticles.com.

The Qualiflyer Group and Revelex.com sign marketing agreement (2001). *PR Newswire*, January 31, [On-line], available: www.findarticles.com.

Turkish Airlines (2001). *Travel Agent*, April 30, [On-line], available: www.findarticles.com.

Turkish Privatization Administration (2002). Government shares in Turkish Airlines to be privatized. [On-line], available: www.oib.gov.tr/announcements2.htm.

Value-at-Risk (VaR) Computations Under Various VaR Models and Stress Testing

Suat Teker

M. Baris Akçay

SUMMARY. Bank for International Settlements (BIS) proposes that all banks calculate and report amount of market risk they incur and allocate sufficient amount of capital starting at the beginning of year 2002. BIS also suggests that value-at-risk (VaR) models in computing market risk should be used. The Turkish Bank Regulation and Supervision Agency already required all Turkish banks to compute and periodically report market risk and reserve adequate amount of capital since January, 2002. This study mimics an average trading marketable securities portfolio subject to market risk of the four largest Turkish banks. The publicly available quarterly financial reports of year 2001 for Isbank, Garanti, Yapi Kredi and Akbank are examined, and a mimicking portfolio composition is determined as bond investments; 60% in Turkish currency (TRL), 20% in American dollar (USD) and 20% in Euro (EUR). The VaR amounts of the

---

Suat Teker is affiliated with the Department of Accounting and Finance, Istanbul Technical University, Faculty of Management, Macka Campus, 80680 Istanbul, Turkey (E-mail: tekers@itu.edu.tr).

M. Baris Akçay is affiliated with Oyakbank, Department of Market Risk Management, Maslak, Istanbul, Turkey.

[Haworth co-indexing entry note]: "Value-at-Risk (VaR Computations Under Various VaR Models and Stress Testing." Teker, Suat, and M. Baris Akçay. Co-published simultaneously in *Journal of Transnational Management Development* (The International Business Press, an imprint of The Haworth Press, Inc.) Vol. 9, No. 2/3, 2004, pp. 47-67; and: *Islam and Business: Cross-Cultural and Cross-National Perspectives* (ed: Kip Becker) The International Business Press, an imprint of The Haworth Press, Inc., 2004, pp. 47-67. Single or multiple copies of this article are available for a fee from The Haworth Document Delivery Service [1-800-HAWORTH, 9:00 a.m. - 5:00 p.m. (EST). E-mail address: docdelivery@haworthpress.com].

mimicking portfolio are computed by applying Historical Simulation, Monte Carlo Simulation, Delta-Normal and Standard Methods. Finally, stress test is applied for each of the models by using crisis scenarios. The Turkish financial crises of November 2000 and February 2001 are simulated as stress scenarios. The results of stress testing reveal that all methods except standard method can stand the crisis in November 2000, but none of the models can stand the crisis in February 2001. *[Article copies available for a fee from The Haworth Document Delivery Service: 1-800-HAWORTH. E-mail address: <docdelivery@haworthpress.com> Website: <http://www.HaworthPress.com> © 2004 by The Haworth Press, Inc. All rights reserved.]*

KEYWORDS. International banking, international settlements, BIS, market risk, value-at-risk, Turkish Bank Regulation and Supervision Agency, Turkish banks

Financial markets and institutions have operated in a fast changing economic environment in recent years. There may be more than 100 crises cited in the economic literature over the last 20 years. This makes, on the average, five financial crises per year. Therefore, one might argue that the importance of risk management for financial institutions has kept increasing at an increasing rate. Lately, the overview of banks about risk management has been proactive. As a result, banks have heavily concentrated on identifying all kinds of risks which likely affect banks' financial position, and measuring and managing financial risks by applying various value-at-risk (VaR) models. The crises that have often occurred in recent years have led financial managers to be precautious. Then, the need for questioning stress testing of VaR models applied has come across. Stress testing attempts to identify the weakest points of a portfolio by pinpointing the crucial risk factors causing the heaviest losses. Stress testing is applied for banks' portfolio by simulating likely worst case scenarios (Christoffersen, Hahn, and Inoue, 2001). Financial crises that actually occurred in the past might be a good approximation for the worst case scenarios.

This research computes the amount of VaR of a mimicking portfolio under various VaR models and examines the effects of stress scenarios on banks' capital adequacy. By using publicly available quarterly financial reports of year 2001 of the four largest Turkish banks (namely Garanti, YapiKredi, Isbank and Akbank), a mimic trading marketable securities portfolio is composed. The examination of a marketable securities portfolio of the underlying banks reveals that their trading portfolios on the average included 1.5 units of securities denominated in Turkish currency (TRL) for every 0.5 unit of security denominated in US dollar (USD) and 0.5 unit of security denominated in Euro (EUR). Based on this analysis and knowing that the trading securities portfolios of the Turkish banks are almost completely composed of bond investments, it is assumed that a mimic bond portfolio (nominal value of 2,500 trillion TRL) is currently held, which is composed of 60% TRL, 20% USD and 20% EUR denominated bonds. The bonds invested in the portfolio are chosen as the ones traded most heavily in the secondary market. The definition of the bonds invested in the mimic portfolio is presented in Table 1. Fifteen bonds with various maturities are included in the portfolio and five bonds in each currency at the predetermined amount invested.

METHODOLOGY AND DATA

This study employs Historical Simulation, Monte Carlo Simulation, Delta-Normal and Standard Methods for market risk computations of the mimicking bond portfolio. Among these, Delta-Normal and stan-

TABLE 1. Investments in Bonds in the Mimic Portfolio

Code of Bond		Type of Bond	Curr	Maturity (dd.mm.yy)	Time to Mat. (Month)	Nominal Amount (Mil. USD/EUR, Bil. TRL)	Present Value
Bond 1	US900123AL40	Eurobond	USD	15.01.2030	335.4	66	340,688
Bond 2	US900123AM23	Eurobond	USD	27.11.2006	53.7	66	153,741
Bond 3	US900123AP53	Eurobond	USD	19.03.2008	69.6	66	158,811
Bond 4	US900147AB51	Eurobond	USD	15.06.2010	96.9	66	187,872
Bond 5	XS0086996310	Eurobond	USD	12.05.2003	10.5	66	117,565
Bond 6	DE0001972354	Eurobond	EURO	06.02.2003	7.4	72	127,435
Bond 7	DE0002938727	Eurobond	EURO	15.03.2004	20.8	72	136,217
Bond 8	DE0003544904	Eurobond	EURO	17.12.2002	5.7	72	128,661
Bond 9	DE0007751752	Eurobond	EURO	07.02.2005	31.8	72	148,421
Bond 10	DE0008553470	Eurobond	EURO	08.05.2007	59.1	72	155,609
Bond 11	TRB231002T17	T-Bill	TRL	23.10.2002	3.8	300,000	261,207
Bond 12	TRT050203T18	T-Bond	TRL	05.02.2003	7.3	300,000	220,557
Bond 13	TRT210104T18	T-Bond	TRL	21.01.2004	19.0	300,000	319,865
Bond 14	TRT170304T12	T-Bond	TRL	17.03.2004	20.9	300,000	334,577
Bond 15	TRB050303T17	T-Bill	TRL	05.03.2003	8.3	300,000	211,439
Total					**TRL**	**2,500,000**	**3,002,665**

dard methods are called as parametric models whereas Historical and Monte Carlo models are based on simulations.

BIS suggests that market risk computations under VaR models should use 10-day holding period and 99% confidence level. On the other hand, J.P. Morgan suggests that a 1-day holding period and 95% confidence level should be used. This study employs both 95% and 99% confidence level, and 1-day and 10-day holding period intervals in all VaR computations.[1] BIS also suggests that one-year historical observations on the asset returns should be utilized in VaR computations (J.P. Morgan, 1996). This study uses 200 working day historical observations (exchange and interest rates), which approximates one calendar year. The KVaR 3.6 software program developed by Reuters is applied for the computation of VaR values of the mimicking portfolio under Historical Simulation and Monte Carlo Simulation models. J.P. Morgan Riskmetrics methodology is employed for variance-covariance matrix computations in Delta-Normal model. The maturity interval form PR200A required by the Turkish Bank Regulatory and Supervisory Agency for market risk calculations is used to apply the standard model.

Historical Simulation Method does not assume any specific distribution for asset returns. It presumes that a defined portfolio is held at a particular point in time and previously observed various return scenarios are applied to the portfolio in order to measure the value changes of the portfolio. First, an expected interest rate for each of bond in the portfolio considering its time to maturity is determined using a previously developed yield curve. Then, daily changes in bond values are computed by using daily historical changes in interest rates. Considering the weights of each group of bonds in the portfolio and the correlations among the bonds, daily profits/losses are computed backward for 200 days for each bond and the whole portfolio. As a result of this process, a number of different portfolio values are obtained and these values are mapped from highest to lowest. Then, the VaR value of the portfolio is read on the map for a given confidence level and holding period. The VaR value is determined to be the worst loss in the portfolio on the 190th observation at 95% confidence level and on the 198th observation at the 99% confidence level. Graph 1 presents the expected profits/losses of the portfolio for 1-day and 10-day holding periods under Historical Simulations. Graph 2 shows the variations from normal distribution at 95% and 99% confidence level for 1-day and 10-day holding periods (see Table 2).

Monte Carlo Simulation model uses historical observations to identify the correlations among risk factors and then computes variance-covariance matrix. By utilizing this computed variance-covariance ma-

GRAPH 1. Distributions Under Historical Simulation

Holding Period = 1-Day

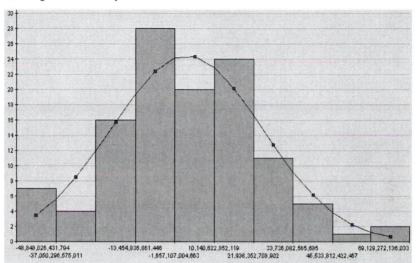

Holding Period = 10-Day

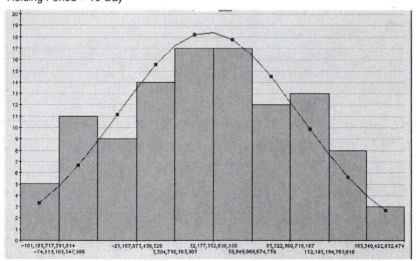

GRAPH 2. Variations from Normal Distribution Under Historical Simulations

CL = 95%, T = 1-Day

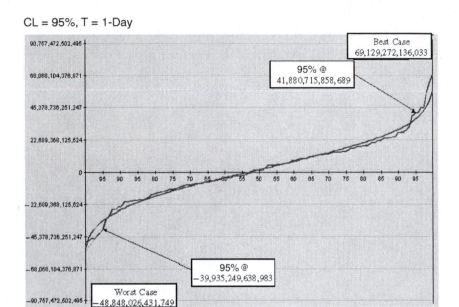

CL = 99%, T = 1-Day

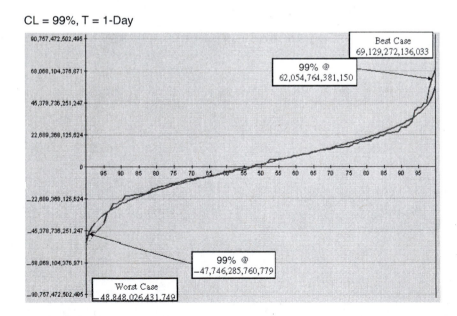

CL = 95%, T = 10-Day

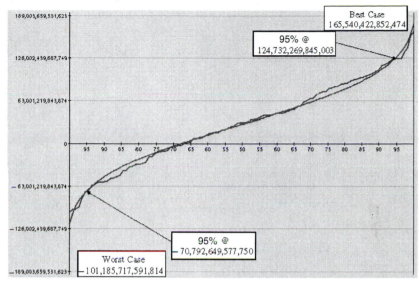

CL = 99%, T = 10-Day

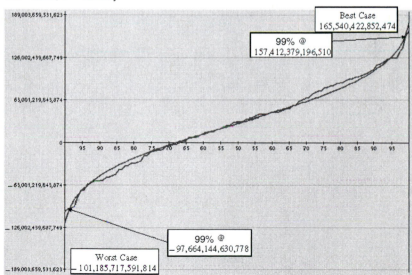

TABLE 2. VaR Values by Type of Risks Under Historical Simulation

HISTORICAL SIMULATION

Risk Type	USD CL: 95% 1-Day	10-Day	USD CL: 99% 1-Day	10-Day	EUR CL: 95% 1-Day	10-Day	EUR CL: 99% 1-Day	10-Day	TRL CL: 95% 1-Day	10-Day	TRL CL: 99% 1-Day	10-Day	TOTAL CL: 95% 1-Day	10-Day	TOTAL CL: 99% 1-Day	10-Day
Interest Risk	8,245	26,664	11,107	30,024	896	2,349	1,156	3,499	13,215	36,648	16,602	47,499	12,468	29,471	18,440	36,337
Currency Risk	17,605	32,677	25,951	38,321	14,473	34,615	19,788	44,077	0	0	0	0	33,430	65,043	43,043	82,047
Residual Risk	65	341	129	629	12	52	21	123	0	0	0	0	67	366	132	678
Total	25,915	35,682	37,187	68,974	15,381	37,016	20,695	47,699	13,215	36,648	16,602	47,499	45,965	94,880	61,615	119,062
Portfolio VaR	21,714	53,451	27,886	62,570	15,017	35,264	20,038	45,688	13,215	36,648	16,602	47,499	39,935	70,793	47,746	97,664

trix, randomly produced expected asset returns are generated. The asset returns generation process is repeated 300 times, and daily expected profits/losses of each bond and the whole portfolio are computed. The resulted VaR values at 95% and 99% confidence level are obtained. Graph 3 shows the expected profits/losses of the portfolio for 1-day and 10-day holding periods under Monte Carlo Simulation. Graph 4 presents the variations from normal distribution at 95% and 99% confidence level for 1-day and 10-day holding period (see Table 3).

Delta-Normal Method was developed by J.P. Morgan known as riskmetrics. Although the application is very simple for a single asset, it gets very complicated as more assets added to the portfolio because of correlations among asset returns. The most restricted assumptions of the model are that all asset returns are distributed normally and linear function of time. This parametric model uses mean and standard deviation of the distribution of the portfolio for computation of VaR amount. The model can be formulized as follows;

$$\text{VaR} = (\text{Market Value of Port.})(\text{Volatility of Port.})(\text{Confidence Level})(\text{Hold. Period})$$
$$= (MV_p)(\sigma_p)(CL)(\sqrt{t}) \tag{1}$$

First, the time to maturity of each bond is determined. Then, all bonds in the portfolio are placed in the standard time intervals of riskmetrics. Next, the interest rates related to time intervals are determined using the derived yield curves. Later, the correlation matrix is computed representing the correlations among various interest rates for various time intervals (see Table 4). Since the number of assets (bonds) in the portfolio exceeds two, the portfolio VaR can be computed only in a vector solution (J.P. Morgan, 1996):

$$\sigma_p = \sqrt{(w_1, w_2, w_3, w_4, \ldots w_n) \times \begin{pmatrix} \text{Covariance} \\ \text{Matrix of} \\ \text{Portfolio} \end{pmatrix} \times \begin{pmatrix} w_1 \\ w_2 \\ w_3 \\ w_4 \\ \cdot \\ \cdot \\ w_n \end{pmatrix}}$$

$$\sigma^2_p = (V)(R)(V^T) \tag{2}$$

where V is the (n × 1) vector of weight of each bond, R is the (n × n) correlation matrix, and V^T is the (1 × n) transpose of vector V.

GRAPH 3. Distributions Under Monte Carlo Simulation

Holding Period = 1-Day

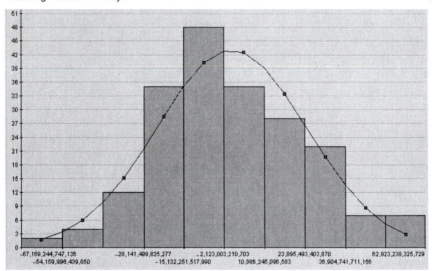

Holding Period = 10-Day

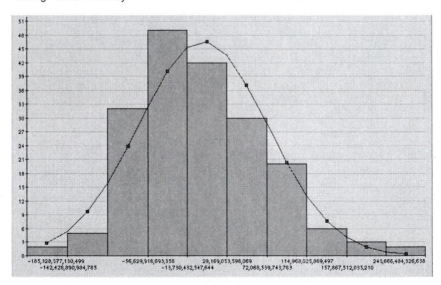

GRAPH 4. Variations from Normal Distribution Under Monte Carlo Simulations

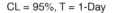

CL = 95%, T = 1-Day

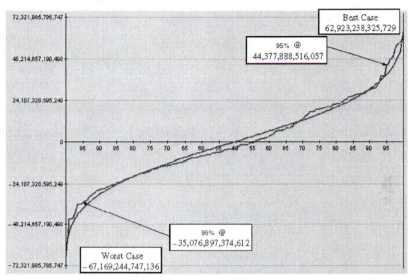

CL = 99%, T = 1-Day

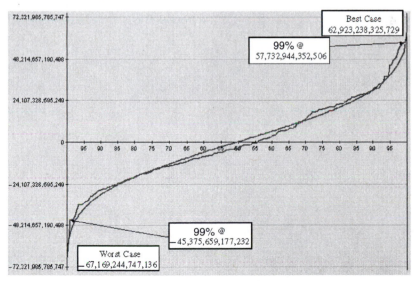

GRAPH 4 (continued)

CL = 95%, T = 10-Day

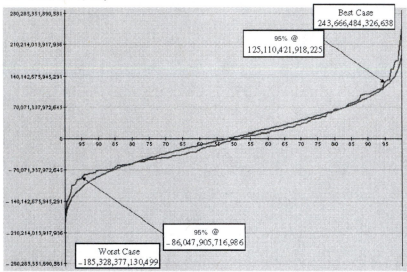

CL = 99%, T = 10-Day

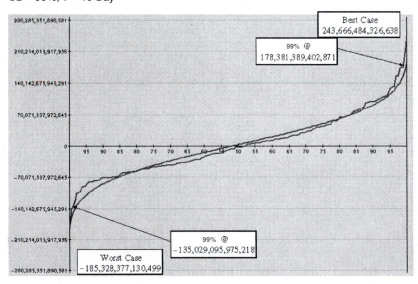

TABLE 3. VaR Values by Type of Risks Under Monte Carlo Simulation

MONTE CARLO SIMULATION

Risk Type	USD				EUR				TRL				TOTAL			
	CL: 95%		CL: 99%		CL: 95%		CL: 99%		CL: 95%		CL: 99%		CL: 95%		CL: 99%	
	1-Day	10-Day	1-Day	10-Day	1-Day	10-Day	1-Day	10-Day	1-Day	10-Day	1-Day	10-Day	1-Day	10-Day	1-Day	10-Day
Interest Risk	7,306	26,577	8,476	33,016	999	2,147	1,177	2,790	9,371	32,983	13,443	39,420	12,849	38,392	16,512	49,138
Currency Risk	19,019	47,178	26,518	64,976	14,336	33,154	22,140	45,343	0	0	0	0	31,981	76,378	46,943	114,440
Residual Risk	93	970	141	1,373	7	75	17	126	0	0	0	0	99	991	157	1,437
Total	26,418	74,725	35,135	99,365	15,342	35,376	23,334	48,259	9,371	32,983	13,443	39,420	44,929	115,761	63,612	165,015
Portfolio VaR	21,258	63,066	29,284	94,793	15,070	33,659	22,563	44,655	9,371	32,983	13,443	39,420	35,077	86,048	45,376	135,029

TABLE 4. Correlation Matrix Under Delta-Normal Method

Period	TL BOND RATES				USD BOND RATES								EUR BOND RATES						
	3M	6M	1Y	2Y	6M	1Y	4Y	5Y	7Y	9Y	20Y	30Y	3M	6M	1Y	2Y	3Y	5Y	10Y
3M	1.000	0.170	0.736	0.868	0.668	0.412	0.474	0.368	0.454	0.171	-0.147	-0.028	-0.435	-0.207	-0.511	-0.550	-0.299	0.100	0.443
6M	0.170	1.000	0.043	0.179	0.145	0.272	0.246	0.275	0.252	0.298	0.287	0.298	-0.048	0.259	0.136	0.119	-0.079	-0.043	0.310
1Y	0.736	0.043	1.000	0.969	0.213	-0.133	-0.064	-0.185	-0.087	-0.398	-0.634	-0.558	-0.754	-0.697	-0.328	-0.836	-0.179	-0.056	-0.154
2Y	0.868	0.179	0.969	1.000	0.378	0.055	0.123	0.003	0.100	-0.212	-0.486	-0.392	-0.695	-0.554	-0.756	-0.775	-0.232	-0.014	0.053
6M	0.668	0.145	0.213	0.378	1.000	0.885	0.932	0.869	0.921	0.745	0.421	0.556	-0.016	0.449	0.180	0.136	-0.279	0.101	0.711
1Y	0.412	0.272	-0.133	0.055	0.885	1.000	0.993	0.989	0.996	0.908	0.642	0.760	0.311	0.714	0.468	0.422	-0.240	0.098	0.805
4Y	0.474	0.246	-0.064	0.123	0.932	0.993	1.000	0.989	1.000	0.895	0.614	0.737	0.243	0.672	0.419	0.374	-0.250	0.102	0.803
5Y	0.368	0.275	-0.185	0.003	0.869	0.989	0.989	1.000	0.993	0.929	0.682	0.794	0.342	0.743	0.512	0.468	-0.222	0.100	0.812
7Y	0.454	0.252	-0.087	0.100	0.921	0.996	1.000	0.993	1.000	0.903	0.629	0.750	0.262	0.687	0.438	0.393	-0.244	0.102	0.806
9Y	0.171	0.298	-0.398	-0.212	0.745	0.908	0.895	0.929	0.903	1.000	0.901	0.961	0.411	0.827	0.673	0.638	-0.138	0.139	0.831
20Y	-0.147	0.287	-0.634	-0.486	0.421	0.642	0.614	0.682	0.629	0.901	1.000	0.986	0.480	0.805	0.777	0.760	-0.004	0.149	0.693
30Y	-0.028	0.298	-0.558	-0.392	0.556	0.760	0.737	0.794	0.750	0.961	0.986	1.000	0.464	0.833	0.755	0.731	-0.056	0.149	0.763
3M	-0.435	-0.048	-0.754	-0.695	-0.016	0.311	0.243	0.342	0.262	0.411	0.480	0.464	1.000	0.626	0.644	0.633	0.030	0.145	0.301
6M	-0.207	0.259	-0.697	-0.554	0.449	0.714	0.672	0.743	0.687	0.827	0.805	0.833	0.626	1.000	0.899	0.875	-0.037	0.045	0.569
1Y	-0.511	0.136	-0.328	-0.756	0.180	0.468	0.419	0.512	0.438	0.673	0.777	0.755	0.644	0.899	1.000	0.998	0.086	-0.017	0.317
2Y	-0.550	0.119	-0.836	-0.775	0.136	0.422	0.374	0.468	0.393	0.638	0.760	0.731	0.633	0.875	0.998	1.000	0.105	-0.030	0.273
3Y	-0.299	-0.079	-0.179	-0.232	-0.279	-0.240	-0.250	-0.222	-0.244	-0.138	-0.004	-0.056	0.030	-0.037	0.086	0.105	1.000	0.022	-0.170
5Y	0.100	-0.043	-0.056	-0.014	0.101	0.098	0.102	0.100	0.102	0.139	0.149	0.149	0.145	0.045	-0.017	-0.030	0.022	1.000	0.297
10Y	0.443	0.310	-0.154	0.053	0.711	0.805	0.803	0.812	0.806	0.831	0.693	0.763	0.301	0.569	0.317	0.273	-0.170	0.297	1.000

The volatility of portfolio is calculated by multiplying above three matrixes (see Table 5). Then, the portfolio VaR value is obtained by multiplying the market value of the portfolio, volatility of the portfolio, square root of holding period and z value of confidence level.

The use of *standard method* is mandatory for all Turkish banks for reporting market risk to the Turkish Bank Regulatory and Supervisory Agency since January, 2002. This method places each asset into a time interval considering its time to maturity. Next, the present values of bonds placed into time intervals are multiplied by predetermined risk percentages. After a few steps of netting short and long positions and differencing time intervals, the portfolio VaR is computed. The portfolio VaR under this method is actually a simple addition of VaR amount of each bond (see Table 6).

STRESS TESTING

VaR models measure the maximum amount of losses incurred in a portfolio for a given confidence level over a period of time. However, the models must be tested for cases of unexpected and extraordinary conditions. Stress testing is a technique to measure the strength of the model for sharp variations in prices and correlations among asset returns. Initially, it is to be decided what kind of a scenario (changes in correlations and prices) is applied for stress testing. The scenarios to be applied for stress testing may be chosen as the crises actually happened in the past. This way, the strength of the portfolio can be measured when the behaviour of risk factors changes in the periods of crisis. On the other hand, the stress scenarios could be the sensitivity of the portfolio for the portfolio's specific risks (Dimson & Marsh, 1997).

In this study November 2000 and February 2001 financial crisis of Turkey are applied as stress scenarios on the mimicking portfolio. The examination of financial data supports that the extraordinary behaviour of risk factors during these crisis periods can be analyzed over a 10-day period. By utilizing Monte Carlo Simulation, a variance-covariance matrix for each crisis is computed considering changes in returns and correlations over the 10-day crises period. Based on this computed variance-covariance matrix, the expected returns in simulated crisis are derived by repeating the simulation 300 times. Finally, the stress VaR values are obtained (see Table 7).

TABLE 5. Covariance Matrix Under Delta-Normal Method

Period	TL BOND RATES				USD BOND RATES								EUR BOND RATES						
	3M	6M	1Y	2Y	6M	1Y	4Y	5Y	7Y	9Y	20Y	30Y	3M	6M	1Y	2Y	3Y	5Y	10Y
3M	**8.E-03**	4.E-04	5.E-03	5.E-03	1.E-04	1.E-04	1.E-04	1.E-04	1.E-04	4.E-05	-4.E-05	-7.E-06	-1.E-04	-5.E-05	-1.E-04	-1.E-04	-4.E-04	7.E-06	6.E-05
6M	4.E-04	**8.E-04**	9.E-05	3.E-04	7.E-06	3.E-05	2.E-05	3.E-05	2.E-05	2.E-05	2.E-05	2.E-05	-4.E-06	2.E-05	9.E-06	8.E-06	-3.E-05	7.E-06	1.E-05
1Y	5.E-03	9.E-05	**5.E-03**	4.E-03	3.E-05	-3.E-05	-1.E-05	-5.E-05	-2.E-05	-7.E-05	-1.E-04	-5.E-05	-2.E-04	-1.E-04	-1.E-04	-1.E-04	-2.E-04	-3.E-06	-2.E-05
2Y	5.E-03	3.E-04	4.E-03	**3.E-03**	4.E-05	1.E-05	2.E-05	7.E-07	2.E-05	-3.E-05	-8.E-05	-6.E-05	-1.E-04	-8.E-05	-1.E-04	-1.E-04	-2.E-04	-7.E-07	5.E-06
6M	1.E-04	7.E-06	3.E-05	4.E-05	**3.E-06**	5.E-06	3.E-06	5.E-06	5.E-06	9.E-06	6.E-06	7.E-06	3.E-06	6.E-06	4.E-06	3.E-06	-1.E-05	1.E-07	2.E-06
1Y	1.E-04	3.E-05	-3.E-05	1.E-05	5.E-06	**1.E-05**	9.E-06	1.E-05	9.E-06	8.E-06	6.E-06	6.E-06	4.E-06	3.E-06	4.E-06	3.E-06	-1.E-05	3.E-07	1.E-06
4Y	1.E-04	2.E-05	-1.E-05	2.E-05	3.E-06	9.E-06	**7.E-06**	9.E-06	7.E-06	6.E-06	5.E-06	5.E-06	2.E-06	3.E-06	3.E-06	2.E-06	-9.E-06	3.E-07	3.E-06
5Y	1.E-04	3.E-05	-5.E-05	7.E-07	5.E-06	1.E-05	9.E-06	**1.E-05**	9.E-06	1.E-05	6.E-06	7.E-06	3.E-06	4.E-06	4.E-06	3.E-06	3.E-07	3.E-07	4.E-06
7Y	1.E-04	2.E-05	-2.E-05	2.E-05	5.E-06	9.E-06	7.E-06	9.E-06	**8.E-06**	6.E-06	6.E-06	5.E-06	2.E-06	5.E-06	3.E-06	2.E-06	1.E-06	2.E-07	3.E-06
9Y	4.E-05	2.E-05	-7.E-05	-3.E-05	5.E-06	8.E-06	6.E-06	1.E-05	6.E-06	**6.E-06**	6.E-06	3.E-06	3.E-06	3.E-06	3.E-06	3.E-06	-5.E-06	-3.E-06	3.E-06
20Y	-4.E-05	2.E-05	-1.E-04	-8.E-05	6.E-06	6.E-06	5.E-06	6.E-06	6.E-06	6.E-06	**8.E-06**	6.E-06	4.E-06	5.E-06	4.E-06	4.E-06	-5.E-06	3.E-07	3.E-06
30Y	-7.E-06	2.E-05	-5.E-05	-6.E-05	7.E-06	6.E-06	5.E-06	7.E-06	5.E-06	5.E-06	7.E-06	**7.E-06**	3.E-06	6.E-06	5.E-06	5.E-06	-1.E-06	3.E-07	3.E-06
3M	-1.E-04	-4.E-06	-2.E-04	-1.E-04	3.E-06	3.E-06	2.E-06	3.E-06	2.E-06	3.E-06	4.E-06	3.E-06	**8.E-06**	4.E-06	5.E-06	4.E-06	1.E-06	3.E-07	1.E-06
6M	-5.E-05	2.E-05	-1.E-04	-8.E-05	6.E-06	3.E-06	3.E-06	4.E-06	5.E-06	3.E-06	4.E-06	6.E-06	4.E-06	**6.E-06**	5.E-06	4.E-06	-1.E-06	9.E-08	2.E-06
1Y	-1.E-04	9.E-06	-1.E-04	-1.E-04	4.E-06	4.E-06	3.E-06	4.E-06	3.E-06	3.E-06	5.E-06	5.E-06	5.E-06	5.E-06	**6.E-06**	5.E-06	3.E-06	-3.E-08	1.E-06
2Y	-1.E-04	8.E-06	-1.E-04	-1.E-04	6.E-07	3.E-06	2.E-06	4.E-06	2.E-06	3.E-06	5.E-06	4.E-06	6.E-07	6.E-07	6.E-06	**5.E-06**	3.E-06	-5.E-08	9.E-07
3Y	-4.E-04	-3.E-05	-2.E-04	-2.E-04	-1.E-06	-1.E-05	-9.E-06	3.E-07	1.E-06	-5.E-06	-5.E-06	-1.E-06	1.E-06	-1.E-06	3.E-06	3.E-06	**2.E-04**	2.E-07	-3.E-06
5Y	7.E-06	7.E-06	-3.E-06	-7.E-07	3.E-07	3.E-07	2.E-07	3.E-07	2.E-07	3.E-07	3.E-07	3.E-07	-3.E-08	9.E-08	-3.E-08	-5.E-08	2.E-07	**6.E-07**	4.E-07
10Y	6.E-05	1.E-05	-2.E-05	5.E-06	1.E-06	3.E-06	3.E-06	4.E-06	3.E-06	3.E-06	3.E-06	3.E-06	1.E-06	2.E-06	1.E-06	9.E-07	-3.E-06	4.E-07	**2.E-06**

62

TABLE 6. VaR Values by Types of Bonds

Bond Type		Historical Simulation				Monte Carlo Simulation				Standard Method	Delta Normal Method			
		CL: 95%		CL: 99%		CL: 95%		CL: 99%			CL: 95%		CL: 99%	
		1-Day	10-Day	1-Day	10-Day	1-Day	10-Day	1-Day	10-Day		1-Day	10-Day	1-Day	10-Day
Bond 1	USD	9,972	26,907	10,655	31,530	8,511	29,220	11,570	42,087	20,442	8,288	26,210	11,704	37,012
Bond 2	USD	3,207	6,537	4,271	7,876	3,156	8,310	4,438	12,275	4,228	2,575	8,142	3,636	11,498
Bond 3	USD	3,346	7,192	4,440	8,755	3,211	8,736	4,646	13,435	5,161	2,653	8,390	3,747	11,848
Bond 4	USD	4,080	9,334	5,314	10,826	3,989	11,107	5,594	17,230	7,045	3,265	10,325	4,611	14,580
Bond 5	USD	2,213	4,081	3,222	4,876	2,357	5,726	3,314	7,751	823	1,849	5,848	2,611	8,258
Bond 6	EUR	2,657	6,336	3,647	8,106	2,602	6,122	4,072	8,313	892	2,209	6,985	3,119	9,864
Bond 7	EUR	2,926	6,881	3,910	8,936	2,922	6,550	4,393	8,704	1,703	2,366	7,483	3,342	10,567
Bond 8	EUR	2,677	6,394	3,671	8,156	2,646	6,092	4,087	8,370	515	2,194	6,939	3,099	9,799
Bond 9	EUR	3,193	7,575	4,285	9,841	3,275	7,215	4,859	9,500	2,597	2,820	8,916	3,982	12,591
Bond 10	EUR	3,276	8,273	4,591	10,802	3,460	7,772	5,211	10,030	4,279	2,726	8,619	3,849	12,172
Bond 11	TRL	1,138	2,279	1,889	3,230	1,037	3,085	1,374	3,844	1,045	880	2,783	1,243	3,930
Bond 12	TRL	1,257	5,164	2,284	6,516	1,365	3,664	1,739	4,741	1,544	1,304	4,123	1,841	5,822
Bond 13	TRL	3,542	11,038	5,504	15,098	3,108	10,513	3,956	12,863	3,998	2,691	8,509	3,800	12,016
Bond 14	TRL	4,063	12,712	6,355	17,398	3,547	12,088	4,573	14,779	4,182	3,484	11,017	4,920	15,558
Bond 15	TRL	1,438	5,669	2,377	6,959	1,358	4,183	1,968	5,131	1,480	1,131	3,578	1,598	5,052
Total		48,985	126,372	62,425	158,905	46,544	130,389	65,794	179,053	59,934	40,436	127,870	57,101	180,568
Portfolio VaR		39,935	70,793	47,746	97,664	35,077	86,048	45,376	135,029	59,934	31,671	100,152	44,723	141,426
Reduction in VaR		18.47%	43.98%	23.51%	38.54%	24.63%	34.01%	31.03%	24.59%	0.00%	21.68%	21.68%	21.68%	21.68%
VaR as % of Port. Value		1.33%	2.36%	1.59%	3.25%	1.17%	2.87%	1.51%	4.50%	2.00%	1.05%	3.34%	1.49%	4.71%

TABLE 7. Results of Stress Testing

Bond Type		Present Value (TRL)	Stress Testing		% Loss in Bonds	
			Shock 1	Shock 2	Shock 1	Shock 2
Bond 1	USD	340,688	12,678	39,205	3.72%	11.51%
Bond 2	USD	153,741	4,337	6,677	2.82%	4.34%
Bond 3	USD	158,811	4,517	7,872	2.84%	4.96%
Bond 4	USD	187,872	5,409	11,000	2.88%	5.86%
Bond 5	USD	117,565	2,615	3,368	2.22%	2.86%
Bond 6	EUR	127,435	3,016	3,609	2.37%	2.83%
Bond 7	EUR	136,217	3,545	4,281	2.60%	3.14%
Bond 8	EUR	128,661	3,015	3,630	2.34%	2.82%
Bond 9	EUR	148,421	4,064	5,441	2.74%	3.67%
Bond 10	EUR	155,609	4,516	7,692	2.90%	4.94%
Bond 11	TRL	261,207	2,724	24,890	1.04%	9.53%
Bond 12	TRL	220,557	4,460	14,700	2.02%	6.66%
Bond 13	TRL	319,865	20,825	51,519	6.51%	16.11%
Bond 14	TRL	334,577	23,869	58,999	7.13%	17.63%
Bond 15	TRL	211,439	5,562	17,452	2.63%	8.25%
Total		3,002,665	105,153	260,335	3.50%	8.67%
Portfolio VaR			89,162	165,411	2.97%	5.51%

Shock 1 = The Turkish financial crisis of November 2000.
Shock 2 = The Turkish financial crisis of February 2001.

ANALYSIS OF COMPUTATIONS

The VaR computations for each model are repeated for 95% and 99% confidence level, and 1-day and 10-day holding period except the standard model (see Table 6). The application results for Historical Simulation and Monte Carlo Simulation are presented in Table 2 and Table 3. The simulation results are analyzed by risk type (interest, currency and residual risk) and by currency type (USD, EUR and TRL). Comparing bond investments in USD, EUR and TRL, the largest VaR values are produced for currency risk in USD and EUR under both methods. The currency risk of TRL is zero since TRL is not subject to currency risk. It also appears that bond investments in TRL are subject to the highest interest rate risk compared to other two currencies. However, bond investments in USD have the largest total VaR and portfolio VaR although USD bonds have only 20% weight in the whole portfolio. Notice that total VaR values are considerably lower than the portfolio VaR since correlations among the bonds in the portfolio have balance-off effect in risk reduction. The computed portfolio VaR values at 99% confidence level and 10-day holding period are about 98 trillion TRL under Historical Simulation and 135 trillion TRL under Monte Carlo Simulation methods.

Table 4 and 5 show correlation and covariance matrices for Delta-Normal method. Table 6 summarizes the VaR values of all four methods by type of bonds. The VaR values of individual bonds under different methods could considerably vary. For instance, the VaR value of Bond 4 at 99% confidence level and 10-day holding period is 10.8 trillion TRL under Historical Simulation, 17.2 trillion TRL under Monte Carlo Simulation, 14.6 trillion TRL under Delta-Normal method and only 7 trillion TRL under standard method. The portfolio VaR values at 99% confidence level and 10-day holding period are about 98 trillion TRL under Historical Simulation, 135 trillion TRL under Monte Carlo Simulation, 60 trillion TRL under standard method and 141 trillion TRL under Delta-Normal Method. Similarly, the portfolio VaR values as a percentage of the present value of the portfolio are 3.25%, 4.50%, 2% and 4.71%, respectively. It appears that the Delta-Normal Method requires the highest amount of capital reserve while the standard method requires the lowest amount of capital reserve for the same mimicking portfolio.

Table 7 presents the results of the stress testing. It is viewed that each bond responds the shocks differently. For example, Bond 5, 6, 7 and 8 respond each shock similarly by making nearly same amount of losses. However, the response of Bond 1, 13 and 14 are highly different for each shock. The first shock causes only 3.72% losses in Bond 1 while the second shock wipes 11.51% of the bond value. Overall effects of Shock 1 and Shock 2 are about 89 and 165 trillion TRL losses in the bond portfolio, respectively.

CONCLUDING REMARKS

The summary of results of all VaR models applied at 99% confidence level and 1-day holding period is presented in Table 8. Shock 1 representing November 2000 financial crises period produces a loss of about 89 trillion TRL or 2.97% of the portfolio value, while Shock 2 representing February 2001 crises period causes a loss of rounding 164 trillion TRL or 5.48% of the portfolio value. The portfolio VaR values are about 48 trillion TRL for Historical Simulation, 45 trillion

TABLE 8. Summary of VaR Results

	Historical Simulation	Monte Carlo Simulation	Delta Normal	Standard Methods	Stress Testing	
					Shock 1	Shock 2
Portfolio VaR	47,746	45,376	44,722	59,934	89,162	164,411
VaR as % of Portfolio Value	1.59%	1.51%	1.49%	2.00%	2.97%	5.48%

TRL for Monte Carlo Simulation, 45 trillion TRL for Delta-Normal and 60 trillion TRL for the standard method. None of the models can apparently stand any of these shocks since the expected VaR values of all models are much less than losses caused by Shock 1 and Shock 2. However, the regulatory agency requires that the calculated VaR values for market risk must be multiplied by a factor of three. Then, all VaR models can stand the Shock 1 and show a good amount of resistance for Shock 2, while the standard model shows no resistance for any of the shocks.

NOTE

1. Except standard model since standard model does not specify confidence level and holding period.

REFERENCES

Beltratti, A., Morano, C. (1999), "Computing Value at Risk with High Frequency Data," Journal of Empirical Finance, May, 6, 431-455.

Bis (1996), "Overview of the Amendment to the Capital Accord to Incorporate Market Risk," Bank for International Settlements, Basle, January.

Cardenas, J., Walters, K. (1999), "Value at Risk–the Monte Carlo Way," Global Investment Management, April, 38, 57-72.

Christoffersen, P., Hahn, J., Inoue, A. (2001), "Testing and Comparing Value-at-Risk Measures," Journal of Empirical Finance, March, 8, 325-342.

Diebolt, F. X, Hickman, A., Inoue, A., Schuermann, T. (1997), "Converting 1-Day Volatility to h-Day Volatility: Scaling by Root-h is Worse Than You Think," Working Paper 34, Wharton Financial Institutions Center, The Wharton School, University of Pennsylvania, July

Diebolt, F. X., Schuermann, T., Stroughair, J.D. (1998), "Pitfalls and Opportunities in the Use of Extreme Value Theory in Risk Management," Working Paper 10, Wharton Financial Institutions Center, The Wharton School, University of Pennsylvania, April.

Dimson, E., Marsh, P. (1997), "Stress Tests of Capital Requirements," Journal of Banking and Finance, December, 21, 1515-1546.

Fallon, W., (1996), "Calculating Value-at-Risk," Working Paper 49, Wharton Financial Institutions Center, The Wharton School, University of Pennsylvania.

Froot, K. A., Stein, J. C., (1998), "Risk Management, Capital Budgeting, and Capital Structure Policy for Financial Institutions: An Integrated Approach," Journal of Financial Economics, Vol. 47, 55-82.

Hendricks, D., (1999), "Evaluation of Value-at-Risk Models Using Historical Data," FRBNY Economic Policy Review, April, 39-69.

Holton, G. A. (2000), "Closed Form Value at Risk," www.contingencyanalysis.com/frame/framevar.htm

Holton, G. A., (2000), "Volatility and Horizon," www.contingencyanalysis.com/frame/framevar.htm

J.P. Morgan & Co., (1996), "Riskmetrics–Technical Document. Third Edition," May 26, www.riskmetrics.com.

J.P. Morgan & Co., (2001), "Return To RiskMetrics®: The Evolution of a Standard", March 01, www.riskmetrics.com

Jorion, P. (1996), "Risk: Measuring the Risk in Value at Risk," Financial Analysts Journal, November, 52, 47-56.

Jorion, P. (2000), Value at Risk: The New Benchmark for Controlling Market Risk, McGraw-Hill, New York.

Kunreuther, H., Novemsky, N., Kahneman, D., (2001) "Making Low Probabilities Useful," Journal of Risk and Uncertainty, Vol. 23: 103-120.

SECTION II:
BUSINESS IN JORDAN

The Effect of Financial Liberalization on the Efficiency of Financial Institutions: The Case of Jordanian Commercial Banks

Aktham Maghyereh

SUMMARY. Jordan undertook major financial sector liberalization starting in the early of 1990s. The effect of this reform on the efficiency of the banking sector is evaluated. A non-parametric method of Data Development Analysis (DEA) has been used to arrive at the efficiency scores for a panel data sample covering eight Jordanian commercial banks over the period 1984 to 2001. The findings suggest that liberalization program was followed by an observable increase in efficiency. Another finding of the study is that large banks demonstrated the faster productivity growth during the liberalization. The study has important implications such as guiding the government policy regarding deregulation and liberalization. *[Article copies available for a fee from The Haworth Document Delivery Service: 1-800-HAWORTH. E-mail address: <docdelivery@ haworthpress.com> Website: <http://www.HaworthPress.com> © 2004 by The Haworth Press, Inc. All rights reserved.]*

KEYWORDS. Jordan, Data Development Analysis, financial institutions, Jordanian commercial banks, commercial banks, financial liberalization

Aktham Maghyereh is affiliated with the Faculty of Economics & Administrative Sciences, Hashemite University, P.O. Box 150459, Zarqa, Jordan (E-mail: maghyreh@ hu.edu.jo).

[Haworth co-indexing entry note]: "The Effect of Financial Liberalization on the Efficiency of Financial Institutions: The Case of Jordanian Commercial Banks." Maghyereh, Aktham. Co-published simultaneously in *Journal of Transnational Management Development* (The International Business Press, an imprint of The Haworth Press, Inc.) Vol. 9, No. 2/3, 2004, pp. 71-106; and: *Islam and Business: Cross-Cultural and Cross-National Perspectives* (ed: Kip Becker) The International Business Press, an imprint of The Haworth Press, Inc., 2004, pp. 71-106. Single or multiple copies of this article are available for a fee from The Haworth Document Delivery Service [1-800-HAWORTH, 9:00 a.m. - 5:00 p.m. (EST). E-mail address: docdelivery@ haworthpress.com].

From the early 1970s through the 1980s, Jordanian banking institutions essentially served as agents of the government, channeling investment funds to selected sectors under the country's economic development policy. The government's extensive involvement in the banking sector during this period led to serious imbalances in the financial markets and in the structure of the economy. As overall financial repression intensified, the deadweight costs associated with excessive regulation adversely impacted the efficiency of the financial system and resource allocation more generally. Restrictions on bank lending, with favored loans to large family controlled firms and strategic projects, caused small and medium sized firms to turn to the informal sector for financing. An additional and perhaps more important implication of excessive government involvement in the banking system was the erosion of effective credit evaluation and risk assessment policies. As has been well documented, Jordanian banks had little discretion in allocating funds, and therefore little incentive to screen and monitor the activities of corporate customers. As a result, the banking sector became increasingly vulnerable to unbridled corporate expansion. When the economy experienced the recent downturn Jordanian banks suffered immensely. The subsequent ballooning of non-performing loans on bank balance resulted in banking crises. For example, by the end of the 1980s, the share of uncollectible loans of Jordanian banks' portfolios was estimated at 30 percent.

Beginning in the early 1990s the government, in response to the IMF and World Bank economic adjustment program, undertook a series of steps to liberalize the financial system. Key among the steps were: removal of restrictions on interest rates, reduction of government direct lending, expanded product deregulation, and reduction of restrictions on foreign exchange transactions, among others. Additional reforms were implemented in 1997 to further liberalize the finance system: interest rates were further deregulated, greater autonomy was given to bank managements, increased capital adequate requirements, promoted bank mergers and acquisitions, induced the inter-bank market, and further liberalization of foreign exchange transactions and foreign investment was undertaken. Despite this important reform, there have been no attempts to investigate the impact of the liberalization program on the efficiency of the Jordanian banking sector.

Further, in spite of the significant structural changes and deregulations which have taken place within emerging economies banking sectors, however, it remains relatively under-researched in comparison to the vast amount of research into the efficiency of industrialized countries' banking sectors. Recent examples of this type of research in industrialized countries include Berg et al. (1991), Elyawsiani and Mehdian (1995), Hunter and Timme (1995), Mitchell and Onvural (1996), Griefel-Tatje et al. (1996, 1997), Humprey and Pulley (1997), Avkiran (1999, 2000), Ragunathan (1999), Drake (2001), and Sathye (2002).

Although the primary goal of deregulation and liberalization in emerging economies has been to improve banks' efficiency, earlier results have been mixed; in particular, the short-term effects of liberalization have been discouraging (Leightner and Lovell, 1998; Harker and Zenios, 2000). Zaim (1995) reports efficiency gains in Turkish banks after the 1980s liberalization program. Leightner and Lovell (1998) investigated the Thai banking industry from both the banks' and the government's perspective from 1989-1994. They found that the average Thai bank had a rapid productivity gain based on its own objectives, but that during this period productivity gains from the liberalization program could not help advance the government objectives (overall economic growth). Gilbert and Wilson (1998) and Hao et al. (1999) examined Korean banking institutions and found that most Korean banks experienced efficiency gains during this period as government controls were lifted. On the other hand, it was found that in Tunisia (Cook et al., 2000) and in Turkey (Yildirim, 2002) liberalization and deregulation does not affect efficiency.

It will be prudent to keep in mind that the consequences of liberalization may differ across countries and may also depend on the sectoral deregulation. In addition, the economic environments are likely to differ significantly across countries and these differences could induce important differences of bank efficiency through different channels. For instance, differences of the per capita, or differences of the density of population across countries could produce significant differences in the nature of the household's demand for banking products and services (Dietsch and Lozano-Vivas, 1996). Furthermore, it should be noted that most of these studies investigated the efficiency after and during the deregulation period without covering the period before and after liberalization programs. This may have altered the real impact of such programs. Extending the evaluation to before and after liberalization could show the real impact of liberalization programs on efficiency.

In this paper, we use a non-parametric mathematical programming model (DEA) for each year from 1984 to 2001 to determine whether or not the liberalization program has improved the efficiency of the Jordanian banking sector. It is hypothesized that after liberalization with the new entries and relaxed regulation competition will intensify, which in turn will discipline banks in resource management and force them to be more efficient. In this paper we also investigated the determinants of efficiency in the Jordanian commercial banks using second-stage regressions. Specifically, we considered the effect of bank size, profitability, loan quality, market power, and capital adequacy ratio on the efficiency.

The examination of efficiency in banking has important public policy implications in the Jordanian context. Firstly, the principal aim of the liberalization program is to achieve a more competitive and efficient financial system. The banking industry is a vital part of the financial system in any country. Thus, its successes or failures strongly affect the health of the economy. Secondary, it is interesting to study the determinants of efficiency, as it is extremely useful for managers in improving organizational performance and it also helps the policy-making bodies create, if needed, an appropriate regulatory environment. Lastly, despite the importance of efficiency studies, the literature on efficiency in Jordanian banking does not exist. So a great work is needed on measuring and comparing the efficiency of Jordanian banks. In view of the above, a study of efficiency in Jordanian banks is useful to various interest groups such as the Government, Central Bank of Jordan, and the community. Hence, the present project proposes to address this important issue in Jordanian banks.

The rest of the paper is organized as follows. The second section gives a brief overview on the Jordanian banking system. The third section introduces the methodology. The selection variables and the reasons behind the selection are presented in the fourth section. The fifth section reports the empirical results. The paper's conclusions are summarized in the sixth section.

A BRIEF OVERVIEW
ON THE JORDANIAN BANKING SYSTEM

In Jordan, there were 28 banks, of which 14 were commercial, 5 branches of foreign banks, and the rest were development and investment banks. These 28 banks had 466 branches and 144 banking offices. That means approximately one branch for each 10,000 inhabitants in 2001. Commercial banks are the dominant institution in the Jordanian banking system. The commercial banks in Jordan are completely private ownership. Because of less developed capital markets, the banks are the main source of funding for the industrial and commercial business. Although the newly developing capital markets are able to compute with the banking sector, banks are still dominant in the financial system, as in other developing countries' financial systems. Development banks, on other hand, obtain funds from the government or other international institutions like the World Bank. The acquired funds have traditionally been used to make medium and long term loans to selected economics sectors.

The Jordanian banking system was heavily regulated with respect to market entry and interest rates before the 1990s. To increase efficiency and create competition in the financial system, the Jordanian government announced and undertook a series of steps to liberalize the financial system in 1993. The main objective of this program was to establish a Western-type free market economy and competition. Key among the steps were: removal restrictions on interest rates, reduction of government direct lending, expanded product deregulation, and reduction of restrictions on foreign exchange transactions, among others. Additional reforms were implemented in 1997 to further liberalize the finance system: interest rates were further deregulated, greater autonomy was given to bank managements, increased capital adequate requirements, promoted bank mergers and acquisitions induced the inter-bank market, and further liberalization of foreign exchange transactions and foreign investment was undertaken.

There have been also several important technological developments in the industry in recent years. Banks have started computerizing all their operations and have introduced Automatic Teller Machines (ATMs), on-line system of communication and PC banking. They have also changed their product mix and introduced new products to the markets. Therefore, the period between 1984 and 2001 seems to be most suitable for studying the effect of the liberalization program on the performance of the Jordanian banking system in terms of efficiency, since the fundamental institutional changes was established approximately in the middle of this period.

METHODOLOGICAL ISSUES

The DEA Methodology

There are two basic approaches to the measurement of efficiency: parametric (or econometric) and non-parametric (mathematical programming).[1] These two approaches employ different techniques to develop a data set with different assumptions for random noise and for the structure of production technology. These assumptions generate the strengths and weaknesses of both approaches. Firstly, the econometric approach is stochastic and attempts to distinguish the effects of noise from the effects of inefficiency; it is based on sampling theory for the interpretation of essentially statistical results. The programming approach is non-stochastic, and hence groups noise and inefficiency together and calls this combination "inefficiency." It is built on the findings and observation of population and assesses efficiency relative to other observed units. Secondly, the econometric approach is parametric and confounds the effects of misspecification of functional form with inefficiency. The programming approach is non-parametric and population-based and hence less prone to this type of specification error.

In this paper we used the non-parametric frontier approach to estimate the efficiency of Jordanian banking sector. The parametric approach includes stochastic frontier analysis, the free disposal hall, thick frontier and the Distribution Free Approaches (DFA), while the non-parametric approach is Data Development Analysis (DEA). In this paper, the DEA approach is used. This approach has been used since "recent research has suggested that the kind of mathematical programming procedure used by DEA for efficient frontier estimation is comparatively robust" (Seiford and Thrall, 1990). Again, DEA will be the chosen methodology in preference to stochastic estimation, since it has been applied in prior studies when the sample size of banks was small.

DEA is a linear programming technique initially developed by Charnes et al. (1978) to evaluate the efficiency of public sector non- profit organizations. Furthermore, after Charnes et al. (1978), a "large number of papers have extended and applied the DEA methodology" (Coelli, 1996). "Sherman and Gold (1985) were the first to apply DEA to banking" (Molyneux et al., 1996).[2] This technique is non-parametric since it's constructed through the envelopment of the decision making units (DMUs).

With DEA methodological framework it is possible to decompose relative efficiency performance into the categories initially suggested by Farrel (1957). Farrel's categories are best illustrated for the two inputs-single output case in the unit frontier diagram (Figure 1). A firm at E is productivity efficient in choosing the cost minimizing production process given the relative input prices represented by the slope of WW'. If a firm uses quantities of inputs, defined by the point R, to produce a unit of output, the technical inefficiency of that firm could be represented by the distance QR, which is the amount by which all inputs could be proportionally reduced without a reduction in output. This can

FIGURE 1. Farrell Efficiency

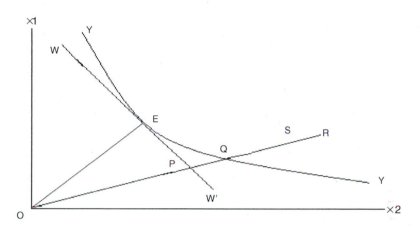

be expressed in percentage terms by the ratio QR/OR, which represents the percentage by which all inputs could be reduced. The allocative efficiency of a firm operating at R is defined to be the ratio OP/OQ. Thus, a firm at R is both allocatively inefficient (in the ratio OQ/OR), and technically inefficient (in the ratio OQ/OR) because it requires an excessive amount of input compared with a firm at Q producing the same level of output. The use of the unit frontier implies the assumption of constant returns to scale. However, a firm using more of both inputs than the combination represented by Q may experience either increasing or decreasing returns to scale. Thus, the technical efficiency ratio OQ/OR may be farther decomposed into scale efficiency (OQ/OR) and pure technical efficiency (OS/OR), with point Q representing the case of constant returns to scale. While scale efficiency is the measure of the ability to avoid waste by operating at or near to the most productive scale, pure technical efficiency is the measure of the ability of a firm to avoid waste by producing as much output as input usage will allow, or using as little input as output level will allow.

The following equation sets out the progression of efficiency measures outlined above. In the following, these concepts are defined in terms the DEA linear programming technique (Drake, 2001).

Productive Efficiency (OP/OR) = Allocative Efficiency (OP/OQ) × Scale Efficiency (OQ/OS) × Pure Technical Efficiency (OS/OR)

Equation (1) below sets out the linear programming problem corresponding to the basic DEA specification of Charnes et al. (1978). The objective function of this program seeks to minimize the efficiency score, θ, which represents the amount of radial reduction in the use of each input. The constraints on this minimization apply to the comparable use of outputs and inputs. Firstly, the output constraint implies that the production of the rth output by observation i cannot expect any linear combination of output r by all firms in the sample. The second constraint involves the use of input s by observation i, and implies that the radially reduced use of input s by firm i (θx_{is} cannot be less than the same linear combination of the use of input s by all firms in the sample. In other words, to reduce the use of all inputs by observation i to the point where input usage lies on the "frontier" defined by the linear combination of inputs and output usage by the "best" firms in the sample.

Considering a sample containing K inputs, M outputs and N firms, where the sets of inputs and outputs for the ith observation are x_{ik}, $k = 1, \ldots, K$ and y_{im}, $m = 1, \ldots, M$, the input-oriented constant return to scale (CRS) DEA for observation i has the form:

$$\min_{\theta, \lambda} \theta = \theta_{CRS}$$

$$such\ that: -y_{ir} + \sum_{j=1}^{N} \lambda_j y_{jr} \geq 0,\ r = 1, \ldots, M$$

$$\theta x_{is} - \sum_{J=1}^{N} \lambda_j X_{js} \geq 0, s = 1, \ldots, K$$

$$\lambda_j \geq 0,\ j = 1, \ldots, N \qquad (1)$$

where θ is a scalar and λ is an $N \times 1$ vector of constants. The value of θ obtained from the linear program is the efficiency score for the ith observation, and will lie in the region (0, 1). An efficiency score of 1 indicates a point on the frontier and hence a technical efficient observation relative to the sample.

Equation (1) must be solved N times, once for each observation in the sample. The efficiency scores indicate, given a level of output, by how much inputs can be decreased for an inefficient observation to be comparable with similar, but more efficient, members of the sample. The efficiency is often referred to as technical efficiency.

Equation (1), however, represents the case in which the assumption of constant returns to scale is imposed on every observation in the sample. In this formulation no account is taken of factors which may make firms unique beyond the sample input-output mix, such as inefficiencies which result from operating in areas of increasing or decreasing returns to scale due to size constraints. To further decompose the efficiency scores from this equation it is necessary to use additional DEA formulations which relax the constant returns to scale assumption embodied in the basic DEA equation.

To determine scale efficiency, the technical efficiency problem (Equation (1)) is solved without the constraint that the requirement set be convex, i.e., the constraint $\Sigma_j \lambda_j = 1$ is dropped. This allows firms to exhibit both increasing and decreasing returns to scale in addition to constant returns. Figure 2 illustrates this for the case of a single input and a single output.

In Figure 2, the production possibility set under constant returns to scale is the region to the right of the ray, OC, through the leftmost input-output observation. Any scaled up or down version of the observations are also in the production possibility set under this assumption of constant return to scale. Imposing the convexity constraint, $\Sigma_j \lambda_j = 1$ ensures the production possibility set is the area right of the piecewise linear frontier VV', which does not assume constant returns to scale. The resulting technical and pure technical efficiency ratios, AQ/AR and AS/AR, are illustrated for one of the observations. Scale efficiency is the ratio of the two results.

In the case of Equation (1), the efficiency ratios with and without the convexity constraint may labeled θ_{VRS} (pure technical efficiency, PTE) and θ_{CRS} (technical efficiency, TE), and scale efficiency (SCALE), θ_{SC},

FIGURE 2. Scale and Technical Efficiency

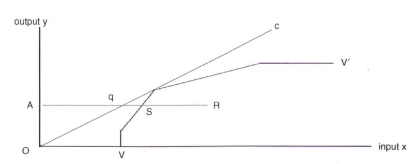

is then $\theta_{CRS}/\theta_{VRS}$. Where scale inefficiency is established, the nature of the returns to scale (i.e., increasing or decreasing) can be established by running Equation (1) under non-constant or variable returns with the convexity constraint, $\Sigma_j \lambda_j = 1$, and contrasting the results with those obtained from running Equation (1) under non-increasing returns, $\Sigma_j \lambda_j \leq 1$. If the pure technical efficiency results are the same under the two different constraints sets then the scale inefficient DMU will be operating under decreasing returns to scale (DRS). Alternatively, if the two resulting measures are different then the DMU will be deemed to be operating under increasing returns to scale (IRS).[3]

To analyze the changes in efficiency over time using a panel of firms, it is necessary to adapt the methods mentioned previously to allow for inter-temporal comparisons (such as comparing the input-output mix for a particular time period with the production technology implied by input and output usage for an adjacent time period). The following outlines this process, using the Farrell (1957) definition of micro level efficiency and the Malmquist index approach to efficiency measurement of Fare et al. (1994).

The input distance function for firm i with respect to two time periods, t and s, is defined using Equation (2), where $S^t = \{(x^t, y^t): x^t \Rightarrow y^t\}$ is the production technology that governs the transformation of inputs for period t:

$$d_i^t(x^s, y^s) = \min_{\theta > 0} \{\theta: (y^s, \theta x^s) \in S^t\} \qquad (2)$$

The distance function in Equation (2) measures the minimum proportional change in input usage at period s required to make the period s input-output set, (x^s, y^s), feasible in relation to the technology S^t at period t. the Malmquist productivity index comparing periods t and $t + 1$ can then be defined using distance functions representing the four combinations of adjacent time periods:

$$m_i(y^{t+1}, x^{t+1}, y^t, x^t) = \sqrt{\frac{d_i^t(x^{t+1}, y^{t+1}) \, d_i^{t+1}(x^{t+1}, y^{t+1})}{d_i^t(x^t, y^t) \, d_i^{t+1}(x^t, y^t)}} \qquad (3)$$

Following Fare et al. (1994), an equivalent way of writing Equation (3) is

$$m_i(y^{t+1}, x^{t+1}, y^t, x^t) = \frac{d_i^{t+1}(x^{t+1}, y^{t+1})}{d_i^t(x^t, y^t)} \sqrt{\frac{d_i^t(x^{t+1}, y^{t+1}) \, d_i^t(x^t, y^t)}{d_i^{t+1}(x^{t+1}, y^{t+1}) \, d_i^{t+1}(x^t, y^t)}} \qquad (4)$$

where the ratio outside the parentheses measures the change in relative efficiency between periods t and $t + 1$ and the geometric mean of the ratios in the perentheses measures the shift in technology between the two periods.

Using the link between the Farrel distance function and DEA efficiency scores it is possible to calculate the required distance function in Equation (4) using DEA of the following form (assuming input orientation and CRS):

$$[d_i^s (x^r, y^r)]^{-1} = \min_{\theta, \lambda} \theta$$

$$such\ that: -y_i^s + \sum_{j=1}^{N} \lambda_j y_{jk}^r \geq 0,\ k = 1, \ldots, M$$

$$\theta x_i^s - \sum_{j=1}^{N} \lambda_j x_{jl}^r \geq 0,\ l = 1, \ldots, K$$

$$\lambda_j \geq 0,\ j = 1, \ldots, N \tag{5}$$

where r and s represent the possible combinations of time periods t and $t + 1$.

Using this technique, we can calculate a Malmquist total factor productivity change index for each observation for each pair of time periods being compared. If the index for a year, other than the base year, is above 1, there has been an efficiency improvement. On the other hand, if the index value for the year is below 1 there has been efficiency regress.

Production technology may change over time, resulting in shifts in the best practice technical frontiers, better production techniques, new innovations, financial liberalization or heightened competition. Malmquist index allows us to distinguish between shifts in the production frontier (technological change, TECHCH) and movements of banks towards the frontier (efficiency change, EFFCH). Thus, Malmquist total factor productivity change index (TFPCH) is simply the product of efficiency change (EFFCH), how much closer a bank gets to the efficient frontier (catching up or falling behind), and technological change (TECHCH), how much the benchmark production frontier shifts at each bank's observed input mix (innovation or shock).

We obtain the TECHCH and EFFCH indexes under the assumption of CRS, i.e., assuming that banks operate at an optimum scale for cost minimization. However, in reality, banks could face scale inefficiencies due to DRS or IRS. When we relax the CRS assumption and adopt the more realistic VRS, we become able to decompose EFFCH index into pure efficiency change (PECH) and scale efficiency change (SECH) components. PECH index measures the changes in the proximity of firms to the frontier, devoid of scale effects. SECH shows whether the movements inside the frontier are in the right direction to attain the CRS point, where changes in output result in proportional changes in costs.

Second-Stage Regression Methodology

To further investigate whether determine whether the liberalization program improved the efficiency of the Jordanian commercial banks and to understand what banks can do to increase their efficiency, we employ a two-stage procedure as suggested by Coelli et al. (1998); we obtained the point estimates efficiency measures for each bank for each year in the sample period derived from the DEA estimations (first stage), and then regress the resultant scores on a set of relevant variables (second stage) that describe the characteristics being investigated.

As we know from above, the DEA score falls between the interval 0 and 1, making the dependent variable a limit dependent variable. A commonly held view in previous studies is that the use of Panel Data Tobit Model can handle the characteristics of the distribution of the efficiency measures and thus provide results that can guide policies to improve efficiency. Using the efficiency measures for each bank for each year in the sample period derived from the DEA estimation as the dependent variable, we then estimate the following Panel Data Tobit Model:

$$y_{it}^* = \beta' x_{it} + \varepsilon_{it}$$
$$y_{it} = \begin{cases} y_{it}^* & if \quad y_{it}^* > 0 \\ 0 & otherwise \end{cases} \quad i = 1, \ldots, N, t = 1, \ldots, T, \tag{6}$$

where the bank is indexed by i, the time period by t. x_{it} is a $(1 \times K)$ vector of exogenous explanatory variables, β is a $(K \times 1)$ vector of the parameters interest. The y_{it}^* is a latent variable and y_{it} is the DEA score. As in the standard Tobit model, the error term ε_{it} is assumed to be serially uncorrelated and homoscedastic for each bank i such that: $\varepsilon_{it} \sim N(0, \sigma^2)$.

As is well known that when the dependent variable is censored, as in our case, performing Ordinary Least Squares (OLS) on the observed $y_{it}s$ yields biased and inconsistent parameter estimates. Applying Maximum Likelihood Estimation (MLE) to the appropriate likelihood function exploits the information contained in the distribution of the unobserved $y^{it}s$ and produces consistent and asymptotically efficient parameter estimates. In addition, MLE yield consistent and asymptotically efficient parameter estimates of β and σ assuming that $E(\varepsilon_{it}/x_{it}) = 0$. In panel data, however, it is usually inappropriate to assume that error-term ε_{it} is serially uncorrelated and homoscedastic for each bank. Banks have different histories, structure, etc., that likely affect the efficiency. This generates heterogeneity in the error-term structure across banks. To control for possible bank-specific effects, we model unobserved, persistent bank-specific heterogeneity with a one-factor random-error components model:

$$\varepsilon_{it} = \eta_i + \upsilon_{it} \tag{7}$$

where $\eta_i \sim N(0, \sigma_\eta^2)$, $\upsilon_{it} \sim N(0, {}_\upsilon^2)$ and that η_i and υ_{it} are mutually uncorrelated, i.e., $E(\eta_i\,\eta_j) = 0$ and $E(\upsilon_{it}\,\upsilon_{js}) = 0$ if $i \neq j$ and $s \neq t$. This means that $\sigma_\varepsilon^2 = \sigma_\eta^2 + \sigma_\upsilon^2$, and implies that for any given time period the latent variables y_{it}^* are independent.

The persistent, unobserved heterogeneity η_i, however, introduces serial correlation within each bank's error structure and generates a non-scalar variance-covariance matrix. In panel data models, this serial correlation yields parameter estimates that are not only inefficient, but also biased and inconsistent. This "incidental parameters problem" is typically resolved by employing fixed-effects or random-effects estimation. Given about the relationship between efficiency and its determinants beyond the sample, we postulate a random-error structure as in Equation (7). We then integrate over the random-error component η_i for each individual bank's conditional function in order to obtain consistent and asymptotically efficient estimates of β and Σ_ε assuming $E(\eta_i/x_{it}) = 0$ and $E(\upsilon_i/x_{it}) = 0$.

The consistency of the parameter estimates under the error-term specification of Equation (6) or (7) requires that explanatory variables to be strictly exogenous. The equation model we estimate here contains unobservable firm-specific effects, which may relate with the explanatory variables as well as the endogenous variables. Hence, the orthogonality conditions between the error terms and the variables are not likely to be met to produce consistent estimators.

To correct for the possible endogeneity among the regressors in the random-effects estimation to obtain consistent and asymptotically efficient estimates of β and $E(\eta_i/x_{it}) = 0$ and $E(\upsilon_{it}/x_{it}) = 0$, we instrument the possible endogeneity variables employing Newey (1987) method. Newey formalizes a consistent and asymptotically efficient estimation technique for estimating the parameters of limited-dependent variable models that have endogenous, linear explanatory variables. The Newey methodology entails performing several estimations on the system of simultaneous equations. In brief, when first estimating the model, reduced-form expression of efficiency measures the repressors, including the residuals from reduced-form linear estimation of the endogenous explanatory variables. By applying Amemiya (1979) Generalized Least Squares (AGLS) to the resulting reduced-form parameter estimates, one obtains an efficient estimate of β. However, to recover an efficient estimate of σ or σ_η and σ_υ, we then employ a modified Minimum Chi-Square (MCS) technique.

VARIABLES SELECTION AND DATA SOURCES

It is commonly acknowledged that the choice of variables (input/output variables) in efficiency studies significantly affects the results. There are, however, certain limitations on variables selection due to the reliability of the data. For example, the variables may present different information, although they carry the same label, or the same information may be reported under different labels. This variation stems from the lack of reporting standards in banking industry. In this project the variables selection will rely mainly on classical banking theory.

Another important difficulty in bank efficiency studies that affects the inputs and outputs selection and hence the results in the definition of a bank's function. Two main approaches to the classification of inputs and outputs can be discerned in the literature; the production approach and the intermediation approach (see Athanassopoulos, 1997; Cinca et al., 2002). Under the production approach, a financial institution is defined as a producer of services for account holders; that is, they perform transactions on deposit accounts and process documents such as loans. Hence, according to this approach, the number of accounts of different loan and deposits categories are generally taken to be appropriate definitions of output (see, e.g., Gilligan et al., 1984; Ferrier et al., 1993; Berg et al., 1993; Zenios et al., 1999; Drake, 2001), and interest costs are excluded from total operating costs.

In contrast, under the intermediation approach, financial intermediaries are institutions that convert and transfer financial assets between surplus units and deficit units. For this methodology, therefore, outputs are defined as the values of the various categories of interest bearing assets on the balance-sheet while deposits and borrowed funds are included with capital and labour as inputs (see, e.g., Sealey and Lindley, 1977; Drake et al., 1992; Miller and Noulas, 1996; Drake, 2001).

As pointed out by Ferrier and Lovell (1990) and Fried et al. (1993), the production approach is preferable when one is interested in cost efficiency as this approach focuses on the operating costs of banking. On the other hand, the intermediation approach concerns the overall costs of banking and is preferable when studying the economic viability of banks (Yildirim, 2002).[4] Since the main interest is in assessment of overall efficiency performance of the Jordanian banking sector within a period (1984-2001) characterized by changes in the regulatory and economic environment, the intermediation approach is adopted.

In this study, the analysis is carried out employing the intermediation approach in which banks are viewed as financial intermediaries employing inputs such as labor, capital and deposits to produce outputs such as earning assets (loans and liquid assets and investments), "off-balance" sheet business, and other services. Following Cinca et al. (2002), three outputs and three inputs are included in the analysis. The category of "other income" (generating from "off-balance" sheet activities and fee income) is included as an output along with two categories of earning assets, loans and liquid assets and investments. With respect to inputs, labor is proxied by total number of staff while capital is proxied by the value of fixed assets. The final input used is the total value of deposits (both retail and managed funds). All variables expressed as monetary variables, such as loans, "other income," etc., are in Jordan dinars (JD) millions and in constant 1995 prices with the Consumer Price Index in each year used as the appropriate deflator. This adjustment does not apply to the labor input as this is measured in physical units by the number of staff employed.

At the end of 2001, the banking sector in Jordan comprised twenty-eight banks of which fifteen are commercial, five branches of foreign banks, two Islamic and six financial corporations. As the locally commercial banks are subject to similar regulatory requirements, the sample is drowning from these banks. Availability of data is dictated the inclusion of banks in the sample. Accordingly, the sample of 10 out of 14 total locally commercial banks over the years 1984 to 2001 is used. The data are collected from the banks and their annual reports. The banks are categorized as the Big Three, and Other Banks. The Big Three banks are the dominant banks in the Jordanian banking sector, with 69.02% of total banks assets in 1984 and 62.03% of total banks assets in 2001.[5] Table 1 provides some relevant statistics of key variables in the sample. Panel A of Table 1 shows the overall descriptive statistics (mean and standard deviation), while Panels B and C show, respectively, the segmented descriptive statistics for the Big Three and Other Banks. An important feature of the data is that these are enormous variations among banks in the sample. Even through the largest banks are only three, it appears that they dominate the sample period.

EMPIRICAL RESULTS

Analysis Efficiency Results

Using the proceeding DEA methodology and data on the eight Jordanian commercial banks, Table 2 provides the summary statistics of effi-

TABLE 1. Descriptive Statistics of the Relevant Variables (in million JD)

	Total Assets	Liquid Assets and Investments	Loans	Other Income	Number of Employees	Fixed Assets	Deposits
Panel A: All Banks							
Mean	544.0009	59.92596	204.2660	2.285888	878.5000	8.088291	481.5889
Maximum	3,811.225	412.4974	964.9763	29.87437	3,199.000	56.15924	3,513.222
Minimum	13.21627	2.049325	5.389478	0.000000	29.00000	0.029479	8.984986
Std. Dev.	699.4183	69.93689	215.0700	3.457142	801.8664	9.845863	635.7456
Panel B: Big Three Banks							
Mean	1,135.676	123.8877	417.5651	4.493603	1,710.192	15.39195	1,006.990
Maximum	3,811.225	412.4974	964.9763	29.87437	3,199.000	56.15924	3,513.222
Minimum	131.5776	17.50465	77.53697	0.261324	808.0000	3.412281	131.4086
Std. Dev.	956.4120	86.47061	253.0236	5.118951	729.9417	12.77408	886.4263
Panel C: Other Banks							
Mean	257.9946	28.37644	100.7020	1.241465	444.6852	4.524759	225.2110
Maximum	930.1208	141.8161	323.1495	7.354524	1,499.000	21.84454	753.8906
Minimum	13.21627	2.049325	5.389478	0.000000	29.00000	0.029479	8.984986
Std. Dev.	206.5643	26.36871	78.14867	1.416175	355.9789	5.406199	180.2785

TABLE 2. Average DEA Efficiency Scores (Standard deviations in parentheses)

Year	1984	1985	1986	1987	1988	1989	1990	1991	1992	1993	1994	1995	1996	1997	1998	1999	2000	2001	All years
Panel A: All Banks (9 banks and 162 observations)																			
TE	0.930	0.859	0.847	0.909	0.959	0.862	0.916	0.847	0.912	0.938	0.932	0.940	0.935	0.944	0.955	0.957	0.987	0.974	0.918
	(0.102)	(0.149)	(0.175)	(0.123)	(0.071)	(0.125)	(0.120)	(0.206)	(0.131)	(0.109)	(0.054)	(0.138)	(0.131)	(0.148)	(0.115)	(0.075)	(0.037)	(0.120)	(0.041)
PTE	0.960	0.934	0.925	0.979	0.996	0.862	0.936	0.916	0.951	0.981	0.986	0.985	0.974	0.965	0.976	0.984	0.987	0.986	0.960
	(0.083)	(0.110)	(0.103)	(0.039)	(0.007)	(0.125)	(0.111)	(0.151)	(0.098)	(0.050)	(0.033)	(0.036)	(0.102)	(0.104)	(0.060)	(0.046)	(0.036)	(0.041)	(0.034)
SCALE	0.969	0.923	0.917	0.929	0.963	0.903	0.977	0.928	0.959	0.956	0.975	0.950	0.967	0.956	0.967	0.972	0.999	0.978	0.951
	(0.070)	(0.135)	(0.162)	(0.126)	(0.068)	(0.116)	(0.036)	(0.164)	(0.094)	(0.084)	(0.040)	(0.116)	(0.070)	(0.104)	(0.094)	(0.062)	(0.001)	(0.117)	(0.025)
Panel B: Big Three Banks (3 banks and 54 observations)																			
TE	0.841	0.781	0.753	0.860	0.920	0.805	0.898	0.835	0.905	0.915	0.967	0.964	0.965	0.997	1.000	1.000	1.000	1.000	0.911
	(0.140)	(0.190)	(0.228)	(0.161)	(0.124)	(0.172)	(0.099)	(0.285)	(0.165)	(0.147)	(0.057)	(0.062)	(0.061)	(0.006)	(0.000)	(0.000)	(0.000)	(0.000)	(0.082)
PTE	0.916	0.901	0.904	0.970	0.998	0.805	0.945	1.000	1.000	1.000	1.000	0.993	0.997	1.000	1.000	1.000	1.000	1.000	0.968
	(0.145)	(0.172)	(0.167)	(0.053)	(0.004)	(0.172)	(0.096)	(0.000)	(0.000)	(0.000)	(0.000)	(0.012)	(0.005)	(0.000)	(0.000)	(0.000)	(0.000)	(0.000)	(0.054)
SCALE	0.923	0.879	0.849	0.890	0.926	0.870	0.951	0.835	0.905	0.918	0.967	0.971	0.968	0.997	1.000	1.000	1.000	1.000	0.936
	(0.122)	(0.192)	(0.259)	(0.178)	(0.119)	(0.173)	(0.056)	(0.285)	(0.165)	(0.142)	(0.057)	(0.050)	(0.055)	(0.006)	(0.000)	(0.000)	(0.000)	(0.000)	(0.056)
Panel C: Other Banks (6 banks and 108 observations)																			
TE	0.975	0.898	0.895	0.934	0.980	0.891	0.925	0.854	0.916	0.951	0.960	0.898	0.905	0.888	0.874	0.936	0.981	0.917	0.921
	(0.041)	(0.125)	(0.143)	(0.109)	(0.024)	(0.102)	(0.137)	(0.189)	(0.130)	(0.100)	(0.058)	(0.165)	(0.157)	(0.174)	(0.122)	(0.087)	(0.046)	(0.143)	(0.037)
PTE	0.982	0.951	0.937	0.985	0.997	0.891	0.933	0.874	0.927	0.972	0.979	0.982	0.949	0.948	0.965	0.977	0.982	0.979	0.956
	(0.031)	(0.081)	(0.075)	(0.037)	(0.009)	(0.102)	(0.128)	(0.175)	(0.116)	(0.061)	(0.041)	(0.044)	(0.125)	(0.128)	(0.073)	(0.057)	(0.044)	(0.051)	(0.034)
SCALE	0.992	0.946	0.952	0.949	0.983	0.920	0.990	0.975	0.987	0.976	0.980	0.910	0.952	0.937	0.906	0.959	1.000	0.938	0.958
	(0.013)	(0.114)	(0.105)	(0.108)	(0.023)	(0.094)	(0.015)	(0.053)	(0.031)	(0.046)	(0.036)	(0.138)	(0.081)	(0.127)	(0.104)	(0.075)	(0.001)	(0.144)	(0.029)

Notes: TE: Technical Efficiency, PTE: Pure Technical Efficiency, SCALE: Scale Efficiency.

ciency measures for each year over the period 1984 to 2001 together with the decomposition into pure technical and scale efficiency, while Figure 3 graphs the summaries drawn from Table 2. In Table 3, the sources of scale inefficiency for each year of study is also provided. As shown in Table 2, geometric mean of technical efficiency for all banks over the sample period is 91.8%. This value is similar to those found in developed countries but higher than what is found in some developing countries. For example, Fukuyama (1993), Altunbas et al. (1994), Favero and Papi (1995), Miller and Noulas (1996), and Sathye (1999) found that overall technical efficiency of Japanese, Germany, Italian, U.S., and Australian banks are around of 94%, 92%, 90%, 95%, and 88%, respectively. However, Bhattacharyya et al. (1997), Taylor et al. (1997), Chaffai (1997), Darrat et al. (2002) and Yildirim (2002) estimated technical efficiency of Indian, Mexican, Tunisian, Kuwaiti and Turkish banks at about 79%, 75%, 72%, 86% and 89%, respectively.[6]

Examination of Table 2 indicates the main source of technical inefficiency is scale inefficiency, with average scale efficiency for all banks over the sample period being 93.1%, meaning that inefficiency due to the divergence of the actual scale of operation for the most productive scale size is about 6.9%. Average pure technical efficiency, on the other hand, is 96%, implying that banks could, on average, have produced the same amount of outputs with approximately 4% fewer resources than they actually employed. Thus, the major source of overall technical inefficiency is scale rather than pure technical.[7] Consistent with these results, Table 3 shows that about 70.9% of banks give evidence of pure technical efficiency whereas only about 53.3% banks experience scale efficiency. Of the total sample, about 28.3% of banks exhibit increasing returns comparing with only about 18.5 of banks experiencing decreasing returns to scale.

Some differences in the efficiency measures of banks are evident according to their size statues. The results in Table 2 show that the Big Three banks have lower scale efficiency on average than that of Other Banks (small banks). However, the Big Three banks also have higher pure technical efficiency. Thus, the Big Three banks are operating at a scale size in excess of that for optimal technical efficiency. This result is consistent with the fact that large banks in Jordan during the earlier deregulation period considerably increased spending on branch infrastructure as a barrier to entry to the new entrants. It can be seen from this study that the impact of this strategy was to expand the major banks to a size beyond that needed for efficient operation. This can be seen strongly when considering the results of average technical efficiency,

FIGURE 3. Average DEA Effficiency Scores

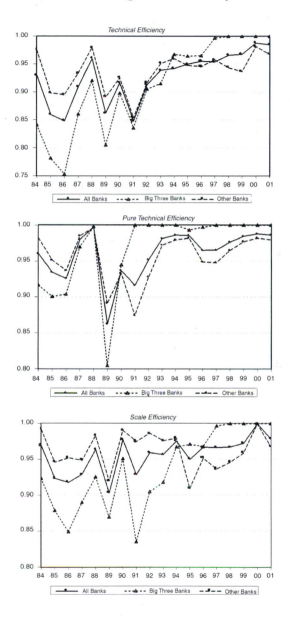

TABLE 3. Number and Percentage of Banks with Pure Technical Efficiency (PTE), Scale Efficiency (DRS), IRS and CRS

Year	1984	1985	1986	1987	1988	1989	1990	1991	1992	1993	1994	1995	1996	1997	1998	1999	2000	2001	Total
Panel A: All Banks (9 banks and 162 observations)																			
PTE	6	6	5	7	7	5	6	6	7	7	7	7	7	8	7	8	8	8	115
	(66.6)	(66.6)	(55.5)	(77.7)	(77.7)	(55.5)	(66.6)	(66.6)	(77.7)	(77.7)	(77.7)	(77.7)	(77.7)	(88.9)	(77.7)	(88.9)	(88.9)	(88.9)	(70.9)
DRS	2	3	2	2	2	2	4	1	2	1	2	2	0	1	1	0	1	2	30
	(22.2)	(33.3)	(22.2)	(22.2)	(22.2)	(22.2)	(44.4)	(11.1)	(22.2)	(11.1)	(22.2)	(22.2)	(0.00)	(11.1)	(11.1)	(0.00)	(11.1)	(22.2)	(18.5)
IRS	5	4	4	4	4	3	0	3	1	2	2	2	3	2	3	3	0	1	46
	(55.5)	(44.4)	(44.4)	(44.4)	(44.4)	(33.3)	(0.00)	(33.3)	(11.1)	(22.2)	(22.2)	(22.2)	(33.3)	(22.2)	(33.3)	(33.3)	(0.00)	(11.1)	(28.3)
CRS	2	2	3	3	3	4	5	5	6	6	5	5	6	6	5	6	8	6	86
	(22.3)	(22.3)	(33.4)	(33.4)	(33.4)	(55.6)	(55.6)	(55.6)	(66.7)	(66.7)	(55.6)	(55.6)	(66.7)	(66.7)	(55.6)	(66.7)	(88.9)	(66.7)	(53.2)
Panel B: Big Three Banks (3 banks and 54 observations)																			
PTE	2	2	2	2	2	2	2	3	3	3	3	3	3	3	3	3	3	3	46
	(66.7)	(66.7)	(66.7)	(66.7)	(66.7)	(66.7)	(66.7)	(100)	(100)	(100)	(100)	(100)	(100)	(100)	(100)	(100)	(100)	(100)	(85.2)
DRS	2	2	1	1	1	2	2	1	1	0	1	0	0	1	0	0	0	0	15
	(66.7)	(66.7)	(33.3)	(33.3)	(33.3)	(66.7)	(66.7)	(33.3)	(33.3)	(0.00)	(33.3)	(0.00)	(0.00)	(33.3)	(0.00)	(0.00)	(0.00)	(0.00)	(27.8)
IRS	0	0	1	1	1	0	0	1	1	1	0	1	1	0	0	0	0	0	8
	(0.00)	(0.00)	(33.3)	(33.3)	(33.3)	(0.00)	(0.00)	(33.3)	(33.3)	(33.3)	(0.00)	(33.3)	(33.3)	(0.00)	(0.00)	(0.00)	(0.00)	(0.00)	(14.8)
CRS	1	1	1	1	1	1	1	1	1	2	2	2	2	2	3	3	3	3	31
	(33.3)	(33.3)	(33.3)	(33.3)	(33.3)	(33.3)	(33.3)	(33.3)	(33.3)	(66.7)	(66.7)	(66.7)	(66.7)	(66.7)	(100)	(100)	(100)	(100)	(57.4)
Panel C: Other Banks (6 banks and 108 observations)																			
PTE	4	4	3	5	5	3	4	3	4	4	2	4	4	5	4	5	5	5	73
	(66.7)	(66.7)	(50.0)	(71.4)	(71.4)	(50.0)	(66.7)	(50.0)	(66.7)	(66.7)	(33.3)	(66.7)	(66.7)	(71.4)	(66.7)	(71.4)	(71.4)	(71.4)	(67.6)
DRS	2	2	1	1	1	2	2	0	1	0	1	1	0	0	1	0	1	2	18
	(33.3)	(33.3)	(16.7)	(16.7)	(16.7)	(33.3)	(33.3)	(0.00)	(16.7)	(0.00)	(16.7)	(33.3)	(0.00)	(0.00)	(16.7)	(0.00)	(16.7)	(33.3)	(16.7)
IRS	1	2	2	2	2	2	1	3	2	3	2	2	3	2	2	3	2	3	33
	(16.7)	(33.3)	(33.3)	(33.3)	(33.3)	(33.3)	(16.7)	(50.0)	(33.3)	(50.0)	(33.3)	(33.3)	(50.0)	(33.3)	(33.3)	(50.0)	(33.3)	(50.0)	(30.6)
CRS	3	3	3	3	3	3	3	4	3	4	3	3	4	4	3	4	3	1	57
	(50.0)	(50.0)	(50.0)	(50.0)	(50.0)	(50.0)	(50.0)	(66.7)	(50.0)	(66.7)	(50.0)	(50.0)	(66.7)	(66.7)	(50.0)	(66.7)	(83.3)	(50.0)	(52.7)

Notes: PTE: Pure Technical Efficiency, DRS: Decrease Return to Scale, IRS: Increase Return to Scale, CRS: Constant Return to Scale.

which do not find the Big Three banks to be the most efficient (91.1 %, 94.1 for the Big Three banks and Other Banks, respectively).[8] This would indicate that the use of size as a barrier to entry was most re-flected in the branch networks employed in these banks. It is interesting to note that in the last four years of this study, the Big Three banks oper-ate at constant return to scale (see Table 3) with scale efficiency scores close to 1 (see Table 2). Furthermore, as discussed below, the Malm-quist Index results found that the Big Three banks tended to improve their scale efficiency toward the end of the sample period; thus, the scale inefficiencies of the earlier post-deregulation period are now declining.

Further, the DEA study found that 1989 through 1991 were the years of lowest average efficiency scores. This result indicates the impor-tance of negative external shocks, such as the economy downturns ex-perienced in the 1980s and 1990s, in effecting negatively on banks operation. During this period increased provisions for bad debts were experienced by the Jordanian banking sector.

Recall that the main hypothesis of the study was that the liberaliza-tion policies would have a positive impact on banking sector efficiency. If the liberalization had a positive impact on the efficiency, it is ex-pected that annual average efficiency scores would increase post-liber-alization period. It is clear from Table 2 as well as Figure 3 that from 1984 to 1993 the average technical efficiency of Jordanian banking fluctuated widely a high 95.9% to a low 84.7%. After 1994, the effi-ciency of the banking system appeared to be much more stable than prior liberalization, with an average efficiency range from 93.2% to 98.7%. The results of efficiency of the Jordanian banking as shown in Figure 3 suggest that the annual average efficiency of the banking sys-tem as a whole followed an upward trend, which suggests that the liber-alization program did fulfill its promise in terms of efficiency gains for all banks. Looking at the decomposition of technical efficiency, Figure 3 shows an upward trend of pure technical and scale efficiency of all Jordanian banks suggesting positive effect of liberalization on all banks. In other words, the slope of the pure technical and scale efficiency scores are steeper for post-policy adjustment period. These results lead one to confirm that the liberalization program did increase the effi-ciency of the Jordanian banking system to higher levels as anticipated.

The results also indicate that although all banks were positively af-fected by liberalization, large banks' (Big Three banks) productivity gains (in both the pure technical and scale efficiency) outweigh those of small banks (Other Banks). As shown from the results, that starting from the immediate post-deregulation period there was considerable improvements in average efficiency measures in the Big Three banks. This may well reflect the response of large banks in recent years to the increasing completion in the Jordanian banking system. As maintained above, large banks in Jordan during the earlier deregulation period considerably spending on branch infrastructure. Given that large Jordanian banks during that period may suffered from excess capacity in respect of infrastructure and branching, it is quite possible that the measures taken in recent years to reduce both branching and staffing level may have resulted in an improvement efficiency measures (especially scale efficiency). Indeed, large Jordanian banks have introduced a direct telephone banking operation which is argued to exhibit much greater economies of scale than traditional branch banking. Furthermore, one of largest Jordanian bank recently has made a significant move into home banking based around the use of personal computer. Hence, in Figure 3 we may be picking up the first tentative evidence of structural change in the efficiency measures as large banks increasingly begin to rationalize branch networks, infrastructure and staff and introduce new form of delivery channels such as telephone banking and home computer based banking.

Further analysis can be developed by applying statistical tests to test whether the increase in the annual average of efficiency scores post-liberalization are statistically significant. Three tests are reported in Table 4. The Median test and Kurskall-Wallis H test assume that the variable under consideration is continuous and that it was measured on at least an ordinal (rank order) scale. These tests assist the hypothesis that the different samples in the comparison were drawn from the same distribution or from distribution with the same median. The analysis of variance (ANOVA) is a parametric test on the differences between means, requiring the assumption that underlying distributions are normal. All tests for all the three subscribed samples reject the null hypothesis of equity of distribution of technical efficiency and its decompositions post-liberalization period, providing information that the increase in the average efficiency measures post-liberalization period appear to be statistically significant. The reported increase in efficiency measures may indicate that banks are becoming more efficient overtime in the post-liberalization period. This observation is highly consistent with our expectations. Following the liberalization, most Jordanian banks started a race to establish their own communications networks, information systems and ATMs. Since these new practices are subject to "learning by doing," Jordanian banks' efficiency might increase over time.

TABLE 4. Statistical Tests of Equality Between the Distributions of Annual Efficiency Scores

	Median X_2 (Prob > X2)	Kuskal-Wallis X_2 (Prob > X2)	ANOVA F (Prob > F)
Panel A: All Banks			
TE	14.666	14.877	65.506
PTE	$(0.002)^a$	$(0.001)^a$	$(0.000)^a$
SCALE	6.923	9.054	18.865
	$(0.0314)^b$	$(0.0108)^b$	$(0.000)^b$
	9.111	12.758	14.805
	$(0.058)^b$	$(0.012)^b$	$(0.000)^a$
Panel B: Big Three Banks			
TE	15.333	14.549	12.918
PTE	$(0.009)^a$	$(0.012)^b$	$(0.000)^a$
SCALE	9.000	8.4571	6.034
	$(0.041)^b$	$(0.041)^b$	$(0.034)^b$
	11.800	14.773	24.599
	$(0.018)^b$	$(0.005)^a$	$(0.000)^a$
Panel C: Other Banks			
TE	5.428	9.406	29.869
PTE	$(0.066)^b$	$(0.009)^a$	$(0.000)^a$
SCALE	6.0181	7.307	5.112
	$(0.052)^b$	$(0.050)^b$	(0.020)
	6.200	7.510	4.278
	$(0.057)^b$	(0.497)	$(0.038)^a$

Note: H_0: $E^{1994} = E^{1995} = ... E^{2001}$. The numbers in parenthesis are p-value. ^{a},^{b}, indicate statistically significant at 1% and 5%, respectively

To investigate further whether the liberalization improved the efficiency of the Jordanian banking system, we study year by year results for the Malmquist Index of productivity change. The yearly Malmquist Index for each of technical efficiency change (EFFCH), technological change (TECHCH), pure technical efficiency change (PECH), scale efficiency change (SECH) and total factor productivity change (TFPCH) are presented in Table 5, while Figure 4 graphs the summaries drawn from Table 5. Consistent with the above results, the Malmquist Index results found that the post-deregulation period studies were generally one of overall efficiency improvement, with productivity improvements of 5% over the sample period. It can also be seen that the main source of productivity improvement is the growth in scale efficiency with an average value of 3.2% over the sample period. Furthermore, the results show that . . . the late 1980s and early 1990s saw efficiency re-

TABLE 5. Malmquist Index Means

Year	1985	1986	1987	1988	1989	1990	1991	1992	1993	1994	1995	1996	1997	1998	1999	2000	2001	All years
Panel A: All Banks (9 banks and 153 observations)																		
EFFCH	0.955	0.983	1.090	1.067	0.895	1.070	0.923	1.109	1.038	1.034	0.955	1.023	0.997	0.997	1.052	1.038	0.957	1.011
	(0.116)	(0.092)	(0.104)	(0.103)	(0.092)	(0.128)	(0.187)	(0.157)	(0.124)	(0.102)	(0.140)	(0.189)	(0.065)	(0.084)	(0.071)	(0.106)	(0.117)	(0.060)
TECHCH	1.080	1.109	1.198	1.055	0.947	0.843	0.840	0.891	1.057	0.934	1.178	0.873	1.093	1.124	0.929	0.915	1.192	1.015
	(0.227)	(0.123)	(0.499)	(0.247)	(0.087)	(0.204)	(0.167)	(0.083)	(0.171)	(0.164)	(0.366)	(0.197)	(0.105)	(0.164)	(0.147)	(0.085)	(0.194)	(0.124)
PECH	0.974	0.994	1.100	1.018	0.958	0.983	0.975	1.054	1.040	1.007	0.999	0.980	0.999	1.017	1.009	1.005	0.998	1.006
	(0.054)	(0.071)	(0.157)	(0.037)	(0.067)	(0.116)	(0.100)	(0.110)	(0.119)	(0.065)	(0.011)	(0.115)	(0.004)	(0.065)	(0.019)	(0.068)	(0.005)	(0.033)
SECH	0.981	0.989	1.023	1.049	0.934	1.096	0.945	1.054	0.997	1.026	0.956	1.038	0.981	0.982	1.042	1.032	0.959	1.005
	(0.106)	(0.058)	(0.083)	(0.105)	(0.070)	(0.124)	(0.147)	(0.135)	(0.023)	(0.070)	(0.135)	(0.095)	(0.081)	(0.051)	(0.057)	(0.077)	(0.117)	(0.044)
TFPCH	1.024	1.086	1.283	1.117	0.851	0.901	0.769	0.993	1.097	0.967	1.130	0.885	1.088	1.122	0.980	0.950	1.137	1.022
	(0.218)	(0.125)	(0.459)	(0.221)	(0.141)	(0.229)	(0.186)	(0.200)	(0.214)	(0.190)	(0.421)	(0.224)	(0.102)	(0.172)	(0.156)	(0.133)	(0.221)	(0.128)
Panel B: Big Three Banks (3 banks and 51 observations)																		
EFFCH	1.023	0.957	1.169	1.082	0.870	1.136	0.938	1.137	1.014	1.071	1.000	1.001	1.035	1.003	1.000	1.000	1.000	1.026
	(0.082)	(0.104)	(0.147)	(0.076)	(0.124)	(0.166)	(0.342)	(0.237)	(0.024)	(0.122)	(0.107)	(0.001)	(0.061)	(0.006)	(0.000)	(0.000)	(0.000)	(0.075)
TECHCH	1.034	1.090	0.931	0.936	0.965	0.919	0.920	0.892	1.078	0.896	0.991	1.020	1.094	1.210	0.882	0.922	1.152	0.996
	(0.023)	(0.125)	(0.013)	(0.040)	(0.051)	(0.162)	(0.148)	(0.081)	(0.094)	(0.064)	(0.073)	(0.052)	(0.096)	(0.260)	(0.178)	(0.152)	(0.105)	(0.099)
PECH	0.987	1.005	1.093	1.031	0.932	1.018	1.066	1.000	1.000	1.000	0.993	1.004	0.999	1.000	1.000	1.000	1.000	1.008
	(0.022)	(0.008)	(0.161)	(0.054)	(0.117)	(0.031)	(0.115)	(0.000)	(0.000)	(0.000)	(0.012)	(0.007)	(0.000)	(0.000)	(0.000)	(0.000)	(0.000)	(0.034)
SECH	1.035	0.952	1.078	1.051	0.934	1.117	0.869	1.137	1.014	1.071	1.007	0.997	1.012	1.003	1.000	1.000	1.000	1.016
	(0.068)	(0.099)	(0.145)	(0.085)	(0.073)	(0.177)	(0.261)	(0.237)	(0.024)	(0.122)	(0.098)	(0.006)	(0.021)	(0.006)	(0.000)	(0.000)	(0.000)	(0.065)
TFPCH	1.056	1.035	1.089	1.012	0.841	1.036	0.830	1.018	1.093	0.959	0.991	1.021	1.132	1.213	1.088	1.092	1.152	1.017
	(0.061)	(0.077)	(0.140)	(0.033)	(0.146)	(0.168)	(0.194)	(0.255)	(0.100)	(0.128)	(0.120)	(0.053)	(0.100)	(0.259)	(0.178)	(0.152)	(0.105)	(0.106)

Year	1985	1986	1987	1988	1989	1990	1991	1992	1993	1994	1995	1996	1997	1998	1999	2000	2001	All years
Panel C: Other Banks (6 banks and 102 observations)																		
EFFCH	0.921	0.997	1.050	1.061	0.908	1.038	0.915	1.095	1.050	1.017	0.934	1.036	0.979	0.994	1.079	1.058	0.936	1.004
	(0.122)	(0.094)	(0.057)	(0.121)	(0.084)	(0.108)	(0.097)	(0.129)	(0.155)	(0.098)	(0.159)	(0.239)	(0.064)	(0.107)	(0.075)	(0.130)	(0.143)	(0.062)
TECHCH	1.104	1.119	1.331	1.115	0.939	0.805	0.807	0.891	1.048	0.954	1.272	0.800	1.093	1.082	0.954	0.911	1.213	1.026
	(0.284)	(0.134)	(0.579)	(0.291)	(0.105)	(0.227)	(0.175)	(0.092)	(0.208)	(0.200)	(0.425)	(0.206)	(0.119)	(0.097)	(0.142)	(0.049)	(0.234)	(0.161)
PECH	0.968	0.989	1.105	1.013	0.971	0.966	0.930	1.081	1.061	1.012	1.002	0.969	1.000	1.027	1.014	1.009	0.997	1.007
	(0.066)	(0.090)	(0.171)	(0.031)	(0.033)	(0.142)	(0.080)	(0.129)	(0.146)	(0.082)	(0.010)	(0.144)	(0.006)	(0.081)	(0.023)	(0.087)	(0.007)	(0.044)
SECH	0.954	1.008	0.996	1.048	0.934	1.086	0.984	1.013	0.989	1.004	0.930	1.059	0.966	0.972	1.064	1.048	0.939	1.000
	(0.117)	(0.017)	(0.007)	(0.123)	(0.077)	(0.109)	(0.049)	(0.026)	(0.019)	(0.016)	(0.152)	(0.114)	(0.098)	(0.062)	(0.061)	(0.094)	(0.144)	(0.048)
TFPCH	1.008	1.112	1.380	1.170	0.856	0.834	0.739	0.982	1.100	0.971	1.200	0.818	1.067	1.077	1.030	0.965	1.130	1.026
	(0.272)	(0.143)	(0.545)	(0.260)	(0.153)	(0.239)	(0.193)	(0.195)	(0.264)	(0.227)	(0.051)	(0.252)	(0.106)	(0.117)	(0.132)	(0.135)	(0.272)	(0.159)

Notes: EFFCH: Efficiency Change, TECHCH: Technological Change, PECH: Pure Technical Efficiency Change, SECH: Scale Efficiency Change, TFPCH: Total Factor Productivity Change.

gress due mainly to technological regress, indicating the importance of negative external shock in slowing down the process of innovation.

Further, the Malmquist Index results show that the Big Three banks are conclusively more efficient than smallest banks (Other Banks) especially during the last four years after the liberalization. Examination of Table 5 and Figure 4 this was due mainly to the rapid improvement in scale efficiency by the Big Three banks during this period. Particularly, the Malmquist found evidence of superior scale efficiency by the Big Three banks, with annual average scale efficiency changes for about 10% during this period. As we have noted above, this may reflects the impact of the intensification of completion and consequence desire of the largest banks to eliminate wasteful excess capacity. This would tend to produce productivity gains which would emerge as frontier shifts in the Malmquist analysis.

Overall the results of the Malmquist analysis suggests that all banks somewhat benefited from the more liberal environment in Jordan. The above results also indicate that the major source of productivity gains in Jordanian banking was scale improvements, especially in large banks.

Determinants of Bank Efficiency: Second-Stage Regression Results

This section reports on our attempt to examine the determinants of Jordanian commercial banks' efficiency after implementing Panel Data Tobit Model. First, we suggest a number of potential determinants and then continue to discuss the empirical results.

We consider the effects of bank size, profitability, market power, capital adequacy ratio, loans quality, and the liberalization on efficiency. There are two main themes about the relationship between bank and performance. The so-called *shakeout theory* posits that smaller banks may not be able to obtain enough capital and management ability to successfully operate updates, thus suggesting a positive relation between size and performance. Alternatively, the *divisibility theory* holds that there will be no such operational advantage accruing to large banks, if the technology is divisible, that is, small-scale banks can produce financial services at costs per unit output comparable to those of large banks, suggesting no (or a negative) association between size and efficiency. The bank size is measured by the logarithm value of total assets. In addition, it's widely argued that higher profitable banks are more able to raise enough capital, thus suggesting a positive relation between profitability and performance. Following Miller and Noulas (1996), we use operating income to total assets as measure profitability.

FIGURE 4. Average Malmquist Index Scores

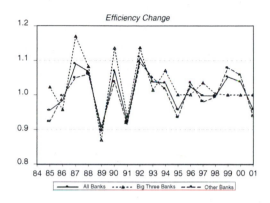

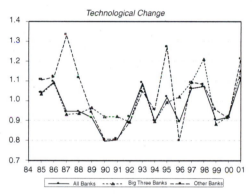

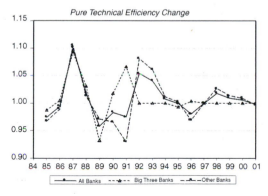

FIGURE 4 (continued)

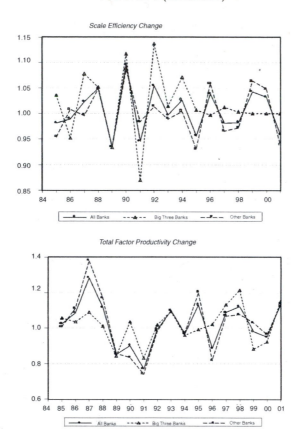

Studies by Edwards and Heggestad (1973) show that in highly con-centrated markets (higher market power), uncertainty avoidance or risk aversion rather than efficiency becomes the objectives of some banks. Market power (lack of competition) can thus lead to reduced efficiency. The efficient structure hypothesis of Demsetz (1973), however, states that market concentration leads to superior performance. We use the ratio of bank deposits to aggregate bank deposits to reflect market power. The capital adequacy ratio indicates the coverage of banks by owners' funds. This variable is computed as the ratio of shareholders equity and net income to total deposits and non-deposit funds. In addition, as Favero and Papi (1995, pp. 390) point out, failure to take into account the quality of outputs and, in particular, neglecting the risk factor, especially for loans, is a significant shortcoming of studies on bank efficiency. In this respect, therefore, it is worthwhile to examine the effect of loan quality on bank efficiency. Following Abrams and Huang (1987), Berger and De Young (1997), and Resti (1997) we used the value of loan loss provisions to total loan as a proxy for loan quality. In this context, a high allowance for possible loan losses may indicate that a large share of loans issued is expected to default. It is also possible, however, that a high ratio of provisions to total loans may be a sign of conservative accounting procedures (Abrams and Huang, 1987). The dummy structure variable is formed to examine whether there is a significant structural jump in Jordanian bank efficiency between the prior liberalization period (1984-1992) and the post-liberalization period (1993-2001) as the reforms were adopted.

Newey-based parameter estimates for the random-effects Panel Data Tobit Model under heterogeneous error-term structures for each of technical efficiency, pure technical efficiency and scale efficiency for all banks class (All banks, Big Three banks, and Other Banks) appears in Table 6. The parameters estimates reflect the AGLS estimation procedure.

The Newey-based determinants of banks' efficiency in Table 6 are similar to the three definitions of efficiency and the three different banks class. Consistent with the *shakeout theory* bank size has significant positive effects on all types of efficiency, indicating that the large banks have higher efficiency. This result suggests that large banks enjoy several advantages compared to small banks. These include the ability of large banks to utilize more efficient technology with less cost, the ability of these banks to set up more specialized staff for more profitable activities and the ability of these banks to provide better quality of output.

Consistent with our prior expectation, we find also that higher profitable banks have higher efficiency. On the other hand, the market power variable is significantly negatively related to all types of efficiency. Such evidence is consistent with the Edwards and Heggestad (1973) hypothesis, which suggests that in highly concentrated markets, uncertainty avoidance or risk aversion rather than efficiency become the objectives of some banks. Market power (lack of competition) can thus lead to reduced efficiency. The policy implication for this result suggests that mergers between banks could strengthen the market power. With a high degree of concentration it is possible that, in Jordan, the "quiet life" hypothesis will come into play. This hypothesis predicts a reverse causation, that is, as firms enjoy greater market power and con-

TABLE 6. Second-Stage Regression Results

	Technical Efficiency			Pure Technical Efficiency			Scale efficiency		
	All Banks	Big Three	Other Banks	All Banks	Big Three	Other Banks	All Banks	Big Three	Other Banks
Constant	1.104 (4.66)[a]	1.020 (2.08)[b]	1.700 (5.93)[a]	0.749 (4.26)[a]	0.827 (3.16)[a]	1.662 (7.58)[a]	1.262 (6.73)[a]	1.002 (2.23)[b]	0.994 (4.89)[a]
Size	1.335 (5.20)[a]	2.078 (3.02)[a]	3.528 (7.21)[a]	0.369 (1.93)[b]	0.180 (2.00)[b]	1.709 (4.59)[a]	1.004 (4.82)[a]	2.177 (3.59)[a]	1.585 (4.58)[a]
Profitability	0.732 (1.58)[b]	0.2331 (1.210)	2.605 (3.90)[a]	0.744 (2.05)[b]	0.3029 (1.70)[b]	1.417 (2.76)[a]	0.012 (0.92)	0.039 (0.56)	1.022 (2.15)[b]
Market Power	−1.369 (−5.28)[a]	−2.104 (−3.21)[a]	−3.617 (−7.48)[a]	−0.361 (−1.87)[b]	−0.175 (−1.50)	−1.805 (−4.90)[a]	−1.048 (−4.99)[a]	−2.203 (−3.83)[a]	−1.586 (−4.64)[a]
Capital Adequacy Ratio	−0.642 (−2.38)[b]	−0.371 (−2.74)[a]	−1.727 (−5.03)[a]	−0.559 (−2.76)[b]	−0.358 (−1.83)[b]	−1.124 (−4.27)[a]	−0.386 (−1.79)[b]	−0.591 (−1.35)	−0.759 (−3.11)[a]
Loans Quality	0.735 (3.16)[a]	0.336 (2.50)[b]	0.856 (2.38)[b]	0.1431 (0.837)	0.524 (1.83)[b]	0.651 (2.40)[b]	1.374 (2.52)[b]	1.657 (0.98)	0.999 (3.91)[a]
Liberalization	0.073 (3.28)[a]	0.114 (3.22)[a]	0.101 (4.92)[a]	0.035 (2.12)[b]	0.012 (1.138)	0.1143 (7.23)[a]	0.045 (2.49)[b]	0.124 (3.89)[a]	−0.004 (−0.30)
Number of Observations	162	54	108	162	54	108	162	54	108
Log-Likelihood (2SIV)	119.86	153.25	301.48	89.914	60.57	84.493	163.71	56.505	10.337
Likelihood-Ratio Test $(H_0: \beta = 0)$	13.837	30.635	78.67	15.240	12.111	63.01	14.887	10.638	22.728
Likelihood-Ratio Test $(H_0:$ joint exogeneit)	5.215	4.381	7.930	5.238	4.802	5.703	6.016	5.927	5.209
Estimation Condition on									
$\sigma_\eta =$	0.0120 (16.3)[a]	0.0216 (12.3)[a]	0.651 (11.8)[a]	0.719 (18.6)[a]	0.179 (1.07)	0.916 (78.9)[a]	1.041 (49.5)[a]	1.31 (10.7)[a]	0.715 (3.97)[a]
$\sigma_v =$	0.0144 (21.7)[a]	0.097 (5.36)[a]	0.0249 (5.62)[a]	0.032 (9.37)[a]	0.045 (4.87)[a]	0.004 (6.59)[a]	0.097 (2.08)[b]	0.165 (4.84)[a]	0.015 (1.58)

Notes: Size is the bank size measured by the logarithm value of total assets. Profitability is measured by operating income to total assets. Market power measured by the ratio of bank deposits to aggregate bank deposits. The capital adequacy ratio is computed as the ratio of shareholders' equity and net income to total deposits and non-deposit funds. Loan quality is measured by the value of loan loss provisions to total loan. Liberalization is measured by a dummy variable which takes a unit value post-liberalization period and zero otherwise. The number in parenthesis are t-statistics. [a],[b], indicate statistical significant at 1% and 5%, respectively.

centration, inefficiency follows not because of non-competitive pricing but more so because of a relaxed environment with no incentives to minimize costs. Thus, if market concentration is leading to lower efficiency, the government policy of encouraging the bank mergers between banks needs to be approached with caution.

Another significant variable is capital adequacy, which shows a negative and significant relationship to all types of efficiency across banks categories. This adverse effect on efficiency may reflect a risk-return trade-off in the sector. Banks with low-risk portfolios, as measured by a higher capital adequacy ratio, are likely to be less efficient. This may be because they rather prefer safer and lower-earning portfolios over riskier but higher-earning portfolios. Interestingly, the loans quality, measured by loan loss provisions to total loans, yields negative and significant coefficients, suggesting that banks with more problem loans are less efficient. This adverse effect for this variable may reflect a risk-return trade-off in the banking sector. This may also be due to the fact that banks that spend less resources on credit underwriting, and loan monitoring is more efficient but at the expense of more problem loans.

Next is considered the effect of the financial liberalization on efficiency. Consistent with the DEA results presented in the previous sub-section, the results suggest that the financial liberalization exerts a positive and significant impact upon all efficiency measures across the three different banks categories. Consistent with the above conclusion, the results also show that the efficiency of Big Three banks (large banks) are typically much more affected by the liberalization than Other Banks (small banks). This may due to the fact that large banks in Jordan have more experience than smaller banks in adapting to the conditions of a new environment and in assimilating the new technology.

CONCLUSIONS

Financial market deregulation and liberalization have transformed the banking systems of a large number of countries over the last two decades. The reforms are sure to have a profound effect on the development of the financial system in these countries, and their overall macroeconomic performance. Jordan was one such country which, post-1993, very substantially de-regulated interest rates and the allocation of credit, liberalized entry into the sector, and introduced modern prudential regulation and supervision.

In this paper, we use a non-parametric mathematical programming model (DEA) for each year from 1984 to 2001 to determine whether or not the liberalization program improved the efficiency of the Jordanian banking sector. In this paper we also investigated the determinants of efficiency of the Jordanian banking sector using second-stage regressions. Specifically, we considered the effect of profitability, asset quality, bank size, market power, and the degree of capitalization on banks' efficiency.

The results indicate that average efficiency score of Jordanian banks compares well with the efficiency score of banks in developed countries. Every phase of the analysis, the total efficiency scores suggests that the liberalization has provided the anticipated efficiency gains. All the efficiency scores displayed consistent increases after the introduction of the policy. For all measures, the scores became more stable. Thus, the expected result that the liberalization would have motivated management materialized. Another important result is that large banks strongly outperform small banks in terms of efficiency. Our results show that large banks demonstrated the faster productivity growth during the liberalization. In fact, the largest banks have been the pioneers of many new products and practices in the system, as they introduced credit cards, leasing, factoring and forfeiting, and a market-oriented management philosophy. During the liberalization period, the largest banks in Jordan also started to use high technology such as establishing ATM networks, associating to the SWIFT system and using on-line computer systems. Because these transfers were mostly to the largest banks, they appear to have benefited more from this diffusion than the smallest banks.

The factors that may influence efficiency have been identified in this study and could aid banks and policy makers in devising suitable strategies. First, consistent with the above results, large banks are found to be more efficient than small banks. Therefore, small banks should be encouraged to become larger. Second, banks' profitability is positively related to efficiency. Third, the market power plays an important role in efficiency. Therefore, motivating the competitive environment in the market will eventually lead to more efficiency. Fourth, the significance of capital adequacy ratio in explaining efficiency implies that banks with higher capital adequacy ratio are less efficient since they are risk-averse and prefer safer and lower-earning portfolios. The quality of loans variable is significant and negatively related with efficiency. Banks with higher loan loss provisions are found to be less efficient. Finally and more importantly, the liberalization is positively related to efficiency, suggesting that a further liberalization in the market will eventually lead to more efficiency in the Jordanian banking sector.

NOTES

1. Berger et al., (1993) and Berger and Mester (1997) provided a survey of these methods.

2. Beger and Humpherey (1997) identified over 60 studies that have applied DEA to the banking industry.

3. For more detail see for example Coelli et al. (1998).

4. Sathye (2001) also noted that this approach is more relevant to financial institutions as it is inclusive of interest expenses which often account for one-half to two-thirds of total costs.

5. Central Bank of Jordan Bulletin, various issues.

6. We should take care when comparing efficiency scores drawing from different samples, even when the same method of estimation is applied. This is because the efficiency estimates are sensitive to the specification of inputs and outputs.

7. This conclusion is inconsistent with most empirical results–in a global context–which found that input X-inefficiencies, such as technical inefficiencies, dominate output inefficiencies, such as economies of scope, when determining overall efficiency (see, for example, Allen and Rai, 1996).

8. This finding is not agreement with Berger et al. (1993) and Drake (2001), who concluded that large banks in the U.S. and U.K., respectively, are on average are more efficient than small banks.

REFERENCES

Abrams, B. A. and Huang, C. J. (1987). Predicting bank failures: The role of structure in affecting recent failure experiences in the USA. Applied Economics, 19, 1291-1302.

Allen, L. and Rai, A. (1996). operational efficiency in banking: An international comparison. Journal of Banking and Finance, 20, 655-672.

Altunbas, Y., Evans, L. and Molyneux, P. (1994). Universal banks, ownership and efficiency–A stochastic frontier analysis of the German banking market. Working Paper, Institute of European Finance.

Amemiya, T. (1979). The estimation of a simultaneous-equation Tobit model. International Economic Review, 20, 169-181.

Athanassopoulos, A. D., (1997). Service quality and operating efficiency synergies for management control in the provision of financial services: Evidence from Greek bank branches. European Journal of Operational Research, 98, 300-313.

Avkiran, N. (1999). The evidence on efficiency gains: the role of mergers and benefits to the public. Journal of Banking and Finance, 23, 991-1013.

Avkiran, N. (2000). Rising productivity of Australian trading banks under deregulation 1986-1995. Journal of Economic and Finance, 24, 122-140.

Berger, A. N., and DeYoung, R. (1997). Problem loans and cost efficiency in commercial banks. Journal of Banking and Finance, 21, 849-870.

Berg, A. N., Forsund, F. R., Hjalmarrsson, L. and Suominwn, M. (1993). Banking efficiency in the Nordic countries. Journal of Banking and Finance, 17, 371-388.

Berger, A. N. and Gunther, J. W. (1997). Problem loans and cost efficiency in commercial banks. Journal of Banking and Finance, 21, 849-870.

Berger, A. N., Hunter, W. C. and Timme, S. G. (1993). The efficiency of financial institutions: A review of research past, present and future. Journal of Banking and finance, 17, 221-249.

Berger, A. N., Forsund, F. and Jansen, E. (1991). Technical efficiency of Norwegian Banks: A nonparametric approach to efficiency measurement. Journal of Productivity Analysis, 2, 127-142.

Berger, A. N., Forsund, F., Hjalmarsson, L. and Souminen, M. (1993). Banking efficiency in the Nordic countries. Journal of Banking and Finance, 17, 371-388.

Berger, N. A., and Humphrey, D. B. (1997). Efficiency of financial institutions: International survey and direction for future research. European Journal of Operational Research, 98, 175-212.

Berger, N. A., and Mester, L. J. (1997). Inside the black box: What explains differences in the efficiencies of financial institutions. Journal of Banking and Finance, 21, 895-947.

Bhattacharyya, A., Lovell, C.A.K. and Sahay, P. (1997). The impact of liberalization on the productive efficiency of Indian commercial banks. European Journal of Operational Research, 98, 332-345.

Chaffai, M. (1997). Estimating input-specific technical inefficiency: The case of the Tunisian banking industry. European Journal of Operational Research, 98, 314-331.

Charnes, A., Cooper, W. W. and Rhodes, E. (1978). Measuring the efficiency of decision making units. European Journal of Operational Research, 2, 429-444.

Cinca, C. S., Molinero, C. M. and Garcia, F. C. (2002). Behind DEA efficiency in financial institutions. Working Paper, University of Zaragoza, mimeo.

Coelli, T. (1996). A Guide to DEAP version 2.1, a Data Development Analysis (computer) program. CEPA Working Paper 96/08.

Coelli, T., Rao P. and Battese, G. (1998). An introduction to efficiency and productivity analysis. Kluwer, Boston.

Cook, W. D., Hababou, M. and Roberts, G. S. (2000). The effect of financial liberalization on Tunisian banking industry: A non-parametric approach. Working Paper, York University, mimeo.

Darke, L. M. (1992). Economies of scale and scope in U.K. building societies: An application of the translog multi-product cost function. Applied Financial Economics, 2, 211-219.

Darrat, A. F., Topuz, C. and Yousef, T. (2002). Assessing cost and technical efficiency of banks in Kuwait. Paper presented in the ERF's 8th Annual Conference in Cairo, Egypt.

Demsetz, H., (1973). Industry structure, market rivalry, and public policy. Journal of Law and Economics, 16, 1-9.

Dietsch, M., and Lozano-Vivas, A. (2000). How the environment determines banking efficiency: A comparison between French and Spanish industries. Journal of Banking and Finance, 24, 985-1004.

Drake, L. (2001). Efficiency and productivity change in U.K. banking. Applied Financial Economics, 11, 557-571.

Edwards, F. R., and Heggestad, A. A. (1973). Uncertainty, market structure and performance: The Galbraith-Caves hypothesis and managerial motives in banking. Quarterly Journal of Economics, 87, 455-473.

Elyawsiani, E., and Mehdian, S. M. (1995). The comparative efficiency performance of small and large U.S commercial banks in the pre- and post-deregulation eras. Applied Economics, 27, 1069-1079.

Fare, R., Grosskopf, S., Norris, M. and Zhang, Z. (1994). Productivity growth, technical progress and efficiency change in industrialized countries. American Economic Review, 84, 66-83.

Farrell, M. J. (1957). Measurement of productive efficiency. Journal of Royal Statistical Society, 120, 253-290.

Favero, C. A. and Papi, L. (1995). Technical efficiency and scale efficiency in the Italian banking sector: A nonparametric approach. Applied Economics, 27, 385-395.

Ferrier, G. D., Grosskopf, S. and Haynes, K. J. (1993). Economics of diversification in the banking industry. Journal of Monetary Economics, 31, 229-245.

Ferrier, G. D., and Lovell, C. A. K. (1990). Measuring cost efficiency in banking: Econometric and linear programming evidence. Journal of Econometrics, 46, 229-255.

Fried, H. O., Lovell, C. A. K and Eechaut, P. V. (1993). Evaluating the performance of U.S. credit unions. Journal of Banking and Finance, 17, 251-265.

Fukuyama, H. (1993). Technical and scale efficiency of Japanese commercial banks: A non-parametric approach. Applied Economics, 25, 1101-1112.

Gilbert, R. A., and Wilson, P. W. (1998). Effects of deregulation on the productivity of Korean banks. Journal of Economics and Business, 50, 133-166.

Griefel-Tatje, E. and Lovell, C. A. K. (1996). Deregulation and productivity decline: The case of Spanish Saving Banks. European Economic Review, 40, 1281-1303.

Griefel-Tatje, E., and Lovell, C. A. K. (1997). The source of productivity change in Spanish banking. European Journal of Operational Research, 98, 364-380.

Hao, J., Hunter, W. and Yang, W. (1999). Deregulation and efficiency: The case of private Korean banks. Working Paper No. 27, Federal Reserve Bank of Chicago.

Harker, P. T., and Zenios, S. A. (2000). What drives the performance of financial institutions? In Harker, P. T., and Zenios S. A. (eds.), Performance of financial institutions. Cambridge University Press, New York.

Humprey, D. B., and Pulley, L. B. (1997). Banks' responses to deregulation: profits, technology and efficiency. Journal of Money, Credit and Banking, 29,

Hunter, W. C. and Timme, S. (1995). Core deposits and physical capital: A reexamination of bank scale economies and efficiency with quasi-fixed inputs. Journal of Money, Credit and Banking, 27, 165-185.

Leightner, E. J. and Lovell, C. A. K. (1998). The impact of financial liberalization on the performance of Thai banks. Journal of Economics and Business, 50, 115-131.

Miller, S. M. and Noulas, A. G. (1996). The technical efficiency of large bank production. Journal of Banking and Finance, 20, 495-509.

Mitchell, K. and Onvural, N. M. (1996). Economies of scale and scope at large commercial banks: Evidence from the Fourier flexible functional form. Journal of Money Credit and Banking, 28, 178-199.

Molyneux, P., Altunbas, Y. and Gardener, E. (1996). Efficiency in European banking. John Wiley Chichester 198.

Newey, W. K. (1987). Efficient estimation of limited dependent variable models with endogenous explanatory variables. Journal of Econometrics, 36, 231-250.

Parkan, C. (1987). Measuring the efficiency of service operations: An application to bank ranches. Engineering Costs and production Economies, 12, 237-242.

Ragunathan, V. (1999). Financial deregulation and integration: An Australian perspective. Journal of Economics and Business, 51, 505-514.

Resti, A. (1997). Evaluating the cost-efficiency of the Italian banking system: What can learn from the joint application of parametric and nonparametric techniques. Journal of Banking and Finance, 21, 221-250.

Sathye, M. (2001). X-efficiency of Australian banking: An empirical investigation. Journal of Banking and Finance, 25, 613-630.

Sathye, M. (2002). Measuring productivity changes in Australian banking: An application of Malmquist indices. Managerial Finance, 28, 48-59.

Sealey, C. W. and Lindley, J. T. (1997). inputs, outputs, and a theory of production and cost at depository financial institutions. Journal of Finance, 32, 1251-1266.

Seiford, L. M., and Thrall, R. M. (1990). Recent development in DEA: The mathematical programming approach to frontier analysis. Journal of Econometrics, 46, 7-38.

Sherman, D. and Gold, F. (1985). Branch operating efficiency: Evaluation with Data Development Analysis. Journal of Banking and Finance, 9, 297-315.

Taylor, W. M., Thompson, R. G., Thrall, R. M. and Dharmapala, P. S. (1997). DEA/AR efficiency and profitability of Mexican banks: A total income model. European Journal of Operational Research, 98, 332-342.

Yildirim, C. (2002). Evolution of banking efficiency within an unstable macroeconomic environment: The case of Turkish commercial banks. Applied Economics, 34, 2289-2301.

Zaim, O. (1995). The effect of financial liberalization on the efficiency of Turkish commercial banks. Applied Financial Economics, 257-264.

Zenios, C. V., Zenios, A. S., Agathocleous, K. and Soteriou, A. (1999). Benchmarks of the efficiency of bank branches. Interfaces, 29, 37-51.

Management Training
and Development Needs
Assessment Practices
in the Jordanian Private and Public Sectors:
Integrated or Isolated?

Jamal Abu-Doleh

SUMMARY. This paper aims to unveil the current plans, procedures and practices of management training and development (MTD) needs assessment in the Jordanian private and public organizations. Self-completion questionnaires were distributed to 64 training managers of whom 30 were from the private sector, and 34 were from the public sector. The major research findings include that only one-third of the investigated organizations report having a formal and systematic plan for the analysis of their managers' MTD needs; the majority of these organizations have conducted their MTD needs analysis for lower level management; and, even worse, the overwhelming majority of the respondents report assessing their managers training need in the absence of functional and organizational needs analysis. Also, the findings of the study show that in few of the organizations do training managers report having MTD needs as-

Jamal Abu-Doleh is affiliated with the Business Administration Department, Yarmouk University, Jordan.

[Haworth co-indexing entry note]: "Management Training and Development Needs Assessment Practices in the Jordanian Private and Public Sectors: Integrated or Isolated?" Abu-Doleh, Jamal. Co-published simultaneously in *Journal of Transnational Management Development* (The International Business Press, an imprint of The Haworth Press, Inc.) Vol. 9, No. 2/3, 2004, pp. 107-121; and: *Islam and Business: Cross-Cultural and Cross-National Perspectives* (ed: Kip Becker) The International Business Press, an imprint of The Haworth Press, Inc., 2004, pp. 107-121. Single or multiple copies of this article are available for a fee from The Haworth Document Delivery Service [1-800-HAWORTH, 9:00 a.m. - 5:00 p.m. (EST). E-mail address: docdelivery@haworthpress.com].

Digital Object Identifier: 10.1300/J130v09n02_06

sessment procedures linked with managers job description and management performance appraisal schemes. Finally, the author recommends that training managers should monitor effectively their MTD needs assessment plans and procedures. These plans should be related to the organization needs analysis and to the management appraisal scheme. Also, training managers are advised to make simultaneous analysis of the individual, functional and organizational needs before designing any training programme. *[Article copies available for a fee from The Haworth Document Delivery Service: 1-800-HAWORTH. E-mail address: <docdelivery@ haworthpress.com> Website: <http://www.HaworthPress.com> © 2004 by The Haworth Press, Inc. All rights reserved.]*

KEYWORDS. Managers training and development needs assessment, Jordan, private sector, public sector

INTRODUCTION

The impact of management training and development (MTD) needs assessment on the success of conducting management training programmes have become the dominant research issue in the field of management training. Therefore, it is important for Arab trainers and human resource development specialists to chart the future of management training and development in the Arab world, and to consider the themes that will dominate at this new millennium. Admittedly, MTD in the Arab countries, in general, and in Jordan, in particular, has been a subject of increasing interest and debate in recent years (Al-Faleh, 1990; Atiyyah, 1993; Weir, 1994; Abu-Doleh, 2000). However, few would disagree that one of the most critical challenges facing the developing countries is the training and development of their managers. In contrast, in the developed countries it appears to be an increased recognition of the efficacy of MTD as strategies to improve organizational effectiveness and competitiveness. This is consistent with the notion that managers can, and do, have significant impact on organizational effectiveness and efficiency. Therefore, assessment of managers' training and development needs will help in making the training programmes more target oriented. In doing this, all training efforts will be geared towards the same end result of increasing the organization's efficiency and effectiveness. In this paper, the research aim is to investigate the practices of managers' training and development need assessment adopted by the

Jordanian private and public organizations. The assessment of managers' training needs come at the beginning of any MTD design programme. This is important, because training need assessment is basic to exposing the gap between what is happening and what ought to be happening in terms of managerial performance. It determines whether a gap exists between the requirements of a job and the skills of the managers who perform it. As a result, an accurate needs assessment enables the limited training budget to be directed more specifically towards achieving organizational strategy. However, the distinction between organizational needs, operational needs and managers' needs should be taken into account in order to design acceptable MTD programmes that fit the needs of both the organization itself and its human assets.

LITERATURE REVIEW

In the developed countries, MTD needs assessment has received substantial and ongoing contributions from the disciplines of education, psychology and management and, as a result, is perhaps the most multidisciplinary field in the management training and development area. Also, the Arab states have been aware of the positive impact of management training and development on organizational effectiveness, economic and social development and, as a result, the 1980s were declared by these states as "the decade of administrative development" (Zoubi, 1982). Despite the Arab states' recognition of the important role of management training and development to organizational effectiveness, very little empirical research about value-added MTD programmes has been conducted (Abdalla and Al-Homoud, 1995; Abu-Doleh, 1996; Abu-Doleh and Weir, 1997). As far as Jordan is concerned, MTD has recently become an important issue in both the private and public organizations. Despite this concern, very little empirical research has been conducted on managers' training and development need assessment. Therefore, this study will attempt to survey current MTD need assessment practices adopted by the Jordanian private and public (governmental) organizations. In fact, there is an acute shortage of qualified managers in Jordan (Shaikh, 1988). Arguing in a similar vein, Atiyyah (1993) recognized the fact that shortage of qualified managers presents a major obstacle to the development of less advanced countries. Therefore, Atiyyah has further argued that the future of management development in the Arab world largely depends on developments in their political, economic, socio-cultural and organizational systems. Therefore, it is hoped that this study will help to better train and develop Jordanian managers by investigating their actual training and development need from the training managers' points of view. Kubr and Porkopenko (1989) have outlined different techniques that can be used to gather information about managers MTD need assessment. These include interviews, surveys, career planning, self-assessment, performance appraisals, tests and examinations, record and report analysis and the use of assessment centres. A proper needs assessment not only lays the foundation for the application of a systems approach to MTD, but also helps the decision makers to separate training needs from non-training needs, without which human resource training and development is often wasted. A systematic approach to training requires the assessment of training needs, the development/implementation of the programme, and the evaluation and continual modification of the training process (Goldstein, 1986). Thus, training need assessment is a critical component of the training system (Walter, 2000; Moshe, 2000) because it provides data to determine who is to be trained, what training programmes are needed, and how the results of training programmes are to be evaluated. In sum, training needs assessment is considered as one of the fundamental prerequisites of an effective training programme. Undertaking systematic needs assessment before embarking on training has been recommended to organizations for almost forty years. McGehee and Thayer's (1961) model for organization, task, and person analysis has been cited and described in training and industrial/organizational psychology texts. The culmination of the MTD needs assessment phase is a set of objectives specifying the purpose of the training and the competencies desired in trainees after they complete the programme (Fisher et al., 1999). Needs assessment takes effort, time and money. Unfortunately, a great many organizations undertake management training without this necessary preliminary investment. In short, it is worth noting that without managers' training needs analysis it is difficult if not impossible to continue in the application of an MTD systems approach which includes objectives setting, programme design, programme implementation, and programme evaluation and follow-up (Taylor, 1989). In fact, all the aforementioned steps of MTD systematic approaches are mainly based on getting the first step (the manager training needs assessment) right. In other words, it is the most important step in the MTD systems approach. On the other hand, it is equally important to evaluate those MTD programmes. Feedback, reinforcement, and follow-up to the managers' knowledge, skills, and behavior that are taught in the MTD programmes are needed as recognition to encourage the managers to take active steps toward developing their managerial skills.

RESEARCH METHODOLOGY
AND THE INVESTIGATED ORGANIZATIONS:
THE SAMPLE

The research on which this article is based aimed at answering the following seven questions:

1. Do Jordanian private and public organizations have a formal MTD needs assessment scheme for their managers?
2. Do Jordanian private and public organizations have a linkage between managers training need assessment and managers' job description, on the one hand, and managers' performance appraisal scheme, on the other?
3. To find out the managerial levels to which a management needs assessment scheme relates in both sectors of the study.
4. Do Jordanian private organizations have different approaches to be used in conducting their management needs assessment compared to their counterparts in the public sector?
5. Do Jordanian private organizations have different procedures in determining their management needs assessment compared to their counterparts in the public sector?
6. To uncover what training managers think of MTD needs for their managers in both sectors of the study.
7. To provide objective practical suggestions and recommendations for formulating and implementing MTD policies and plans in Jordan.

In order to answer the aforementioned research questions, the present study investigated a selected representative sample from the Jordanian private and public organizations that have a formal and separate training and development department or unit. The selected sample represents more than two-thirds of the total organizations working in the above sectors. However, of these 30 and 34 private and public organizations respectively were identified as a sample subjects. The approached private organizations represent different business sectors. Fourteen organizations out of the 30 were from the financial sector, 10 industrial organizations and 6 organizations from the service sector. The questionnaire of this study was designed to be answered by senior managers in charge of training and development department (often known as administrative development and training units in the public sector). Therefore, over a period of three months in late 2001 the author managed to distribute a self-completion questionnaire to 64 training managers of whom 30 (46.9 per cent) were from the private sector, and 34 (53.1 per cent) were from the public sector. But, it is worth noting that having a separate training and development department/unit is in itself not enough to claim that the organization is really engaged in effective and systematic training approach. For this, respondents were asked to indicate whether or not they conduct training needs assessment for their managers, and if yes, whether that need assessment is being linked to manager's job description and manager's performance appraisal scheme. Also, respondents were asked to comment on the managerial levels to which their management needs assessment plan relates. However, the responses to the above questions as well as to other MTD needs analysis issues are described in the following discussion.

RESULTS OF THE STUDY

As can be seen from Table 1, more than two-thirds of the private organizations (80.0 per cent) and nearly 65 per cent of their counterparts in the public sector report assessing their managers' training and development needs on a regular basis. Be that as it may, this outcome should be taken with caution.

Undoubtedly, it is worth noting that assessing managers' MTD needs by the majority of the investigated organizations is in itself not enough to claim that these organizations are really engaged in effective MTD needs analysis. In support of this argument, respondents were asked to indicate whether or not they assess their managers' MTD needs in connection with the manager's job description and the manager's performance appraisal. It has been often cited that having a clear job description and

TABLE 1. Regular Assessment of Managers MTD Needs (N = 64)

Business sector	Yes	(%)	No	(%)	Total
Private	24	80.0	6	20.0	30 (100.0%)
Public	22	64.7	12	35.3	34 (100.0%)
Total	46	71.9	18	28.1	64 (100.0%)

conducting performance appraisal are the major prerequisites for the successful enhancement of MTD needs analysis. In this context, the responses of the training managers approached reveal that more than half of the private organizations (62.5 per cent) had a clear job description or management competency statement for their managers, whereas less than half of their counterparts in the public sector (45.4 per cent) reported having such a clear managerial job description. This result could be explained by the fact that private organizations involve a high degree of risk and limited resources and therefore the line of responsibilities and authorities are clearly defined and strictly followed. With regard to systematic managerial performance appraisal, 66.6 per cent of the private organizations reported such appraisal, whereas 54.5 per cent of the organizations in the public sector reported that they had such a systematic managerial performance appraisal scheme. As far as the connection between MTD needs assessment and manager's job description and performance appraisal is concerned, the majority of the responding organizations in the private and public sectors, 70.8 per cent and 72.7 per cent, respectively, reported that they had no such connection. This is to say that managers' training and development needs analysis had been conducted in the absence of its core prerequisites. Therefore, training in the investigated organizations can be described as "a knee-jerk" reaction to a perceived problem or as a response to a popular fad in training programmes. Thus any call for training that is undertaken without a careful analysis of whether or not it is needed is likely to be ineffective and a waste of money and resources (Abu-Doleh, 1996; Branine, 1996). In sum, the results of this study has shown that less than one-third of the investigated organizations from each sector are really engaged in real and effective systematic MTD needs analysis for their managers. In line with this, Sarri et al.'s (1988) survey results indicated that only 27 per cent of organizations systematically assessed the training needs of their managers. By the same token, Coopers and Lybrand's (1985) report indicates that few companies have procedures for analysis of managers training and development needs. Likewise with the above discussion, Abdalla and Al-Homoud (1995) considered the difficulties originating from the absence of information in Kuwaiti organizations about the reservoir of basic skills, job descriptions and career planning as a serious obstacle for conducting systematic training needs assessment. Abdalla and Al-Homoud's (1995) survey results show that all government organizations and 96 per cent of private and joint-venture organizations have no specific practices or procedures for determining the training and educational needs of their managerial personnel. Abdalla and

Al-Homoud went on to say that the absence of systematic needs assessment is a serious drawback on the organization's management development efforts.

With regard to management levels to which MTD needs analysis scheme relates, Table 2 outlines these levels.

As can be noticed from the results in Table 2, the vast majority of the investigated organizations conducted their management needs assessment primarily for lower levels of management. Specifically, among organizations that report having MTD assessment procedures, this is done for first-level supervisors in 82.6 per cent of these organizations, whilst nearly 48 per cent and less than one-fifth (19.5 per cent) of these organizations have similar procedures for middle and top management, respectively. This latter finding is in line with other research results (Sarri et al., 1988; Abu-Doleh and Weir, 1997). Time and again, the results in Table 2 indicate that there is a statistically significant difference at the 0.05 level between the private and public sectors in terms of assessing lower management training needs for the private sector, as shown by a mean rank of 25.19. However, the Mann-Whitney non-parametric test indicates no statistically significant mean rank difference in either middle or top management needs assessment in both sectors.

With regard to approaches used in conducting MTD needs assessment, Table 3 summarizes these approaches.

Amazingly, it is clear from Table 3 that all public organizations (100 per cent) and the overwhelming majority of the private organizations

TABLE 2. Mann-Whitney U-Test for Management Level of MTD Needs Assessment (N = 46)[1]

Management level	Private (N = 24)			Public (N = 22)			M-W
	Mean Score[2]	SD	Mean Rank	Mean Score	SD	Mean Rank	U-value
Top level	1.92	.64	16.21	1.31	.81	14.23	154.3
Middle level	2.61	.78	21.23	2.01	.78	17.21	144.5
Lower level	3.92	.72	25.19	2.80	.62	18.79	165.0[3]

Notes:
M-W denotes Mann-Whitney U non-parametric test.
SD denotes standard deviation.
1. The responses were restricted only to organizations which report assessing their managers' MTD need on a regular basis.
2. Respondents rated their answers on a Likert five-point scale, where 1 (very low) to 5 (very high).
3. Significant at $p < 0.05$ by two-tail test.

TABLE 3. Approaches Used in Conducting MTD Needs Assessment (N = 46)

Business sector	Private (N = 24)				Public (N = 22)			
Type of analysis	Yes	(%)	No	(%)	Yes	(%)	No	(%)
Individual analysis	10	41.7	14	58.3	9	40.9	13	59.1
Functional/departmental	11	45.8	13	54.2	8	36.4	14	63.6
Organizational analysis	4	16.7	20	83.3	-	-	22	100.0

(83.3 per cent) which did regularly assess their managers' MTD needs conducted these assessments in the absence of organizational needs analysis. This finding leads us to question the value of managers' training and development needs assessment. Unless managers' MTD need assessment is based on real organizational need analysis little can be said about the usefulness and contribution of these assessments in helping the organizations to achieve their strategic objectives (Abu-Doleh, 1996). Also, as shown in Table 3, much emphasis was placed on the individual analysis and functional analysis rather than organizational analysis. Individual analysis as an approach to MTD needs assessment was cited by less than half of the respondents in both sectors (41.7 per cent and 40.9 per cent in the private and public organizations, respectively). Another 45.8 per cent of the respondents in the private sector and 36.4 per cent of their counterparts in the public sector report using functional/departmental analysis in determining their managers' MTD needs. Amazingly, in a few cases (7 out of 46 organizations), individual analysis and functional analysis were used simultaneously. Not surprisingly, no single organization in the two sectors has used all the three approaches simultaneously in conducting their MTD needs analysis.

As far as the procedures of MTD needs assessment are concerned, Table 4 below outlines these procedures.

The non-parametric M-W test results in Table 4 indicate no statistically significant difference at the 0.05 level between the two sectors in terms of the procedures used in conducting their MTD needs analysis, except on the "asking managers for their training needs" and on the "system failures, technology changes and problematic symptoms" as a procedure to assess MTD needs, where the private organizations placed a statistically higher mean rank of 26.21 and 21.12, respectively, compared to that of 20.90 and 15.16 for the public organizations. Summing up the above, we can state that private organizations usually are more active in asking their managers for their training needs than their counterparts in the public sector. This is to say, private organizations have more trust in letting their managers decide on what training they need. In line with this result, Sarri et al.'s (1988) survey results indicate that managers can nominate themselves in the majority of the companies to attend training and education programmes. However, "asking managers for their training needs" or the "request from line managers" as procedures to make MTD needs assessment are not necessarily an expression of the existence of real managers' training need. Also as shown in Table 4, "a request from the supervisors" as a procedure to determine MTD needs for their employees was highly used by the respondents in both sectors as indicated by a higher mean score of 3.85 and 3.65 for the private and public sectors, respectively. Expectedly, it is worth recalling that private organizations monitor more effectively their "system failures, technology changes and problematic symptoms" than their counterparts in the bureaucratic public sector. This can be justified by the fact that the Jordanian private sector faces a lot of changes and uncertainty in its internal

TABLE 4. Mann-Whitney U-Test for the Procedures of MTD Needs Assessment (N = 46)

Procedures of MTD needs assessment #	Private (N = 24)			Public (N = 22)			M-W
	Mean score	SD	Mean rank	Mean score	SD	Mean rank	U-value
1	2.42	.92	19.11	2.10	.77	17.62	162.5
2	4.12	.84	26.21	3.40	.82	20.90	182.0*
3	3.12	.72	21.84	2.70	.66	18.12	176.0
4	3.85	.87	23.12	3.65	.54	24.60	192.0
5	2.80	.73	21.12	1.90	.76	15.16	135.0*
6	2.76	.65	20.11	3.14	.92	22.11	172.0
7	2.13	.72	18.64	2.70	.74	21.24	146.0
8	1.82	.90	15.41	2.41	.81	18.21	167.5
9	2.16	.68	19.56	1.70	.72	14.16	154.0

Notes: * Significant at $p < 0.05$ by two-tail test.
# Procedures of MTD needs assessment denote:
1 = Regular systematic performance appraisal.
2 = Asking managers for their training needs.
3 = Request from line managers.
4 = Request from the supervisors.
5 = System failures, technology changes, problematic symptoms (e.g., customer complaints).
6 = Ad hoc assessment by T&D staff.
7 = Ad hoc assessment by training committee.
8 = Through the help of external training providers/consultant.
9 = Full training needs analysis.

and external environment. These drivers of changes provide the impetus for the private sector to determine their managers' training need in order to face these changes. However, if mean ratings between 2.50 and 3.50 are interpreted as "moderate" use, then the results in Table 4 indicate that the majority of the respondents in both sectors have used the listed procedures in assessing their MTD needs in a moderate way. Even worse, some procedures like getting "the help of external training providers/consultant" and conducting "full training needs analysis" have not been widely used by the majority of organizations in both sectors, as indicated by a low mean rating. In short, this is indicative of the lack of effective procedures to MTD needs assessment by the majority of the investigated organizations in both sectors.

Training managers were also asked to comment on what they think their line managers need in terms of training and development programmes. Their responses are shown in Table 5.

As shown in Table 5, the topics of developing interpersonal skills, human resource management, leadership, organization change and development, time management and strategic planning and forecasting were cited by more than half of the respondents in both sectors. On the other hand, the topics of motivation and communication, marketing and sales, crisis management, general managerial skills, production and operation management, stress management and total quality management were cited by less than half of the respondents in both sectors as perceived MTD needs for their managers. Expectedly, a topic such as private-public partnership (PPP) was cited by more than half and less than one-third of the respondents in the public and private sectors, respectively. This finding is not surprising since the public sector in Jordan is now undergoing a process of privatization. Public services in Jordan as well as in most countries around the world face many challenges. There is much controversy and even disagreement about how far public services have successfully met the challenges of the last few decades (Alfaouri, 2001). Therefore, since King Abdullah II came to power, he has called for the adoption of the PPP policy in Jordan to reinforce the privatization and the reform of public sector policies and procedures. In this regard, two key points are worth highlighting from the results in Table 5. The first point is related to the strong belief of the overwhelming majority of the respondents in both sectors to the need of their managers to be involved in creative/innovative thinking training programmes. The other significant point is that most of the respondents also believe that their managers have a real need to attend training programmes in organization change and development. Today, creative/innovative thinking can be seen to play a vital role, both in the private sector where it has been an important factor in the drive for efficiency, and in the public sector where the need to maximize resources has also become a political and economic necessity following decades of sustained pressure on government spending.

CONCLUSION AND IMPLICATIONS

As has been pointed out already, only nearly one-third of Jordanian private and public organizations report having a formal and systematic MTD needs analysis for their managers. Interestingly, the majority of these organizations have conducted their MTD needs assessment pri-

TABLE 5. The Perception of Training Managers Towards Their Managers' MTD Need (N = 64)[1]

The perceived MTD needs[2]	Cited by the private organisations (N = 30)	Cited by the public organisations (N = 34)
Developing interpersonal skills	53.3	70.5
Human resource management	80.0	61.7
Private-public partnership	30.0	79.4
Leadership	63.3	73.5
Motivation and communication	40.0	41.1
Organisation change and development	83.3	85.2
Crisis management	46.6	29.1
Time management	86.6	79.4
Finance and accounting	56.6	41.1
General managerial skills	30.0	47.1
Creative/innovative thinking	90.0	88.2
Strategic planning and forecasting	76.6	82.4
Production and operation management	46.6	35.3
Marketing and sales	36.3	26.5
Stress management	33.3	23.5
Total quality management	40.0	44.1

Notes: 1. The responses to the above perceived MTD needs were not restricted to organizations which have only conducted regular MTD needs assessment.
2. Each of the perceived MTD needs rated on a scale of 1 (very low) to 5 (very high).

marily for lower levels of management, whilst nearly one-fifth of the in-vestigated organizations have carried out MTD needs assessment for their top management levels. On the other hand, the overwhelming majority of the private and public organizations of this study have conducted their managers' MTD needs assessment in the absence of organizational need analysis. Accordingly, it can be concluded that managers' MTD needs assessment scheme has been implemented in an *ad hoc* basis rather than comprehensive and systematic analysis. As far as the procedures of MTD needs assessments are concerned, asking managers for their training needs, a request from line managers and a re-quest from the supervisors were the main procedures used in determin-ing MTD needs. On the contrary, conducting a full systematic training needs analysis and getting the help of external training consultants in the analysis of MTD needs were not common practice in the investi-gated organizations. In short, this is indicative of the lack of effective procedures to MTD needs assessment. In general, it seems that manag-ers' MTD needs assessment practices in the Jordanian private and pub-lic sectors are similar and still at an early development stage. Therefore, both sectors of the study need to learn how to make an effective and sys-tematic MTD need analysis. As a result, four main implications can be drawn from the current research findings. First, training managers should monitor effectively their MTD policies and plans. Particular at-tention should be paid to how effectively they translate their training plans into workable and measurable training programmes within their organization context. Management training systems must be pragmatic and should focus upon actual managers' training needs assessments, otherwise training will be carried out without any rational basis and will be doomed to failure. For this to happen, training managers should have long-term MTD policies and plans. In addition, they should strive to re-late their MTD policies and plans to real managers' training needs anal-ysis, and to the overall organization strategy. In this regard, it is urgent to relate simultaneously managers' needs analysis procedures with the analysis of their functional and organizational needs. Thus, all training efforts of the organization will be geared towards the same end result of increasing the organization's efficiency and effectiveness. Second, training managers should relate their MTD needs assessment plan to all management levels rather than focusing on lower level management. Third, given the great impact of MTD needs assessment plan on the suc-cess of training function, the use of full-training needs assessment pro-cedures are recommended rather than merely asking the individual managers about their training needs. In this context, it is worth stressing the importance of relating MTD needs assessment to the managers' job description and to performance appraisal schemes. Fourth, Jordanian organizations should offer special training programmes for managers in the area of innovative/creative thinking, strategic planning and forecasting, time management, organization change and development, human resource management and leadership.

REFERENCES

Abdalla, I.A., and Al-Homoud, M. (1995) "A survey of Management Training and Development Practices in the State of Kuwait," Journal of Management Development, 14 (3): 14-25.

Abu-Doleh, J. (1996) Human Resource Management: Management Training and Development in the Jordanian Private Sector, Unpublished PhD Thesis, University of Bradford Management Centre, England.

Abu-Doleh, J. (2000) "Human Resource Planning in Jordan: A Challenge for the Next Millennium," Middle East Business Review, 4 (1): 57-68, University of London.

Abu-Doleh, J., and Weir, D. (1997) "Management Training and Development Needs Analysis Practices in Jordanian Private Companies," Middle East Business Review, 2 (1): 80-87, University of London.

Al-Faleh, M. (1990) "Training and Development of Business Executives in Jordan," Dirasat, 17 (1), 7-38, University of Jordan.

Alfaouri, R. (2001) "Perspectives of Public Private Partnership Policy in Jordan," Paper Presented at the Seventh Public and Private Sector Partnerships: The Enterprise Governance, 59-70.

Atiyyah, H. (1993) "Management Development in Arab Countries: The Challenges of the 1990s," Journal of Management Development, 12 (1): 3-13.

Branine, M. (1996) "Observations on Training and Management Development in the People's Republic of China," Personnel Review, 25 (1): 25-39.

Coopers and Lybrand Associates (1985) A Challenge to Complacency: Changing Attitudes to Training, MSC/NEDO.

Fisher, C., Schoenfeldt, L., and Shaw, J. (1999) Human Resource Management, Fourth Edition, Boston, Houghton Mifflin Company.

Goldstein, I.L. (1986) Training in Organizations: Needs Assessment, Development, and Evaluation, Second Edition, Monterey, CA: Brooks Cole.

Kubr, M., and Prokopenko, J. (1989) Diagnosing Management Training and Development Needs, Geneva: International Labour Organization.

Mangham, I., and Silver, M. (1986) Management Training–Context and Practice, ESRC/DTI.

McGehee, W., and Thayer, P. (1961) Training in Business and Industry, New York, Wiley.

Moshe, M. (2000) "A Comparative Perspective on Executive Development: Trends in Eleven European Countries," Public Administration, 78 (1): 135-153.

Sarri, L., Johnson, D., Mclaughlin, S., and Zimmerle, D. (1988) "A Survey of Management Training and Education Practices in U.S. Companies," Personnel Psychology, 41: 731-743.

Shaikh, F. (1988) Management Leadership Style in the Private Sector in Jordan, Unpublished PhD Thesis, University of Glasgow, Scotland.

Taylor, D.S. (1989) "Training," in Molander, C., (Ed.), Human Resource Management, Bromley, Kent: Chartwell-Bratt Ltd, 143-169.

Walter, S. (2000) "Rethinking Training," Corrections Today, 62 (6): 100-104.

Weir, D. (1994) "Is There a Basis for a Specifically Arab Approach to Management Development?" Paper Presented at the Arab Management Conference, University of Bradford, July 5-7.

Zoubi, A. (1982) "Towards a Decade of Administrative Development in the Arab world," Arab Journal of Administration, April, 29-41.

Socio-Cultural Values and Organizational Culture

Hala M. Sabri

SUMMARY. This exploratory study examines if certain dimensions of the socio-cultural values could explain certain types of organizational culture. The proposition merits investigation because it has important implications for local as well as international and global companies. The study first investigates employees' perceptions of the existing and preferred cultural orientations in four Jordanian organizations, and then it compares the results with other studies conducted in other cultures (American and South African). In Jordan data were collected by means of Harrison and Stokes survey for diagnosing organizational culture, the same instrument used in the USA and in South Africa. The study concludes by suggesting that in certain countries the national culture's effects may appear in a particular dominant organizational culture, that is desired by the management, but not actually preferred by employees. This implies that it is more beneficial for international and transnational corporations to develop "strong" cultures rather than to encourage local units to adapt to their national cultures. *[Article copies available for a fee from The Haworth Document Delivery Service: 1-800-HAWORTH. E-mail*

Hala M. Sabri is Assistant Professor, Faculty of Economics and Administrative Sciences, Al-Zaytoonah University of Jordan, Amman, Jordan (E-mail: hasabi@yahoo. com).

[Haworth co-indexing entry note]: "Socio-Cultural Values and Organizational Culture." Sabri, Hala M. Co-published simultaneously in *Journal of Transnational Management Development* (The International Business Press, an imprint of The Haworth Press, Inc.) Vol. 9, No. 2/3, 2004, pp. 123-145; and: *Islam and Business: Cross-Cultural and Cross-National Perspectives* (ed: Kip Becker) The International Business Press, an imprint of The Haworth Press, Inc., 2004, pp. 123-145. Single or multiple copies of this article are available for a fee from The Haworth Document Delivery Service [1-800-HAWORTH, 9:00 a.m. - 5:00 p.m. (EST). E-mail address: docdelivery@haworthpress.com].

http://www.haworthpress.com/web/JTMD
© 2004 by The Haworth Press, Inc. All rights reserved.
Digital Object Identifier: 10.1300/J130v09n02_07

123

KEYWORDS. National culture, organizational culture, Jordan, Arab culture, power distance, uncertainty avoidance, achievement, individualism

Human behavior is dominated by culture in the sense that the greater part, perhaps all, of the variation between societies is based on differences in cultural experience. (Wilson, 1977: xiv)

Since the early 1980s culture has become an increasingly important element for academics and practitioners. As organizations seek to manage change in order to maintain advantages and respond to external pressures, the vital role that culture plays in successful change is being realized. Hence, the interest in organizational culture stems from the belief that culture influences behavior, decision-making and organizational strategies and performance (Denison, 1990; Kotter & Heskett, 1992).

Globalization has also heightened awareness of the need to not only understand the organizational culture but also the impact of national and international cultures.

Several management scholars maintain that there is no culture free theory of management (Hofstede, 1980; Al Tayeb, 1988; Handy, 1991; Pheysey, 1993; Gannon 1994; and Hickson & Pugh, 1995). These scholars argue that organizational culture is a product of individuals whose understanding is influenced by societal values, beliefs, work and social experiences. Hofstede (1991), for instance, argued that organizations are culture bound and that managers and organizations are not separable from their indigenous cultures. Ultimately, every manager, one way or another, has been formed by his culture. This means that, individuals working in organizations and the culture they bring with them, influence the way organizations are designed and managed and the way people react to their organizational processes and climates. Hence, people familiar with organizations in different countries are often struck by the variety of organizational solutions to the same task problem. Within this context, Arab customs and values have often been linked to a bureaucratic form of organization structure (Badawy, 1980; Muna, 1980; Hofstede, 1991; Dadfar, 1994; Hickson & Pugh, 1995; and Weir, 1996).

To date, however, there has been little empirical support for this idea. Although Arab organizations exist in a culture that is different from that of the West, its influence may be outweighed by other organizational constraints, including those of size, technology, dependence and external environment.

This study, therefore, has two objectives. The first is to examine the extent to which national culture and organizational culture are intertwined. Specifically, it examines the extent to which organizational culture could be explained by particular dimensions of national culture within the context of an Arab country, namely, Jordan. This is important for Arab businesses and, in particular, for Jordanian organizations. Given the paucity of research-based information coming out of this part of the world, knowledge of the socio-cultural and work related values and the management styles existing in Arab countries should be of great interest for international comparative management researchers. Moreover, Jordan, nowadays, has a strategic and important position for technology transfer and foreign direct investment. In recent years, Jordan has initiated several policies that aimed at stimulating entrepreneurs to actively participate in the economic transformation and encouraging foreign direct investments. Policy makers also realized the need to capitalize in the Jordanian human resources to speed development. The IT field nowadays has become the most popular one for young students and young entrepreneurs alike. Consequently, understanding the internal qualities and the cultures of organizations is vital for enhancing economic development in Jordan (Ali & Sabri, 2001).

The second objective is to test to what extent do the cultural differences between countries (such as Jordan, the USA and South Africa) account for significant variations in the culture of their organizations. This is important because knowledge of the socio-cultural and work related values should be of interest for international comparative management researchers. It also has important implications for the extent to which international and global companies need to take account of national cultures when deciding how much autonomy they should give to units operating in different countries to determine their own culture.

The paper is organized as follows. The next section reviews the literature on national culture and organizational culture. Following that, the research methodology is described and then the research hypotheses are laid out and data is analyzed. The paper concludes with discussion and further directions.

THEORETICAL BACKGROUND

National Culture. Several studies have examined similarities and differences between national cultures in order to identify "culture clusters" and attempt to classify national cultures by surveying the attitudes towards work of people employed in different countries. These studies have emphasized geography, language and religion as the main dimensions that underline these clusters (Ronen & Shenkar, 1985; Smith, 1992). Hofstede (1980) argues that every person carries within himself patterns of thinking, feeling and potential actions, which were learnt throughout his lifetime. He called these patterns "mental programs" and argued that their source lies within the social environment in which one grew up. Mental programs vary, as much as the social environment in which they were acquired. Hofstede elaborated by calling such mental programs the term "culture," which he defined as "the collective programming of the mind which distinguishes the members of one group or category of people from another." The definition applies equally to societies and organizations. It offers simplicity and clarity and is useful for cross-cultural research (Shakelton & Ali, 1990). Hofstede surveyed 116,000 employees working for 72 IBM subsidiaries around the world. The survey ranged over 38 occupations and involved 20 languages. A factor analysis of the responses to a set of standardized questions produced four dimensions of national culture: high versus low Power Distance; strong versus weak Uncertainty Avoidance; Individualism versus Collectivism; and Masculinity versus Femininity. Hofstede argues that these dimensions affected thinking and action in predictable ways.

Power Distance (PD) reflects the extent to which the less powerful people in a culture accept and expect power to be distributed unequally. In high power distance countries, there is a considerable dependence of subordinates on bosses and preference for autocratic or paternalistic boss. Power is based on family, friends and charisma and the ability to use force. In low power distance counties there is a limited dependence of subordinates on bosses and preference for consultations.

Uncertainty Avoidance (UA) reflects the extent to which people become nervous in unstructured, ambiguous situations, and try to avoid such situations by developing rules to guide behavior and a belief in absolute truth. Coping with uncertainty is achieved through the domain of technology, law and religion. Religious beliefs tend to deal with the ultimate uncertainties of life and death. In organizations these take the form of technology, rules and rituals. *The Individualism-Col-*

lectivism (IDV) dimension reflects the extent to which culture encourages individuals as opposed to collectivist, group-centered concerns. In individualistic cultures the emphasis is on personal commitment and achievement. By contrast, in collectivist cultures the interest of group prevails over that of the individual. Hofstede (1991) suggested a negative correlation between the individualism/collectivism index and the power distance index. Countries which are high on power distance are more collectivist cultures, in which people are dependent on in groups and power figures.

The Masculinity-Femininity (MAS) dimension highlights "masculine" cultures where performance is what counts, ambition is the driving force and achievement factors are emphasized. It is believed that to be important is to have an opportunity for higher earnings, to attain recognition by doing a good job with a chance for advancement. Challenging work satisfies the sense of accomplishment. Meanwhile, in feminine cultures there are strong sex role distinctions and women's work is identified as lying within the family domain. Men and women are expected to be concerned with relationships, and to sympathize with whatever is small and weak.

Hofstede suggested that the first two dimensions (Power Distance and Uncertainty Avoidance) describe organizational characteristics, while the other two (Individualism-Collectivism and Masculinity-Femininity) describe individual characteristics.

In this context, management scholars have indicated that the Arab society has its own social and cultural environment, which plays a major role in molding its organizational processes and managerial systems. Several researchers indicated that the driving forces that are related to the study of management in the Arab world are language, history, religion, traditional values and external forces (Attiyah, 1993; Ali, 1995; Weir, 1995). Barakat (1991), for instance, acknowledged that Islamic religion is the most important aspect in the Arab culture. To the Arabs, Islam is a symbol of their identity, aspiration, and glorious achievements. But Islam, he adds, is often used to legitimize the tribal system and protect family interests and shield tribalistic values rather than as a pure belief system. Likewise, Dadfar (1990) argues that even though Islam is against tribalism and pre-Islamic values, the Arabs have skillfully blended the tribal values with the Islamic ones, to the extent that it became difficult to draw a clear borderline between Islamic and pre-Islamic values. Other research on Arab organizations indicated that Arab managers are reluctant to delegate authority; believe that centralization builds respect; avoid responsibility and risk-taking; prefer stable lifestyle over rewarding but challenging work; are highly concerned with job security; and give priority to friendships and personal consider-ations over organizational goals and performance (Al Nimir & Palmer, 1982; and Al Hegelan & Palmer, 1985).

Organizational Culture. Ouchi (1981), Deal and Kennedy (1982), Schein (1985), and Harrison (1990) argue that organizational culture is a distinctive constellation of beliefs; and values work styles and rela-tionships, which distinguish one organization from another. Schein (1990: 111), for instance, defined organizational culture as "a pattern of basic assumptions invented, discovered or developed by a given group, as it learns to cope with its problems of external adaptation and internal integration, that has worked well enough to be considered valid and therefore, to be taught to new members as the correct way to perceive, think, and feel in relation to those problems." When these beliefs and values are widely and deeply held, the culture is considered "strong cul-ture." In this respect there is less need for detailed organizational rules and regulations. In contrast, in "weak organizational culture" rules and regulations are strictly enforced to control behavior.

In the last twenty years many writers have proposed that organiza-tions have cultures (Allen & Kraft, 1982; Peters & Waterman, 1982). Amsa (1986) has related the present preoccupation with organizational culture to socio-economic factors in Western societies. Raelin (1986) and Iwami (1992) asserted that American corporate culture was de-picted originally as a progressive model of organizational practice when compared with bureaucratic models of the late nineteenth and early twentieth centuries and later as a regressive model in comparison with the more successful organizational and economic systems of Germany and Japan. Harrison (1990) and Handy (1991) argue that organizations are as different and varied as the nations and societies of the world. Or-ganizations have different culture-sets of values and norms and beliefs, reflected in different structures and systems. Harrison (1990) identified four cultural orientations inside organizations. He called them: Power, Role, Achievement and Support cultures. In *power culture*, leaders dis-play strength, justice and are paternalistic. Subordinates are submissive and are expected to be compliant, willing and loyal. The *role orienta-tion* requires less direct supervision, assuming that people work most efficiently and effectively when they have clearly defined tasks. Clarity and precision of the roles and procedures are also a must. Unlike the power and role cultures, the *achievement culture* relies on self-motivat-ing strategies and is based on competence. Although people supervise themselves, structure and system are necessary in this culture. Like the achievement culture, the *support-oriented* organization assumes that people want to contribute. Hence, this culture offers its members a satisfaction that stems from relationships, mutuality, connection and belonging.

National Culture and Organizational Culture. As different societies presumably have different cultures, considerable research efforts were and are still expended in search of culture's influence on the structures and processes of organizations, and on the attitudes, needs and motivations of managers (Roberts, 1970; Kraut, 1975; Weinshall, 1977; and Al Tayeb, 1988). Gannon (1994), for example, suggests that in organizational behavior it is of interest to know the extent to which local organizations adopt values commonly held in their society. However, the degree to which researchers were concerned with linking the internal qualities of organizations to the wider cultural context varied greatly (Deal & Kennedy, 1982; Tichy, 1982; Martin & Powers, 1983; Handy, 1985; Sabri, 1995).

Hofstede et al. (1990) recognized that organizational culture differences are composed of other elements than those that make up national culture differences. At the national level cultural differences reside mostly in values, rather than in practices. At the organizational level, cultural differences reside mostly in practices, and less in values. Yet, Hofstede (1993, p. 1) asserts that organizational and national culture do, in fact, overlap and also they affect the different programs in people's minds.

Pheysey (1993) argues that a society's culture expresses how members of the society go about solving their survival problems and that this is reflected in the way organizations located in their society go about solving their problems. She cautions that organizational cultures do not fit inside societal (national) culture. At both levels cultures vary not only in content but also in strength and intensity. In spite of these difficulties, it is our view that the relation between national and organizational cultures should be explored, however tentatively, so that practical concerns for international management can be highlighted. While the author does not offer generalizable certainties on the basis of this study, it is hoped to move the debate that national culture might serve as a useful method for considering organizational behavior, and show how cross-organizational study could be designed. Thus, Pheysey (1993: 15) suggested a link between Hofstede's four dimensions of National cultures and Harrison's (1990) four cultural orientations. From the perspective of Hofstede's (1980) national cultures. Pheysey noticed the organizational cultures, which might exist within every society as follows:

1. *In Power Distance terms*, the organization is seen as embedded with *"Power Culture"* where there is "relatively bounded and stable occurrences of social order based on habits of deference to authority."
2. *In Uncertainty Avoidance terms*, an organization is seen as having a *"Role Culture"* where people work most effectively and efficiently if they have relatively simple and clearly defined tasks. Clarity of roles and procedures fits the parts of organization together like a machine.
3. *In Individualism terms*, people are interested in the work itself; thus, an organization tends to have *"Achievement Culture,"* which assumes that people will be self-motivated and enjoy working at tasks, which are intrinsically satisfying. People also emphasize their personal commitment and achievement.
4. *The Femininity Culture* offers satisfaction through relationships, mutuality, belonging and connection. People contribute out of a sense of commitment to the organization. Thus it would match a *"Support Culture"* in organizations.

METHODOLOGY

This study draws its methodology from three main propositions in the reviewed literature. First, Hofstede's (1980) "culture bound" proposition, which assumes the predominant effect of national culture on organizations and employee behavior inside them; second, Harrison's (1990) four cultural orientations (Power, Role, Achievement and Support); and third, Pheysey's (1993) idea that Hofstede's dimensions of national culture could be useful tools to explain Harrison's four organizational cultures.

The incidence of other studies, which used the same instrument for measuring organizational culture (such as Harrison (1990) in the USA and Serfontein (1990) in South Africa), helped to drew on their results and gain cross-cultural understanding on the similarities/dissimilarities with the Jordanian organizational culture. Therefore, it is suggested that the methodology which this study has adopted for the cross-cultural comparison overcame the cost and time obstacles suggested by Ardent (1985) and Adler (1986).

Measurement of national culture. Hofstede's four dimensions of national culture were selected in this study for several reasons. First: Hofstede probably provides the most comprehensive data available on national cultures that has received widespread acceptance, and still figures prominently in most recent studies on societal cultures. Moreover, by now, there is hardly a cross-national study that does not cite Hofstede. Second: Hofstede (1991) studied the values of 50 countries and 3 regions. His study included samples of the IBM Company from seven Arab countries [Egypt, Iraq, Kuwait, Lebanon, Libya, Saudi Arabia and United Arab Emirates] which were considered as representatives of the Arab culture. Because the sample in each country was small, Hofstede referred to these seven countries as "Arab Group." For the Arab group generally, Hofstede suggested high power distance, moderate uncertainty avoidance, high collectivist and moderate masculine/feminine society. It should be indicated here that Jordan, as an Arab country, also shares basic cultural values with the rest of the Arab world, especially the Arab Gulf States. Although Jordan's economy is not oil based, this does not influence the deeply held cultural values and orientations.

Measurement of organizational culture. The measure of organizational culture used in this study is the Harrison and Stokes Diagnosing Organizational Culture instrument (1992), which assesses respondents' perceptions of existing and preferred organizational cultures in terms of Harrison's constructs of organizational culture. This instrument has been chosen for several reasons. First: it can be used to survey a wide range of employees' perceptions of culture. It was used widely in different societies and found to be reliable (e.g., Anderson, 1995; Al-Salem, 1996). Second: it was the same instrument utilized to measure the organizational culture in the USA by Harrison (1990) and in South Africa by Serfontein (1990). Third: because Pheysey (1993) explicitly links the four constructs of organizational culture measured by this instrument with Hofstede's four dimensions of national culture. The instrument contains 15 statements. Each statement has four possible alternatives (a, b, c and d), each of which represents a particular culture. Alternative "a" refers to the Power culture, alternative "b" assesses the Role culture, alternative "c" describes the Achievement culture and alternative "d" describes the Support culture. There are two columns for each alternative: existing and preferred cultures. Participants are asked to rank each alternative for both columns from 4 (the most dominant view) to 1 (the least dominant view). The current reliability coefficient ranges from .66 to .85.

Hypotheses

In Hofstede's (1991) study of the work values of 50 countries and 3 regions, country scores on each of the four dimensions ranged, from lowest to highest, as follows: On power distance: 11-104. On Uncertainty avoidance: 8-112. On Individualism: 6-91 (the least individualistic to the more collectivist). On Masculinity dimension: 5-95 (the least masculine to the more feminine). Accordingly, Hofstede (1991) assigned rank 1 to the country that scored the highest, and 53 to the one that scored the lowest on each of the four dimensions.

On Power Distance dimension the Arabs scored high, the American scored low and the South African scored high. *On Uncertainty Avoidance dimension*, the Arabs scored moderate, the American scored low and the South African scored low. On *Individualism*, the Arabs scored low, the American scored high and the South African scored high. And finally, on *Masculinity*, the Arabs scored moderate, the Americans scored high and the South African scored high.

According to this classification we can expect Arab managers to be likely to accept greater power distance between individuals, to be uncertainty avoidant, to be collectivist in orientation, and to adopt feminine values (giving greater concern for people than for tasks). The American and South African managers can be expected to value more equality in power, to be more tolerant to uncertainties, to be individualistic, and to adopt masculine values (giving greater concern for tasks than people). These results provide an opportunity to elaborate the following hypotheses, which predict a relationship between Hofstede's four dimensions of national culture and Harrison's four constructs of organizational culture:

H1: Jordanian organizations will be more power and role oriented than organizations in other countries that have different national cultures (such as the USA and South Africa).

H2: Jordanian employees will have a stronger preference for power and role organizational cultures than employees working in organizations in other countries that have different national cultures (such as the USA and South Africa).

Database and Samples

Data on organizational culture for this study were obtained from the following sources. *First:* in Jordan, data were collected from a random sample of employees working for four Jordanian organizations. Two of these represented product organizations, potash and oil refinery. The other two represented service organizations, passenger airline and electricity. The Harrison and Stokes questionnaire "Diagnosing Organizational Culture" was translated from English into Arabic. An Arab language expert, who was fluent in English, checked the translation. The translated questionnaire was then given (separately) to two other independent experts, who were asked to check the translation. Finally the questionnaire was administered to a pilot sample of six employees working at different levels in a Jordanian organization. This group was then interviewed to explore any difficulties they encountered before the questionnaire was distributed on a wider scale. The 360 questionnaires were distributed and 234 (65%) usable questionnaires were returned. 48 from potash, 57 from refinery, 49 from electricity, and 80 from airline. The sample comprised 136 (58%) managerial and 98 (42%) non-managerial positions. Seventy-two percent of the sample were university graduates and the majority of them were males (82%). Over 50% were 40 years of age or older. Table 1 shows the characteristics of Jordanian respondents.

Second: Harrison (1990) provided the USA data from a study he conducted on a sample of 311 managers working for a variety of companies, in the USA, tending towards the technical and professional occupations. Serfontein (1990) provided South Africa's data from a study he conducted on a sample of 451 employees from three engineering companies. Both Harrison and Serfontein used the same instrument of measurement "diagnosing organizational culture."

FINDINGS AND DISCUSSION

In the following comparison of Jordanian, American and South African employees, the discussion will focus on the respondents' perceptions of the existing and preferred organizational culture, in the three societies. It will be seen that there are some significant divergence of views between the three groups on their perceptions of existing and preferred cultural orientations. This is reflected by the inter-related pattern of results produced by the Harrison and Stokes instrument. It should be

TABLE 1. Personal Characteristics of Jordanian Respondents (n = 234)

Variable	Frequency	% Frequency
1. Economic Sector:		
Electricity	49	21
Potash	48	21
Refinery	57	24
Airline	80	34
	-------	-------
Total	234	100
2. Job Level:		
Managers	136	58
Non-Managers	98	42
	-------	------
Total	234	100
3. Educational Level:		
University Graduates	169	72
Non-University Graduates	65	28
	-------	------
Total	234	100
4. Sex:		
Males	191	82
Females	43	18
	-------	------
Total	234	100
5. Age Group:		
20-24	5	2
25-30	22	9
30-34	47	20
35-39	41	18
40-50	97	42
Over 50	22	9
	-------	------
Total	234	100

noted, however, that, as in the other cross-cultural research (Trompenaars & Hampden-Turner, 1999), differences are sometimes a matter of degree rather than contradiction.

Comparing groups on existing organizational culture. Table 2 provides a comparison of Jordanian, American and South African employ-

TABLE 2. Comparison of Jordanian (n = 234), American (n = 311), and South African (n = 451) Employees' Perceptions of Existing Organizational Cultures

Existing Culture	Results	Jordan N = 234 (1)	USA N = 311	Jordan N = 234 (2)	South Africa N = 451
Power	Mean	45.9	36.3	45.9	41.3
	SD	9.7	12.6	9.7	9.2
	t-value	10.1***		12.6***	
Role	Mean	41.5	39.7	41.5	41.3
	SD	6.0	7.3	6.0	5.6
	t-value	3.2***		0.43	
Achievement	Mean	33.6	41.5	33.6	38.9
	SD	6.4	7.7	6.4	6.8
	t-value	13.1***		12.6***	
Support	Mean	29.1	32.3	29.1	28.7
	SD	6.3	11.6	6.3	7.7
	t-value	4.1***		1.1	

*** $p < 0.001$ at two tailed test.
(1) Degrees of Freedom (543).
(2) Degrees of Freedom (683).

ees' responses, giving means, standard deviations and *t-test* results of the existing organizational culture.

On existing cultures, Jordanian organizations are more power and role oriented than American organizations that are more achievement and support oriented and South African organizations that are more achievement oriented. The differences are significant. Achievement and support cultures are less common in Jordanian organizations. These results seem to lend support for *H1*, which assumes that Jordanian organizations will be more power and role oriented than American and South African organizations.

In Jordan the national culture is high on power distance, moderate on uncertainty avoidance. In Jordan, as well as in other Arab countries, power orientation is practiced in the social, political and administrative structures. The Jordanians are known to be polite, obedient and respect authority. This behavior rests on the tribal and patriarchal systems (Abdel-Khaliq, 1984; and Al-Kubaisy, 1985). Tribal orientation in Jordan can be explored in the sense of family commitment and loyalty to the tribe. In this system, power rests in the hands of the tribe's chief (called in Arabic Sheikh). In the business world, the high power distance translates into a strong tendency for authoritative and paternalistic styles resulting in high centralization of decision-making (Attiyeh, 1993). Personal power rather than organizational power is sought. Employees are viewed as incapable of contributing to decision-making. Hierarchy reflects the existential inequality between superiors and subordinates. Top executives demand complete submission of their employees, and subordinates in return do not take initiative and expect to be told what to do. Uncertainty and risks are avoided; survival of business is the primary goal of managers. Perhaps this explains why "role" culture is the second most prevailing culture. Rules and procedures in the "role" oriented organizations are enforced to cope with uncertainty and to avoid undesired behavior. But in Jordan, although rules and laws are seen as ways to prevent uncertainties, the exercise of discretionary power by Jordanian managers, in most cases, replaces the need for these internal rules. The Jordanian culture is also more collectivist and moderately masculine culture. In this culture, management is management of groups and relationship prevails over task. The employer-employee relationship is perceived in moral terms, like a family link, hence allegiance to company growth is secondary to that of the family.

   The tendency of Jordanian organizations towards a role orientation, that is dependent on formalization, confirms the previous research that rules and regulations in Arab organizations appear to be only a reflection of the noteworthy tendency of Arab executives to assign duties according to their personal judgment calling on rules and procedures, that are generally neglected, as a protective tactic to reinforce their power. This result might have pointed to what Dore (1973), for example, has called a late development effect. Dore (1973: 416) argues that:

   In nations that in contemporary economic terms are late developers, it is possible to design organizations from scratch to look like
   those in industrialized nations, adopting straight away the text
   book techniques and principles of scientific management that specialization and formalization scores reflect. The later industrialization begins, the bigger the organizational leap, the more likely
   industry is to begin with rationalized bureaucratic forms of organization including specialist personnel managers, operating objective recruitment and promotion schemes, the more so if, as is

likely, the state plays a direct role in the industrialization process through state corporations or partnership schemes.

In the United States the culture scores low on power distance and weak on uncertainty avoidance. That's why the American management style focuses on role of employees. In low power culture a key idea is "participative management," a situation in which subordinates are involved in decisions at the discretion and initiative of their managers. It is also tolerant of different and innovative ideas and behavior. Motivation is by achievement and esteem or belongingness. The American culture is also more individualistic and masculine culture (it is ranked first among the 50 countries and 3 regions on the individualism index). In individualistic and masculine cultures management is management of individuals, hiring and promotion decisions are supposed to be based on skills and rules only, self-actualization by every individual is an ultimate goal and task prevails over relationship. Performance is what counts. Hence, the emphasis is on personal commitment and achievement.

In South Africa organizations are more dominated by power and role than achievement and support cultures. The tendency towards power orientation could match the high power distance of the South African culture. But the tendency of South African organizations towards role culture (although the national culture of South Africa is weak on uncertainty avoidance) could have resulted in the fact that the sample came from three engineering companies. This result lends support for Harrison's view (1995) that the type of organization's activity, coupled with modern production methods, constrain existing culture. Furthermore, Hofstede (1991: 130) indicates that weak uncertainty avoidance cultures try to integrate minorities and guarantee equal rights, but this doses not hold, obviously, for South Africa. Hofstede (1991: 130) explains that this is because in his study of national cultures data in South Africa were from whites only, but it is the whites who set the policies. The weak inclination of the South African culture towards uncertainty avoidance could at least explain why part of South African whites reject apartheid.

Comparing groups on preferred organizational cultures. Table 3 provides a comparison of Jordanian, American and South African respondents' perceptions of preferred organizational cultures, giving mean scores, standard deviations and t-test results.

On preferred cultures, the comparison shows that Jordanian employees have a significant preference for power and role orientations than

TABLE 3. Comparison of Jordanian (n = 234), American (n = 311) and South African (n = 451) Employees' Perceptions of Preferred Organizational Cultures

Culture	Results	Jordan n = 234 (1)	USA n = 311	Jordan N = 234 (2)	South Africa N = 451
Power	Mean	24.5	20.6	24.5	25.2
	SD	6.8	5.2	6.8	7.7
	t-value	7.3***		1.22	
Role	Mean	43.1	33.4	43.1	36.2
	SD	5.4	5.4	5.4	4.8
	t-value	9.4***		10.0***	
Achievement	Mean	46.8	52.9	46.8	49.4
	SD	5.6	5.1	5.6	7.4
	t-value	13.7***		5.1***	
Support	Mean	35.6	42.0	35.6	39.5
	SD	6.7	8.0	6.7	6.3
	t-value	10.0***		7.1***	

*** $p < 0.001$ at two-tailed test.
(1) Degrees of Freedom (543).
(2) Degrees of Freedom (683).

American and South African groups, who significantly prefer organizations that are more achievement and support oriented. This result also seems to provide support for *H2*, which assumes that Jordanian employees will have a stronger preference for power and role oriented organizations than American and South African employees. Furthermore, the strong preference of American respondents towards achievement and support cultures matches their national culture (that is low on power distance, individualistic and masculine culture). These results seem to offer support for Harrison's (1995) view that the national culture manifests its influence on preferred culture.

In South Africa, respondents expressed their preference for an organization that is more achievement and support oriented. This is also in line with the individualistic and masculine orientations of the South African national culture. It should be noted, however, that although the South African national culture is high on power distance, since apartheid has gone, South African whites recognize that their country can survive only if the blacks play an integral role in the development of the new South Africa (Lewis, 1999).

Moreover, Jordanian respondents' preferred organizational culture is quite different from their perceptions of the existing organizational culture. Mean scores of the preferred cultures shown in Table 4 indicate that Jordanian respondents expressed a preference for an organizational culture that has a strong orientation towards achievement. Few expressed a preference towards support culture, and power was the least preferred orientation.

This result could indicate to that many current employees in Jordanian organizations are being exposed to non-traditional sources of mental programming. Allaire and Firsirotu (1984) refer to Selznick's (1957) argument that organizations are historical products reflecting past and current leaders' efforts to chart and guide the organization's distinctive competence, and they cite Pettigrew's statement that founders:

> . . . may be seen not only as creators of more rational and tangible aspects of organizations such as structures and technologies but also as creators of symbols, ideologies, language, beliefs, rituals, and myths aspects of the more cultural and expressive components of organizational life. (Pettigrew, 1979: 574)

The founders of the four Jordanian organizations in this study may have been more heavily influenced by historical factors, such as tribalism and Ottoman domination, than the majority of current members. These traditional sources of socialization may have had less impact on those organizational members who completed the Harrison and Stokes' instrument because many of them have been exposed to alternative sources of mental programming or what Berger and Luckman (1966) refer to as the processes of secondary socialization. Berger and Luckman (1966: 150) define socialization as the comprehensive and consistent induction of an individual into a society. Through the process of primary socialization the individual has no alternative other than to take on the roles and attitudes of significant others, such as parents, and to take on their world. Secondary socialization is any subsequent process that inducts an already socialized individual into new sectors of the objective world of his or her society. It may affect the individual's construction of reality appertaining to specific institutional context. Calori et al. (1997), for example, highlight education as one of the factors that can affect beliefs about how things ought to be done and how organizations should be managed. Thus, Jordanian employees included in this study may have been influenced by processes of secondary socialization associated with higher education, overseas experience, and employment in multi-national companies in Jordan and other Arab countries and the media. Over 72 percent of all respondents included in this study hold university degrees, and a high proportion of them have worked or studied abroad. This line of argument recognizes the possibility that processes of secondary socialization may have a powerful effect on employees' preferences regarding organizational culture. It also raises the possibility that Hofstede's data for the Arab countries may fail to reflect an accurate picture of the effects of the mental programming or processes of secondary socialization that many current organizational members have been exposed to.

Conclusion

If it is accepted that national culture does exert an influence on organizational culture, this influence might be expected to be weakest on existing culture because it is likely to be more open to influences from immediate contingencies such as market conditions and technological developments. For that reason, further research is required to improve the understanding of the relationship between societal culture and organizational culture and the consequences on management practices and employee behaviors. If culture is viewed in functional or instrumental terms, as an adaptive mechanism that enables individuals and communities to manage problems in ways that satisfy their needs, for example for dependence on power distance and/or uncertainty avoidance, the nature of the match between national culture and organizational culture could have important consequences. In those situations where societal values (which are the focus of the processes of primary and secondary socialization) fail to permeate an organization's culture, organizational members may experience difficulty satisfying their needs and this may be reflected in low levels of job satisfaction, commitment, motivation and performance.

If the relationships between national culture and organizational culture have an effect on commitment, motivation and job satisfaction and performance of organizational members and on the commitment of constituents external to the organization, they may also have important policy implications for the management of international and transnational organizations. Such organizations may need to consider whether promoting a consistent world-wide organizational culture will be more or less beneficial than adapting an organization's culture to match the needs of different national cultures. Marcoulides and Heck (1993) refer to a widely held view that organizations with "strong" cultures perform at higher levels of productivity than organizations with weak cultures. They define a "strong" culture as one that is widely shared and exhibits a well-integrated and effective set of values, beliefs and behavior patterns. Peters and Waterman (1982: 75), in their search for corporate excellence, assert that:

> Without exception, the dominance and coherence of culture proved to be an essential quality of the excellent companies.

This view implies that, in certain cultures, it will be more beneficial for international and transnational companies to develop "strong" corporate cultures rather than to encourage local units to adapt to their national cultures. It is possible, however, that "weak" organizational cultures might be more beneficial when companies are confronted with differentiated environments. This is because weak organizational cultures offer the possibility of greater internal differentiation that, in turn, enables different units of the organization to develop the most appropriate organization-environment interface.

Limitation

When interpreting the results of this study, several limitations should be borne in mind. In measuring the cultural differences and their influences on organizations and management practices, researchers have always faced difficulty. This was not because of lack of instruments but mostly from the excess of instruments that have been tried and are still being tried. Hence, some might argue that a limitation of this study is that it had adopted an instrument of measurement developed in Western cultures and then had it administered in an Arab national setting. The strength of the adopted instrument in this study was in its confirmed validity (by being translated into different languages) and also by being replicated on organizations in different national cultures. Moreover, the use of internationally recognized instrument of measurement is extremely helpful in developing the cross-cultural research and advocates arguments between management practitioners in different cultures especially where cross-cultural research building is required.

Furthermore, ideally, it would have been desirable if the cross-cultural comparison in this study obtained data from organizations in different national cultures over same period of time. Limited resources and time constraints made this difficult. However, this study offered quantitative data and thus overcame a criticism of many cross-cultural studies which Nath (1968: 57) noticed have provided useful insights, but failed to provide rigorous comparative data, because they have mostly been based on impressions or uncontrolled interviews.

It is also important to note that the author does not claim the sample as representative of all Jordanian employees; the intention, however, was exploratory, and it is accepted that further research will be needed to verify the findings of this study. It is recommended that further research should include additional organizations in countries with more diverse cultures, over one period of time, by means of the same instrument of measurement.

Finally, it is possible to learn a lot from the empirical work reported in this study and the theories that have been suggested. Yet, a lot more remains unknown that if researched would contribute to the advancement of organization theory. Therefore, further research and analysis are necessary and warranted.

REFERENCES

Abdel-Khaliq, N. (1984). "Al-Aba'ad Al Bieyah Lil Birocratia Al Kuwaitia" (Environmental Dimensions of Bureaucracy in Kuwait), *Studies in The Gulf and Arabia*, Vol.10, (38), 13-65.

Adler, N. (1986). *International Dimensions of Organizational Behavior*. Boston, MA: Kent Publishing Company.

Al-Hegelan, H. & Palmer, M. (1985). Bureaucracy and development in Saudi Arabia, *Middle Eastern Journal*, 39 (Winter), 48-59.

Al-Kubaisy, A. (1985). "Theory and Practice of Administrative Development in a New Nation," *Dissertation Abstracts* I, A32, 5873-A.

Ali, A & Sabri, H. (2001). Organizational Culture and Job Satisfaction in Jordan, *Journal of Transnational Management Development*, Vol. 6 (1/2), 105-118.

Ali, A. (1995). "Cultural Discontinuity and Arab Management Thoughts," *International Studies of Management and Organization*, Vol. 25 (3), 7-30.

Allaire, Y., & Firsirotu, M. E. (1984). "Theories of Organizational Culture," *Organization Studies*, Vol. 5 (3), 193-226.

Allen, F. R., & Kraft, C. (1982). *The Organizational Unconscious. How to Create The Corporate Culture You Want and Need*. Englewood Cliffs, NJ: Prentice-Hall.

Amsa, P. (1986). "Organizational Culture And Work Group Behavior: An Empirical Study," *Journal of Management Studies*, Vol. 23 (4), 347-362.

Anderson, C. (1995). "The relationship between organizational culture and effectiveness in community college and business partnerships," Doctoral Dissertation (Unpublished), University of San Francisco, Faculty of the School of Education.

Arndt, J. (1985). "On Making Marketing Science More Scientific: Roles of Orientations, Paradigms, Metaphors, And Puzzle Solving," *Journal of Marketing,* Vol. 3, 11-23.

Al-Tayeb, M. (1988). *Organizations and National Culture: A Comparative Analysis,* Newbury Park, CA: Sage.

Attiyah, H. (1993). "Roots of Organization and Management Problems in Arab Countries: Cultural or Otherwise?" A paper presented at The Arab Management Conference, Bradford Management Center, Bradford, July 6-8.

Al-Nimir, S. & Palmer, M. (1982). Bureaucracy and development in Saudi Arabia, *Public Administration and Development,* Vol. 2, 93-104.

Al-Salem, A. A. (1996). "A Case Study of The Organizational Culture of the Makkah Municipality In the Context of Saudi Society," *Ph.D.* Thesis (Unpublished), Temple University, USA.

Badawy, M. K. (1980). "Style of Mideastern Managers," *California Management Review,* Vol. 22, 51-58.

Barakat, H. (1991). *The Modern Arab Society: An Experimental, Social Research* (4th ed.), Center for Arab Unity Studies, Beirut.

Berger, P. L. & Luckman, T. (1966). *The social construction of reality,* Harmondsworth: Penguin.

Calori, R., Lubatkin, M., Very, P. and Veiga, J. F. (1997) "Modeling the origins nationally bounded administrative heritages: A historical institutional analysis of French and British firms," *Organization Sciences,* 8, 6: 681-696.

Dadfar, H. (1990). "Industrial Buying Behavior in the Middle East: A Cross-National Study, Doctoral Dissertation, Linkoping University.

Dadfar, H. (1993). "In Search of Arab Management Direction and Identity," A Paper Presented at The Arab Management Conference, University of Bradford, Bradford, July 6-8.

Deal, T. E., & Kennedy, A. A. (1982). *Corporate Cultures: The Rites and Rituals of Corporate life,* Reading, MA: Addison-Wesley.

Denison, D. R. (1990). *Corporate Culture and Effectiveness.* New York: Wiley.

Dore, R. (1973). *British Factory–Japanese Factory,* London, George Allen and Unwin.

Gannon, M. (1994). *Understanding Global Cultures: Metaphorical Journeys Through 17 Countries,* Thousand Oaks, CA: Sage Publications.

Handy, C. B. (1981). *Understanding Organizations,* Harmondsworth, Penguin, 2nd ed.

Handy, C. B. (1991). *Gods of Management,* London, Penguin, 3rd ed.

Harrison, R., & Stokes, H. (1992). *Working With Organization Culture: A Workbook and Manual for Diagnosing Culture,* Horshman: Roffey Park Institute.

Harrison, R. (1995). A Special Correspondence with the Researcher, (Unpublished).

Hickson, D., & Pugh, D. S. (1995). *Management Worldwide: The Impact of Societal Culture on Organizations Around the Globe,* London: Penguin Books.

Hofstede, G. (1980). *Culture's Consequences: International Differences in Work-Related Values,* London, Sage Publications.

Hofstede, G. (1991). *Cultures and Organizations, Software of the Mind,* London, McGraw-Hill Book Co.

Hofstede, G. (1993). "Inter-Cultural conflict and Synergy in Europe," in Hickson, D. (ed.) *Management in Western Europe: Society, Culture and Organization in Twelve Nations,* Berlin, de Guyter, 1-8.

Iwami, M. (1992). "What is Japanese Style Corporate Management," *Management Japan,* Vol. 23 (1), 24-26.

Kotter, J. P., & Heskett, J. L. (1992). *Corporate Culture and Performance,* Maxwell McMillan International, New York.

Kraut, A. (1975). "Some Recent Advances in Cross National Management Research," *Academy of Management Journal,* Vol. 18, 538-549.

Lammers, C. J., & Hickson, D. J. (eds.) (1979). *Organizations Alike and Unlike: International and Inter-Institutional Studies in The Sociology of Organization,* London: Routledge & Kegan Paul.

Lewis, R. D. (1999). *When Cultures Collide: Managing Successfully Across Cultures,* London: Nicholas Brealey Publishing.

Marcoulides, G. A. & Heck, R. H. (1993). "Organizational cultures and performance: Proposing and testing a model." *Organizational Science,* 4.2: 209-225.

Muna, F. M. (1980). *The Arab Executive,* London, McMillan.

Nath, R. (1968). "A Methodological Review of Cross-Cultural Management Research," *International Social Science Journal,* Vol. 20 (1), 36-62.

Ouchi, W. G. (1981). *Theory Z: How American Business Can Meet the Japanese Challenge,* Reading, MA: Addison-Wesley.

Pheysey, D. (1993). *Organizational Culture: Types and Transformation,* London: Routledge.

Pettigrew, A. M. (1979). "On Studying Organization Culture," *Administrative Science Quarterly,* Vol. 24, 570-581.

Peters, T. J., & Waterman, R. H, Jr. (1982). *In Search of Excellence: Lessons From America's Best-Run Companies,* New York, Harper and Row.

Ronen, S. & Shenkar, O. (1985). "Clustering in attitudinal dimensions: A review and syntheses." *Academy of Management Review,* 10, 3: 435-454.

Sabri, H. M. (1995). The Structure of organizations across nations. A Paper presented at The Arab Management Conference, Bradford Management Center, Bradford, July 4-7.

Schein, E. (1990). "Organizational Culture," *American Psychologist,* February: 109-119.

Schein, E. (1985). *Organizational Culture and Leadership,* San Francisco, Jossey-Bass.

Selznick, P. (1957). *Leadership in administration.* Evanston: Row Peterson.

Shakelton, V. & Ali, A. (1990). "Work-Related Values of Managers," *Journal of Cross-Cultural Psychology,* 21: 109-18.

Smith, P. B. (1992). "Organizational behavior and national culture." *British Journal of Management,* 3: 39-51.

Tichy, N. M. (1982). "Managing Change Strategically: The Technical, Political and Cultural Keys," *Organizational Dynamics,* Autumn, 9-80.

Trompenaars, F. and Hampden-Turner, C. (1999). *Riding the Waves of Culture: Understanding Cultural Diversity in Business,* Corrected reprint. London: Nicholas Brealey.

Weinshall, T. D. (1977). (ed.) *Culture and Management*, Harmondsworth, Penguin.

Weir, D. (1994). "Is There a Basis For a Specificity Arab Approach to Management Development?" A paper presented at The Arab Management Conference, Bradford Management Center, Bradford, July 5-7.

Weir, D. (1995). "The Fourth Paradigm Revisited," A paper presented at The Arab Management Conference, Bradford Management Center, Bradford, July 4-6.

Wilson, R. W. (1977). *Deviance and Social Control in Chinese Society*, New York: Prager.

Wind, Y., & Permutter, H. V. (1973). "On the Cross-Cultural Identification of Frontier Issues in Multinational Marketing," *Columbia Journal of World Business*, Vol 12 (4), 131-139.

SECTION III:
BUSINESS IN EGYPT
AND LEBANON

The Direct and Mediating Effects of Transactional and Transformational Leadership: A Comparative Approach

Mahmoud A. Elgamal

SUMMARY. The purpose of this study is to test a comprehensive model of relationships between transactional and transformational leadership trust in organizations, organizational justice, intention to leave and organizational citizenship behavior. The data were collected from 179 middle and direct levels managers in 17 private Egyptian organizations. The data were analyzed using regression analysis and structural equations analysis. The latter analysis provides the potential of examining the complex model as a whole. The focus of the analysis was on the direct and mediating effects of the leadership variables. The study results showed that transformational leadership has an influence over the outcome variables above and beyond the influence of the contextual

Mahmoud A. Elgamal is affiliated with the Management & Marketing Department, College of Business Administration, Kuwait University, P.O. Box 5486, Safat Code No. 13055, Kuwait.

The author extends his gratitude to Professor Hosni Hamdy, of the Statistics Department of the College of Business Administration, Kuwait University, for his support and advice in the structural equations analysis.

[Haworth co-indexing entry note]: "The Direct and Mediating Effects of Transactional and Transformational Leadership: A Comparative Approach." Elgamal, Mahmoud A. Co-published simultaneously in *Journal of Transnational Management Development* (The International Business Press, an imprint of The Haworth Press, Inc.) Vol. 9, No. 2/3, 2004, pp. 149-169; and: *Islam and Business: Cross-Cultural and Cross-National Perspectives* (ed: Kip Becker) The International Business Press, an imprint of The Haworth Press, Inc., 2004, pp. 149-169. Single or multiple copies of this article are available for a fee from The Haworth Document Delivery Service [1-800-HAWORTH, 9:00 a.m. - 5:00 p.m. (EST). E-mail address: docdelivery@haworthpress.com].

Digital Object Identifier: 10.1300/J130v09n02_08

149

variables. The implications, limitations and the future research directions were discussed. *[Article copies available for a fee from The Haworth
Document Delivery Service: 1-800-HAWORTH. E-mail address:
<docdelivery@haworthpress. com> Website: <http://www.HaworthPress.com>
© 2004 by The Haworth Press, Inc. All rights reserved.]*

KEYWORDS. Transformational leadership, Kuwait, Egypt, Middle
East

This research presents a comprehensive model of relationships between
transactional and transformational leadership, trust in management, trust in
peers, organizational justice, intention to leave and organizational citizenship behaviors. Whereas traditional leadership studies tend to test the concept as an independent variable (Pillai, 1999), others tested it as a mediator
of contextual or antecedent variables and a host of outcome variables, including intention to leave (Bycio, Hackett & Allen, 1995), organizational
commitment (Ferres, Travaglione & Connell, 2002), organization citizenship behaviors (Ferres et al., 2002; Pillai, 1999), and satisfaction (Pillai,
1999).

This study compares and contrasts the leadership style (transactional
and transformational) direct and mediating effects on selected outcome
variables, including intention to leave and organizational citizenship
behaviors. The examination of the mediating effects of the leadership
style is based on identifying the relevant contextual variables. These
contextual variables are those variables that constitute the leadership
environment.

The study model is depicted in Figure 1. The model indicates that the
major objective of the study is to compare the direct effects of the
transactional and transformational leaderships on the outcome variables
of the intention to leave and organizational citizenship behaviors with
the indirect effects or the mediating effects of transactional and
transformational leaderships. In the latter, the leadership style mediates
the effects of the contextual variables on the outcome variables. The
study includes four contextual variables, trust in management trust in
peers, dispositional trust and organizational justice.

It is important to test the networks of the leadership styles that explain the ways these styles work. In his view of transformational leadership theory, Bass (1995) observed that there had been relatively little

FIGURE 1. The Study Model

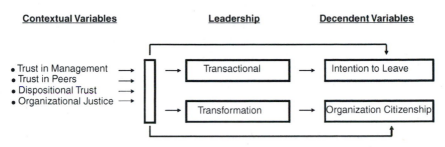

research testing the many networks of linkages expected to explain how transformational leadership works.

The present study thus attempts to follow on previous work on leadership styles and their relationships with contextual and outcome variables. The study does that by presenting and testing the proposed model.

THEORETICAL BACKGROUND

The last two decades witnessed a shift from traditional or transactional models of leadership to a new type of leadership theories, all of which have charisma and inspiration as their central concepts. This may be explained in part by the inherent romantic connotations of charismatic leadership, and in part by their promise of extraordinary individual and organizational outcomes (House & Shamir, 1993; Meindel, 1990).

According to Bass (1985), transactional leaders depend on contingent rewards, that is the transactional leaders clarify for their followers the followers' responsibilities, the expectations the leaders have, the tasks that must be accomplished and the benefits for the followers from compliance. Thus transactional leadership is based on an economic exchange process. On the other hand, Bass (1985) defined transformational leaders, as leaders who motivate their followers to perform beyond expectations by activating followers' high order needs, fostering a climate of trust and inducing followers to sacrifice self-interest for the sake of the organization. In the case of transformational leaders, the followers trust and emotionally identify with the leaders.

There is a tendency among most of the conceptualizations of leadership theories to favor transformational leadership over transactional leadership. Transformational leadership captures much of what is referred to in the literature as desirable-leader-behavior (Parry, 1998). In addition transformational leadership has been linked to outcomes such as leadership effectiveness, satisfaction, innovativeness, quality improvement and both subjective and objective high ratings of performance, although the underlying processes are not entirely clear (Bass, 1995). However, Bass and Avolio (1993) argue that the best leaders are both transactional and transformational. Their view is supported by the results of several studies that show consistently that there is a high intercorrelation between transactional and transformational leaderships, with a correlation coefficient in excess of .7 (e.g., Podsakoff, Mackenzie, Moorman & Fetter, 1990; Yammarino & Dubinsky, 1999).

The effects of the leaders are constrained and shaped by several organizational variables. The reason for this is that leaders cannot control all the organizational variables and that is very true especially for the middle and direct management levels. However, varied research indicates that leaders play a major role in determining the success or failure of the organization learning and success efforts (Prewitt, 2003).

Trust usually occurs as one element in a complicated process of coordinating and controlling organizational relations. Transformational leadership as a construct is frequently associated with trust (Bryman, 1999; Butler, Cantrell & Flick, 1999; Fairholm, 1994; Gillespie & Mann, 2000; Podsakoff, Mackenzie & Bommer, 1996; Sashkin, 1988). The majority of these studies posit transformational leadership as an antecedent to trust. The current study takes a different perspective by testing transactional and transformational leadership as mediators of management trust, peer trust, dispositional trust and organizational justice.

The effects of trust in organizations settings has attracted increasing interest in recent years (Clark & Payne, 1997; Hosmer, 1995; Kramer & Tyler, 1996; Mayer & Schoorman, 1995; Mayer & Davis, 1999). Trust in organizations was conceptualized as determining organizational success, organizational stability and well being of employees (Cook & Wall, 1980; Tyler & Kramer, 1996; Shaw, 1997). All theories posit trust as a central feature of the relationship with transformational leaders. Trust has been linked to the sense of identity that an employee derives from his or her relationships with leaders (Tyler & Degoey, 1996).

Some studies supported the notion that work-place trust is established and developed primarily through the organizational leaders. However, it could be also argued that the existence of trust in management increases the chances of attributing transformational leadership to leaders. In addition to trust in management, it has been noted that trust in peers at work is a highly important ingredient in organizational solidarity and organization effectiveness (Arnold et al., 2000; Clarkson, 1998; Cook & Wall, 1980; Velez, 2000).

Organizational justice focuses on the ways in which employees determine if they have been treated fairly in their jobs and the ways in which those perceptions influence other organizational outcomes (Alexander & Ruderman, 1987; Folger & Konovsky, 1989; Fryxell & Gordon, 1989; Greenberg, 1996; Moorman, 1991). Organizational justice has been conceptualized to include procedural justice and distributive justice (e.g., Robbins, 2001). In most studies of justice, there has tended to be a high correlation between the two of them (Moorman, 1991). Transformational leaders can elicit extraordinary levels of performance if they are perceived as providing inter-personally fair treatment to subordinates. By the same logic, transformational leadership can be more readily attributed to leaders if subordinates perceive the organization's environment to be just.

The construct of Organizational Citizenship Behaviors (OCB) was tied to transformational leadership. OCB are defined as work related behaviors that are discretionary, not related to the formal organizational reward system, and promoting the effective functioning of the organization (Organ, 1988). Thus OCB relates to an employee going beyond the normal job requirements. However, there is a relatively limited number of studies that have focused on the extra role behaviors such as OCB, compared to prescribed role behaviors (Podsakoff et al., 1990). The inherent ambiguity of the OCB construct frees the individual to contribute in a discretionary fashion without thinking that this will be acquiescence to exploitation. OCB was found to be positively related to job satisfaction, trust, perception of fairness and organization commitment (Organ & Konovsky, 1989).

The Podsakoff et al. (1990) study showed a direct relationship between transactional leadership and OCB, but no direct relationship between transformational leadership and OCB. However, since transformational leadership is based on eliciting extraordinary follower outcomes, one could argue that transformational leadership has a direct effect on OCB. In turn from a theoretical and empirical standpoint, it seems fruitful to test this direct relationship.

Organizational justice was also found to influence OCB. Previous research indicates that organizational justice creates the norm of reciprocity, which means that when employees are treated fairly, they in return treat their authorities fairly, and that leads to substantial increases in

OCB (Alexander & Ruderman, 1987; Folger & Greenberg, 1985; Folger & Konovsky, 1989).

Intention to leave is a conscious and deliberate willfulness to leave the organization. Several studies (Tett & Meyer, 1993; Bycio et al., 1995) reported negative relationship between transactional leadership and intention to leave. In general the studies show that high commitment is related to low levels of intention to leave. However, it is important to point out that labor market conditions, expectations regarding alternative job opportunities, and job tenure all act as intervening variables with regard to intention to leave (Robbins, 2001; Schnake & Dumler, 2000). The study of Tansky (1993) found support for the relationship between perceptions of overall organizational fairness and organization commitment, including intentions to remain in the organization. She suggested that cultural fairness was responsible for influencing employee attitudes over time.

The previous review of the literature indicates that direct and indirect effects of leadership style that have to be tested are founded in the literature. However, most of the studies focused on either exploring the different effects of transformational leadership only, or focused on either direct or the mediating effects of leadership style. The present study casts a comparative integrative approach, since it includes both the transactional and transformational leadership and examines both the direct and mediating effects of leadership style.

THE HYPOTHESES

The study hypotheses are designed to test the direct and indirect or mediating effects of the transactional and transformational leadership. To confirm the mediating effects of the leadership style all the three hypotheses below have to be satisfied (James & Brett, 1989).

Hypothesis 1

Hypothesis 1-1: The contextual variables of trust in management, trust in peers, dispositional trust and organizational justice will have a significant effect on levels of transactional leadership.

Hypothesis 1-2: The contextual variables of trust in management, trust in peers, dispositional trust and organizational justice will have a significant effect on levels of transformational leadership.

Hypothesis 2

Hypothesis 2-1: Higher levels of transactional leadership, considered independently from contextual variables, will predict lower intentions to leave and higher OCB.

Hypothesis 2-2: Higher levels of transformational leadership, considered independently from contextual variables, will predict lower intentions to leave and higher OCB.

Hypothesis 3

Hypothesis 3-1: The contextual variables of trust in management, trust in peers, dispositional trust and organizational justice will not impact as strongly on organizational outcomes when the influence of transactional leadership is considered concurrently with the contextual variables.

Hypothesis 3-2: The contextual variables of trust in management, trust in peers, dispositional trust and organizational justice will not impact as strongly on organizational outcomes when the influence of transformational leadership is considered concurrently with the contextual variables.

METHOD

This part of the research discusses the study sample and measurement tool.

Sample

The sample consisted of 179 middle and direct managers in 17 private Egyptian enterprises. These enterprises were in the areas of communication, manufacturing industries and food industry. Data were collected using a questionnaire. Each enterprise contributed between 8 to 12 questionnaires. The sample included 81% male and 19% female respondents. The average age was 37 years, and ranged from 32 to 47 years old. There was about 22% with 5 years or less work experience, 43% with 5 to 10 years of experience, 28% with 10 to 15 years experience and 7% with more than 15 years experience. All respondents worked for their current organization for at least one year.

Questionnaire Measures

Thirty-six questions captured the eight variables under investigation, with four of them utilized to obtain the demographic information of gender, work tenure, organization tenure and age. A 4-point Likert scale (ranging from 1 = to a limited extent to 4 = to a very great extent) was used to measure the following constructs. All questions were developed for the present study. Below we show how each was measured.

Leadership Variables

Transformational Leadership. Five items measured the transformational leadership level of the respondent's immediate managers. Confirmatory factor analysis reduced these items to four. The internal reliability coefficient for the items used in the current study Cronbach Alpha was .88. An example of an item is "My manger is a person to identify with."

Transactional Leadership. Two items measured the transactional level of respondent's immediate managers. Confirmatory factor analysis added one item that was originally envisioned as part of the transformational leadership construct. The internal reliability coefficient for the items used in the current study Cronbach Alpha was .70. An example of an item is "I expect my manager to reward me for doing a good job."

Contextual Variables

Trust in Management. Five items measured trust in management level of respondent's immediate managers. Confirmatory factor analysis showed that all of the five items load highly on one factor. The internal reliability coefficient for the items used in the current study Cronbach Alpha was .82. An example of an item is "Management is sincere in its attempts to meet employees' points of view."

Trust in Peers. Five items measured trust in peers level of respondent's peers. Confirmatory factor analysis showed that all of the five items load highly on one factor. The internal reliability coefficient for the items used in the current study Cronbach Alpha was .84. An example of an item is; "I can trust people I work with to lend a hand if I need."

Dispositional Trust. Two items measured dispositional trust. Confirmatory factor analysis showed that the two items loaded highly on one factor. The internal reliability coefficient for the items used in the current study Cronbach Alpha was .60. An example of an item is "My first reaction is to trust people."

Outcome Variables

Organizational Justice. Five items measured organizational justice level as perceived by the subjects. Confirmatory factor analysis reduced these items to four items. The internal reliability coefficient for the items used in the current study Cronbach Alpha was .75. An example of an item is "In general disciplinary actions taken in this organization are fair."

Intention to Leave. Two items measured the respondent's level of intention to leave their organizations. Confirmatory factor analysis showed that the two items loaded highly on one factor. The internal reliability coefficient for the items used in the current study Cronbach Alpha was .65. An example of an item is "I often think about quitting."

Organizational Citizenship Behavior. Four items measured the respondent's perceived level of their organizational citizenship behavior. Confirmatory factor analysis showed that the four items loaded highly on one factor. The internal reliability coefficient for the items used in the current study Cronbach Alpha was .79. An example of an item is "I am really ready to go the extra mile for my organization."

RESULTS

Levels of Transactional, Transformational, Contextual and Outcome Variables

The descriptive statistics contained in Table 1 show that all variables are close to the midpoint scale. The means ranged between 2.26 and 2.88. The highest means were transactional leadership (M = 2.88), transformational leadership (M = 2.65) and organizational citizenship behavior (M = 2.64).

Relationship Between the Variables

Correlations showing the magnitude and direction of the linear relationships between transactional and transformational leadership and

TABLE 1. Means, Standard Deviations and Ranges for Organizational and Leadership Variables

Variable	M^{ab}	SD
Trust in Management	2.27	.65
Trust in Peers	2.72	.70
Dispositional Trust	2.47	.74
Organizational Justice	2.33	.64
Intention to Leave	2.26	.87
Organizational Citizenship	2.64	.77
Transactional Leadership	2.88	.69
Transformational Leadership	2.65	.83

a. Higher scores indicate higher levels for each variable
b. n = 179 for each variable.

contextual and outcome variables, are presented in Table 2. The correlations between transactional leadership was significant with trust in peers (r = .29, p < .001), organizational justice (r = .19, p < .01) and organizational citizenship (r = .32, p < .001). The correlation between transformational leadership was significant with all contextual and outcome variables with the exception of dispositional trust. Transformational leadership was significantly correlated to trust in management (r = .54, p < .001), trust in peers (r = .46, p < .001), organizational justice (r = .48, p < .001), intention to leave (r = −.29, p < .001) and organizational citizenship behavior (r = .56, p < .001). In addition to having the above indicated significant correlations, these correlations were generally of moderate magnitude, indicating that these relationships were fairly important. The strongest inter-correlation among the contextual variables was between trust in management and organizational justice (r = .61, p < .001). It is to be noted that the correlation between transactional and transformational leadership was .40 (p < .001), rather low when compared to the previously reported correlation of around .7. In addition, higher levels of trust in management, trust in peers and organizational justice were related to lower intentions to leave and higher levels of organizational citizenship behavior.

Regression Analysis

Four stages of standardized regression analyses were performed to test the feasibility of the mediating model of transactional and transfor-

TABLE 2. Reliability Coefficients and Intercorrelation Between Organizational and Leadership Variables

	Variable	alpha	1	2	3	4	5	6	7
1	Trust in Management	.82	1.0						
2	Trust in Peers	.84	.38**	1.0					
3	Dispositional Trust	.60	.14	.28**	1.0				
4	Procedural Justice	.75	.61**	.25**	.03	1.0			
5	Intention to Leave	.65	−.31**	−.26**	−.19*	−.22*	1.0		
6	Organizational Citizenship	.79	.51**	.47**	.20*	.53**	−.30**	1.0	
7	Transactional Leadership	.70	.16	.29**	.06	.19*	−.05	.32**	1.0
8	Transformational Leadership	.88	.54**	.46**	.12	.48**	−.29**	.56**	.40**

*Significant at the .01 level
**Significant at the .001 level

mational leadership. Firstly, the effects of the contextual variables (trust in management, trust in peers, dispositional trust and organizational justice) on transactional and transformational leadership was examined (Hypotheses 1-1 and 1-2). Next, the influence of transactional and transformational leadership on each of the outcome variables (intention to leave and organizational citizenship behaviors) was investigated (Hypotheses 2-1 and 2-2). Third, the effect of the contextual variables on each of the outcome variables, independent of transactional and transformational leadership, was determined. The last stage explored the extenuating effect of transactional and transformational leadership by including all contextual and leadership style as predictors of each of the outcome variables and comparing these results with the variance levels noted in the third stage of regression analysis (Hypotheses 3-1 and 3-2).

Contextual Variables and Leadership Style. The results displayed in Table 3 indicate that the combined contextual variables significantly influenced transactional leadership, $F = 4.5$, $p < .05$, accounting for .07 (adjusted r square) in levels of the variable. Trust in peers was the only significant predictor of transactional leadership ($B = .26$, $p < .001$). With respect to transformational leadership, the results displayed in Table 3 indicate that the combined contextual variables significantly influenced transformational leadership, $F = 28.8$, $p < .001$, accounting for .39 (adjusted r square) in levels of the variable. All contextual variables were significant predictors of transformational leadership except dis-

TABLE 3. Summary of Standard Regression Analysis for Contextual Variables Predicting Transactional and Transformational Leadership

Variable	Transactional Leadership			Transformational Leadership		
	B	SEB	B	B	SEB	B
Trust in Management	−.03	.10	−.03	.36	.10	.28**
Trust in Peers	.26	.08	.26**	.35	.08	.29**
Dispositional Trust	−.01	.07	−.01	−.01	.07	−.01
Procedural Justice	.14	.10	.13	.30	.10	.23**

R = .31 R^2 = .09   R = .63 R^2 = .40
Adjusted R^2 = 07   Adjusted R^2 = .39
F = 4.5*   F = 28.9**
*P < .05   *P <.05
**P < .001   **P < .001

positional trust (trust in management B = .28, p < .001, trust in peers B = .29, p < .001, organizational justice B = .23, p < .001).

The Influence of Transactional and Transformational Leadership on Outcomes. The F values in Table 4 demonstrate the significance of only three of the regression models used to predict outcome variables using transactional then transformational leadership as predictors (independent variables or the direct effect). Transactional leadership was a significant predictor of only organizational citizenship behaviors and explained only .10 of the variance in this outcome variable (adjusted r square = .10). While transformational leadership was a significant predictor of both intention to leave with explained variance of .08 (adjusted r square = .10) and organizational citizenship behaviors, with explained variance of .31 (adjusted r square = .31).

The Influence of the Contextual Variables on Outcome Variables. The regression analysis presented in Table 5 demonstrates that the contextual variables had a direct influence on each of the outcome variables, accounting for between 12 and 42 percent of the total variance of intention to leave and organizational citizenship behaviors respectively (p < .001 for each model). Each of the contextual variables had an effect on at least one outcome variable, with the exception of dispositional trust which does not have any significant effect. Trust in management played a central roles for both intention to leave and OCB, trust in peers influenced OCB significantly, and organizational justice influenced OCB significantly. The explained variance of intention to leave by the

TABLE 4. Summary of Standard Regression Analysis for Transactional and Transformational Leadership Predicting Outcome Variable

Variable	Intention to Leave B	Organizational Citizenship B
Transactional Leadership	−.05	.32**
	R = .05 R^2 = .002 Adjusted R^2 = .003 F = .47	R = .32 R^2 = .10 Adjusted R^2 = .10 F = 19.8**
Transformational Leadership	−.29**	.56**
	R = .29 R^2 = .08 Adjusted R^2 = .08 F = 16.5**	R = .56 R^2 = .31 Adjusted R^2 = .31 F = 80**

*P < .05
**P < .001

TABLE 5. Summary of Standard Regression Analysis for Contextual Variables Prediction the Outcome Variables

Variable	Intention to Leave B	Organizational Citizenship B
Trust in Management	−.21*	.18*
Trust in peers	−.13	.29**
Dispositional Trust	.12	.08
Organizational Justice	−.05	.34**
	R = .37 R^2 = .14 Adjusted R^2 = .12 F = 6.8**	R = .65 R^2 = .42 Adjusted R^2 = .41 F = 32**

* < .05 ** < .001

contextual variables was .12 (adjusted r square = .12) and the explained variance in OCB by the contextual variables was .41 (adjusted r square = .41).

The Mediating Effects of Transactional and Transformational Leadership. If leadership style acted as a mediator, the influence of the contextual variables on outcome variables would presumably decrease significantly if leadership style and contextual variables were added simultaneously as predictor variables. Table 6 illustrates that transactional leadership does not mediate the relationship between contextual variables and OCB. The variance explained in OCB after adding transactional leadership to the contextual variables increased from .41 to .44 and the extended model was significant ($F = 27.7$, $p < .001$). In addition transactional leadership was added as a significant predictor of OCB to the significant contextual variables predictors; namely it was added to trust in management, trust in peers and organizational justice. Table 6 also illustrates that transformational leadership did not mediate the relationship between contextual variables and both the intention to leave and OCB. The explained variance in the intention to leave increased from .14 to .15 and the model was significant ($F = 5.9$, $p < .001$); the explained variance in OCB increased from .41 to .44 and the model was significant ($F = 29.9$, $p < .001$). The addition of transformational

TABLE 6. Summary of Standard Regression Analysis for Contextual and Leadership Variables Predicting the Outcome Variables

Variables	Model 1	Transactional Leadership	Model 2	Transformational Leadership
	Intention to Leave B	Organizational Citizenship B	Intention to Leave B	Organizational Citizenship B
Transactional Leadership	.04	.15*	–	–
Transformational Leadership	–	–	–.13	.26**
Trust in Management	–.21*	.18*	–.18	.10
Trust in Peers	–.14	.25**	–.09	.22**
Dispositional Trust	–.12	.08	–.12	.09
Organizational Justice	–.05	.32**	–0.2	.28**
	$R = .37$ $R^2 = .14$ Adjusted $R^2 = .11$ $F = 5.4**$	$R = .67$ $R^2 = .44$ Adjusted $R^2 = .43$ $F = 27.7**$	$R = .38$ $R^2 = .15$ Adjusted $R^2 = .12$ $F = 5.9**$	$R = .68$ $R^2 = .46$ Adjusted $R^2 = .45$ $F^2 = 29.9**$

*P < .05
**P < .001

leadership to the contextual variables, also changed the pattern of the relationships for the OCB. The influence of trust in management was reduced to insignificance and was substituted by a significant influence of transformational leadership. However, the influence of each of trust in peers and organizational justice remained significant.

Structural Equation Analysis

To test the study model as a whole, structural equation analysis was used through LISREL 9. Figure 2 depicts the results of testing the model and the path coefficients of the variables in the model. The results of testing the validity of the model produced mixed indications. Using the

FIGURE 2. Structural Equation Analysis

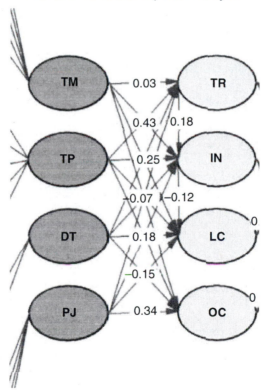

TM = trust in management, TP = trust in peer, DT = dispostional trust, TR = transactional leadership, IN = transformational leadership, LC = intention to leave, OC = organizational citizenship.

criteria of model fit of the Root Mean Square Residual (RMSR) reported by LISREL 9, the model fits the data since the reported RMSR for the study model = .076. Normally, RMSRs of .10 or less are considered indicative of an acceptable model fit. However, other indicators of fit did not show the conventional level of fit. The Goodness of Fit Index (GFI) and the Adjusted Goodness of Fit Index (AGFI) were .076 and .70 respectively. It should be noted that the .90 or higher convention first suggested by Bentier and Boonet (1980) has become the standard in the field (Medsker et al., 1994).

The use of the structural equation analysis allows us to make some conclusions about the causality effect between variables, examining the whole set of the variables at the same time and accounting for the correlations between contextual variables and between leadership variables. The structural equation analysis results indicate that there are only 9 significant paths from among all possible paths in the study model. It is to be noted that the model proposed 4 direct paths for the contextual variables, 4 direct paths for the leadership variables and 8 mediating paths for the leadership variables (that is the model has 16 paths). Figure 3 depicts the significant paths in the study model. The results indicate that trust in management has only one significant path to transformational leadership (with path coefficient of .17). Trust in peers has one significant path coefficient to transactional leadership (with a path coefficient of .17). It also has a significant path coefficient to transformational leadership (with a path coefficient of .30), and has a significant path coeffi-

FIGURE 3. The Study Results

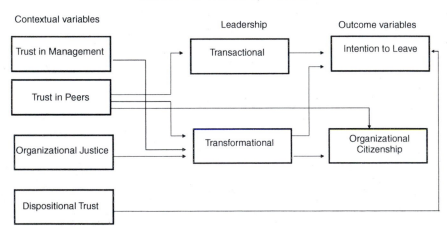

cient to OCB (with a path coefficient of .18). Dispositional trust has a significant path coefficient to intention to leave (with a path coefficient of $-.26$). Organizational justice has a significant path coefficient to transformational leadership (with a path coefficient of .06) and a significant path coefficient to intention to leave (with a path coefficient of $-.04$).

To explore the potentially added influence on outcome variables of the leadership variables over the contextual variables, the standardized path coefficients of the significant direct paths of the contextual variables were compared to the standardized path coefficients of the mediated/indirect paths of the contextual variables–mediated by leadership variables. Two cases emerged. The first case was the direct and mediated effects of the trust in peers and the direct and mediated effect of organizational justice. The standardized path coefficient of the direct effect of the trust in peers on OCB was 2.25, while the standardized path coefficient of trust in peers over transformational leadership was 3.75 and the standardized path coefficient of the over the OCB was 3.1. Thus the indirect effect can be measured by multiplying the last by standardized coefficients, which came to be 11.62, indicating that transformational leadership influence OCB beyond the influence of trust in peers.

The standardized path coefficient of the direct effect of the organizational justice on intention to leave was .33, while the standardized path coefficient of organizational justice over transformational leadership was .5 and the standardized path coefficient of the over intention to leave was 1.2. Thus the indirect effect can be measured by multiplying the last by standardized coefficients, which came to be .6, indicating that transformational leadership influence intention to leave beyond the influence of organizational justice.

DISCUSSION

The results support Hypotheses 1-1 and 1-2 that contextual variables would impact on transactional and on transformational leadership. Each of the contextual variables had a significant influence on at least one of the outcome variables with the exception of dispositional trust. It is to be noted that trust in peers had a significant influence on both of the outcome variables. With respect to Hypothesis 2-1 it was partially supported, transactional leadership was found to be a significant predictor of only OCB.

Hypothesis 2-2, that transformational leadership was a significant predictor of each of the outcome variables, was supported. The results did not support hypothesis 3-1. The addition of transactional leadership to the contextual variables in the regression model increased significantly the variance explained in OCB only. The results did not support hypothesis 3-2, the addition of transformational leadership to the contextual variables in the regression models significantly increased the explained variance in intention to leave and in OCB.

The structural equation analysis indicated that trust in peers is a very potent contextual variable, it has significant effects on transactional leadership, transformational leadership and OCB. The influence of trust in peers over OCB is enhanced by transformational leadership. The importance of trust in peers suggest that leaders should seek to build work group solidarity because that will support the OCB and increase the potential of attributing transformational leadership quality to the leaders.

The role of organizational justice in reducing the intentions to leave is enhanced by transformational leadership. It is important for leaders to support the subordinates' sense of organizational justice. Assessing employee perception of justice/fairness in future research should help us better understand how to build employees' trust and OCB. These contextual variables are significantly and moderately correlated.

The primary objective of this study was to develop and empirically test a model linking transactional and transformational leadership to organization contextual variables and to outcome variables. The degree of fit of the model as indicated by the structural equation analysis provides only partial support for the model. It is clear that the model has to be refined to include other contextual and/or outcome variables, in addition to improving the internal reliability of some of the constructs (transactional leadership, dispositional trust, intention to leave).

The comparatively low correlation between transactional and transformational leadership in the present study of r = .40, compared to the generally reported correlation coefficient of r = .70, is difficult to explain. However it suggests either potential cultural effect or measurement bias. When considering future research directions, the study findings reinforces the integral role of trust in transformational leadership (Butler, Cantrell & Flick, 1999; Jung & Avolio, 2000; Pillai et al., 1999). This suggests that future models should explore the process of the influence of organizational trust, that is trust in management and trust in peers.

To further clarify the effects of transformational leadership and the contextual variables, it is advocated that a comprehensive model of its various determinants and outcomes be formulated to enable management to frame strategies and interventions that consider complex relationships between organization factors. The idea is to adopt and test more holistic approaches/models of the linkages and effects of leadership style.

Future studies should also include more contextual variables. One could claim that the following variables are strong candidates for future models; the employees' perceived organization support and the extent to which employees perceive that they are valued by their organization and that the organization cares about their well being (Eisenberger, Fassolo & Davis-Lamastro, 1990).

The effect of position level on results should be explored, to clarify the influence of the position in the organization hierarchy over the relationships between variables.

The results of the present study are potentially generalizable to middle and direct level managers of private enterprises in Egypt. However, it is not possible to ascertain that, given that the characteristics of the population are not known; nonetheless, the similarity between the private enterprises in developing countries creates a potential to generalize the results of the present study to a wider domain.

The present study did not exclude organizational trust variables—management and peer trust—as consequences of transactional and/or transformational leadership. However this alternative model could also be tested to evaluate its validity. In addition, leadership style could be placed alongside the contextual variables, rather than as a mediator, when testing the effects of leadership styles within an organization. This different conceptualization and model could also be tested.

REFERENCES

Alexander, S. & Ruderman, M. 1987. The role of procedural and distributive justice in organizational Behavior.*Social Justice Research*,1: 177-189.

Bass, B. M. 1985. *Leadership and performance beyond expectations*. New York: Free Press.

Bass, B. M. 1995. Transformational leadership redux. *Leadership Quarterly*, 6: 463-478.

Bass, B. M. & Avolio, B. J. 1993. Transformational leadership: A response to critiques. In M. M. Chemers & R. Ayman (Eds) *Leadership Theory and research: Perspectives and directions*: 49-80. San Diego: Academic Press.

Bryman, A. 1992. *Charisma and Leadership in organizations*, Sage Publications, London.

Butler, J., Cantrell, R. & Flick, R. 1999. Transformational leadership behaviors, upward trust, and satisfaction in self-managed work teams. *Organization Development Journal*, 17(1): 13-28.

Bycio, P., Hackett, R., & Allen, J. 1995. Further assessment of Bass's (1985) conceptualization of transactional and transformational leadership. *Journal of Applied Psychology*, 80: 468-478.

Clarkson, A. 1998. *Relationships at work that help get things done: Social capital in organization settings.* Doctoral Dissertation, Dissertation Abstracts International.

Cook, J. & Wall, T. 1980. New work attitude measures of trust, organization commitment and personal need non-fulfillment. *Journal of Occupational Psychology*, 53: 39-52.

Eisenberger, R., Fassolo, P. & Davis-LaMastro, V. 1990. Perceived organizational support and employee diligence, commitment, and innovation. *Journal of Applied Psychology*, 75(1): 51-59.

Fairholm, G. W. 1994. *Leadership and culture of trust.* Praeger, Westport, Connecticut.

Ferres, N., Travaglione, A. & Connell, J. 2002. Trust: A precursor to the potential mediating effect of transformational leadership? *International Journal of Organizational Behavior*, 5(8): 242-263.

Folger, R. J. & Greenberg, J. 1985. Procedural justice: An interpretive analysis of personnel systems. In K. M. Rowland & G. R. Ferris (Eds), *Research in Personnel and Human Resources Management*, vol.1: 141-183. Greenwich, CT: JAI Press.

Folger, R. & Konovsky, M. 1989. Effects of procedural and distributive justice on reactions to pay raise decisions. *Academy of Management Journal*, 32: 115-130.

Gillespie, N. & Mann, L. 2000. The building blocks of trust: The role of transformational leadership and shared values in predicting team members trust in their leaders. Paper presented at the 2000 Academy of Management Conference, Toronto.

Greenberg, J. 1996. *The quest for justice: on the job: Essays and experiments.* Thousands Oaks, CA: Sage.

Hosmer, L. T. 1995. Trust: The connecting link between organization theory and philosophical ethics. *Academy of Management Review*, 20: 379-403.

House, R. J. & Shamir, B. 1993. Toward the integration of transformational, charismatic, and visionary theories. In M. M. Chemers & R. Ayman (Eds), *Leadership theory and research: Perspectives and directions*: 81-103. San Diego, CA: Academic Press.

James, L. R. & Brett. 1989. Mediators, moderators and tests of mediation. *Journal of Applied Psychology*, 68(2): 307-321.

Jung, D. & Avolio, B. 2000. Opening the black box: An experimental investigation of the mediating effects of trust and value congruence on transformational and transactional leadership. *Journal of Organizational Behavior*, 21(8): 949-964.

Kramer, R. M. & Tyler, T. R. (Eds). 1996. *Trust in organizations: Frontiers of theory and research*, Sage, London.

Mayer, R. & Davis, J. & Schoorman, F. 1995. An integrative model of organizational trust. *Academy of Management Review*, 20(1): 709-734.

Meindel, J. R. 1990. On leadership: An alternative to the conventional wisdom. In B. M. Staw & L. L. Cummings (Eds), *Research in Organizational Behavior*, vol. 12: 159-203. Greenwich, CT: JAI Press.

Moorman, R. H. 1991. Relationship between organizational justice and organization citizenship behaviors: Do fairness perception influence employee citizenship? *Journal of Applied Psychology*, 76: 845-855.

Organ, D. W. &Konovsky, M.1989. Cognitive versus affective determinants of organizational citizenship behavior. *Journal of Applied Psychology*, 74(1): 157-164.

Parry, K. W. 1998. The new leader: A synthesis of leadership in Australia and New Zealand. *Journal of Leadership Studies*, 5(4): 85-95.

Pillai, R. 1999. Fairness perception and trust as mediators fore transformational and transactional leadership: A two sample study. *Journal of Management*. Nov.

Prewitt, V. 2003. Leadership development for learning organizations. *Leadership and Organization Development Journal*, vol. 24(2): 58-61.

Podsakoff, P. M.,Mackenzie, S. B., Moorman, R. H. & Fetter, R. 1990. Transformational leader behaviors and their effects on followers' trust in leader, satisfaction and organizational citizenship behaviors. *Leadership Quarterly*, 1(2):107-142.

Podsakoff, P., MacKenzie, S. B. & Bommer, W. H.1996. Transformational leader behaviors and substitutes for leadership as determinants of employee satisfaction, commitment, trust and organization citizenship behavior. *Journal of Management*, 26(3): 513-563.

Sashkin, M., 1988. The visionary leader. In Conger, J. A. & Kanungo, R. N. (Eds) *Charismatic leadership: The elusive factor in organizational effectiveness*, The Jossey-Bass management series, Jossey-Bass, San Francisco, CA:122-160.

Shaw, R. B., 1997. *Trust in the balance: Building successful organizations on results, integrity and concern*, Jossey-Bass Publishers, San Francisco.

Tett, R. P. & Meyer, J. P. 1993. Job satisfaction, organizational commitment, turnover intention and turnover: Path analysis based on meta-analytic findings. *Personnel Psychology*, 46: 259-293.

Tyler, T. R. & Kramer, R. M. 1996. Wither trust? In Kramer, R. M. & Tyler, T. R. (Eds) *Trust in organizations: Frontiers of theory and research*, Sage Publications, Thousand Oaks, CA.

Tansky, J. W. 1993. Justice and organizational citizenship behavior: What is the relationship? *Employee Responsibilities and Rights Journal*, 6: 195-207.

Velez, P. 2001. Interpersonal trust between a supervisor and subordinate. Doctoral dissertation, Dissertation Abstracts International, 62.

Yammarino, F. J., Spangler, W. Dubinsky A., 1998. Transformational and contingent reward leadership: Individual, dyad and group levels of analysis. *Leadership Quarterly*, 9(1): 27-54.

Factors Affecting the Advancement
of the Lebanese Tourism Industry

Said M. Ladki
Mira W. Sadik

SUMMARY. Lebanon's tourism industry has suffered severe blows resulting from the civil war and political unrest that took place in the country. Despite the increase in the number of arrivals to Lebanon, the industry is experiencing several weaknesses that are directly affecting its advancement. The study identified factors that are hindering tourism advancement in Lebanon. Identified factors serve as a tool to develop future strategies leading to tourism advancement and improved satisfaction. *[Article copies available for a fee from The Haworth Document Delivery Service: 1-800-HAWORTH. E-mail address: <docdelivery@haworthpress.com> Website: <http://www.HaworthPress.com> © 2004 by The Haworth Press, Inc. All rights reserved.]*

KEYWORDS. Lebanon, tourism, tourism satisfaction, Middle East

INTRODUCTION

The purpose of this study is to identify the factors that are hindering the advancement of the Lebanese tourism industry. Specifically, the

Said M. Ladki and Mira W. Sadik are affiliated with the Lebanese American University, Lebanon.

[Haworth co-indexing entry note]: "Factors Affecting the Advancement of the Lebanese Tourism Industry." Ladki, Said M., and Mira W. Sadik. Co-published simultaneously in *Journal of Transnational Management Development* (The International Business Press, an imprint of The Haworth Press, Inc.) Vol. 9, No. 2/3, 2004, pp. 171-185; and: *Islam and Business: Cross-Cultural and Cross-National Perspectives* (ed: Kip Becker) The International Business Press, an imprint of The Haworth Press, Inc., 2004, pp. 171-185. Single or multiple copies of this article are available for a fee from The Haworth Document Delivery Service [1-800-HAWORTH, 9:00 a.m. - 5:00 p.m. (EST). E-mail address: docdelivery@haworthpress.com].

http://www.haworthpress.com/web/JTMD
© 2004 by The Haworth Press, Inc. All rights reserved.
Digital Object Identifier: 10.1300/J130v09n02_09

study identified tourists' reasons for visiting Lebanon, travel related behavior, destination attributes, and country resources and services as affecting overall satisfaction with Lebanon.

Before the 16 years of civil war (1975-1991), Lebanon was perceived
as the ideal tourist destination in the Middle East. Lebanon's scenic
beauty, sunny climate, and historical sites attracted more than 2.4 million visitors annually (Ladki & Dah, 1997). Nevertheless, the damaging
effect of war and political unrest that took place in the country has negatively affected Lebanon's tourism industry. Civil war and military invasion has robbed Lebanon of its prized reputation as the Middle East's
international marketplace and premier financial center, as the region's
educational hotbed and ideal vacation spot, and perhaps most painfully
as an inspiring example of the peaceful coexistence of people from dif-
fering religions and national origins (Meadows, 1994).

Before the civil war, tourism was regarded as the backbone of the
Lebanese economy. This role quickly diminished as Egypt, Jordan,
Syria, and Cyprus captured Lebanon's market share and developed
plans to attract tourists while fiercely competing with Lebanon. During
the prewar years, tourism contributed 20 percent to Lebanon's Gross
Domestic Product. At present, statistics estimate that tourism generates
between 5 and 7 percent of the total GDP (Lebanese Ministry of Tourism, 2001). Though the war brought tourism to a standstill, the constant
increase in the number of visitors demonstrates Lebanon's resilience;
attracting only 180,000 visitors in 1992, one year after the end of the
civil war, and around 1 million visitors in 2001 (Lebanese Ministry of
Tourism, 2001).

According to the World Trade Organization there were 70 million international travelers in the year 2000 out of which 18 million visited the
Middle East, up from 14 million in 1995 (www.wto.org). Arrivals have
increased at an annual average of 6.3 percent since 1983, yet most of the
tourists to the Middle East are from the Middle East (IPR, 2000a). As a
destination, Lebanon is most favored by Arab and especially Kuwaiti
tourists (IPR, 2000b). Despite terrorism and threat of war, it is clear that
the growth potential for tourism in Lebanon and the Middle East is enormous.

With its scenic beauty, its combination of eastern and western cultural values, as well as its rich history, Lebanon has the foundations to
be an ideal tourist destination. However, terrorism and civil war have
severely affected Lebanon's tourism industry. Although serious negative outcomes have resulted from the actual political instability in Lebanon, it is the negative images created in the wake of these prior events

that have deterred tourists from revisiting (Ladki & Dah, 1997). As has been demonstrated many times in the past few years, the tourism sector is the first to suffer from violence and war, and the first to benefit from peace (Aboukhalil, 2002). In 1991, Lebanon began to witness the entry of many international chains, thus increasing competition, exposure, and tourist inflow. By 1998, six years after the end of the civil conflict, Lebanese and international hospitality investors embarked on a $1.2 billion restoration project (Schellen, 2002). The restoration project unavoidably faced many challenges.

Despite the lingering political instability that Lebanon has been witnessing since the end of war, the number of arrivals into the country continues to increase. However, the increase in the number of arrivals has not been paralleled with an increase in investment in hospitality projects. Moreover, issues directly affecting tourists were brought to light and needed the collaboration of key government agencies and the private sector. After all, it is destination offerings and services that drive the tourism industry and nothing will shatter tourists' perceptions of a destination more than inferior, unprofessional service (Gartner, 1996).

Incoming tourists to Lebanon deal with various government agencies, as well as hospitality and service providers, such as airlines, hotels, car rentals, taxi drivers, restaurants, and many others. According to Troels (1995) most incoming tourists leave Lebanon dissatisfied with the service encounters generated from different experiences. To ensure customer satisfaction, Luchars (1996) stated that host countries must provide the benefits that are considered critical to meet expectations.

There exists a general feeling among tourists visiting Lebanon that satisfaction with overall visit is not highly rated (Aboukhalil, 2002). Tourists believe that Lebanon needs to develop a comprehensive approach to tourism development rather than the existing individualistic approach where tourists are required to interact with various service providers in order to achieve satisfaction (Fattoush, 1998). Therefore, the primary objective of this study is to create a better understanding of the forces that hinder tourism advancement in Lebanon. Ultimately, the information provided in this study will help tourism planners develop better offerings that meet the needs of travelers coming to Lebanon.

METHODOLOGY

The study utilizes inferential and descriptive research techniques to investigate the relationship between the variables. The study design employs one dependent variable and four independent variables. The dependent variable is tourists' satisfaction with the visit to Lebanon. The independent variables are (1) tourists' perceived benefits, (2) destination attributes, (3) travel-related behavior, and (4) Lebanon's resources and services.

SAMPLE DESIGN AND PROCEDURE

Sample selection is a very important step in conducting research. Gay (1987) stated that the sample's merit determines the generalizability of the results. Therefore, the most important criterion in this study's sample selection was the ability to increase the validity of the study's conclusions. The random sampling procedure was employed in this study. In simple random sampling, every individual has the same probability of being selected, and the selection of one individual in no way affects the selection of another individual. In other words, all individuals in the defined population had an equal and independent chance of being selected in the sample.

The sample of this study represented a group of (n = 675) tourists who visited Lebanon. Data for the study was collected by responses to a questionnaire designed to measure tourists' benefits, travel related behavior, country resources and services, and destination attributes as affecting satisfaction when visiting Lebanon.

Tourists who participated in the study had their instrument administered by research associates at Beirut International Airport. The instrument was administered at the departure gate for tourists who have concluded their trip to Lebanon. Consideration was given to departing morning and afternoon flights. Most morning flights depart for Europe and North America, while most afternoon flights depart for Asia, the Middle East, and North Africa. Tourists received their instruments and answered their questions while waiting in line to be checked-in at the luggage counter. Each tourist who visited Lebanon in the spring of 2002 had an equal chance of being selected in the sample. There was no follow-up contact with tourists who refused to take part in this study.

INSTRUMENT

A structured questionnaire was used to conduct this survey. Utilizing reviewed literature, a 51-item instrument consisting of five parts was developed. The instrument was designed to measure: (1) tourists benefits in visiting Lebanon, (2) travel-related behavior that tourists engage in while in Lebanon, (3) evaluation of destination attributes, (4) country resources and services, and (5) demographics.

Part one, benefit statements, consisted of eight statements that described reasons for visiting Lebanon, which were mainly developed by McCool and Martin (1994). Answering this section of the instrument required consumers to rate their extent of agreement or disagreement on a five-point Likert type scale (1 = Strongly Disagree and 5 = Strongly Agree). The scale items included statements such as "You came to Lebanon to engage in social nightlife" or "You came to Lebanon to visit religious sites."

Part two, travel-related behavior, consisted of eight statements which were used to test respondents' behavior. The travel-related behavior items were selected from a study by Pizam and Sussman (1995). Tourists were asked to rate their extent of agreement or disagreement. Responses were answered on a five-point Likert type scale (1 = Strongly Disagree and 5 = Strongly Agree). Such statements included "When you came to Lebanon, you planned your own trip" or "While in Lebanon, you participated in structured tours."

Parts three and four gathered information about country resources and services as well as destination attributes. Items were answered using a five point Likert type scale anchored by the bi-polar adjectives (1 = Very Dissatisfied and 5 = Very Satisfied). The variables of interest in this section of the survey included items such as road safety standards, environmental factors, and services. The items in this section were based on attributes and service quality dimensions developed by Pizam and Sussman (1995), Pizam and Jeong (1996), and Pizam and Reichel (1996). Part five was used to collect demographic information such as age, gender, education, and travel patterns.

RESULTS

The questionnaire was distributed to 675 tourists who agreed to participate in the study. The number of usable questionnaires was 213. Thus, the study had a response rate of 31 percent. Of the arrivals to Lebanon, 62 percent reported traveling with two or more companions, and findings revealed that 45 percent of those who visit Lebanon usually travel with friends or family members. The survey revealed that before visiting Lebanon, 37 percent of respondents had visited Europe, and 32 percent had visited other places in the Middle East. Additionally, data showed that 65 percent of the respondents were younger than 35 years. Sixty-two percent of the respondents were male and 44 percent were married. The most popular reason for visiting Lebanon is to engage in social nightlife as reported by 74 percent of respondents. Sixty-one percent of arrivals expressed a desire to know more about available attractions and tourist sites prior to visitation. Of those who visited Lebanon, 32 percent were interested in touring religious sites, and 24 percent were interested in sports-related activities. Brochures, fliers, and guidebooks were used by 49 percent of arrivals, whereas organized structured tours were used by 35 percent of arrivals.

Table 1 summarizes destination attributes and country resources and services available in Lebanon. Respondents were mostly dissatisfied with pollution levels and noise levels, 81 percent and 79 percent respectively. Forty-two percent were mostly dissatisfied with the absence of recycling programs in the country. In terms of services, 75 percent of the respondents were most satisfied with banking services, and 37 percent were least satisfied with the country's price-value relationship. The absence of public restrooms, 67 percent, and public phones, 49 percent, was a big dissatisfier. Sixty-four percent of respondents rated souvenir and gift shops as satisfactory.

Stepwise regression analysis revealed that tourists who travel in groups ($r^2 = 0.37$, $t = 3.74$, $P < 0.001$) and those who get the chance to socialize with other tourists while in Lebanon ($r^2 = 0.41$, $t = 2.10$, $P < 0.001$) were highly satisfied with their visit. Further, tourists were very dissatisfied with local transportation services ($r^2 = 0.15$, $t = 5.98$, $P < 0.001$), road safety and traffic standards ($r^2 = 0.19$, $t = 3.56$, $P < 0.001$), and the abundance of billboards and banners that are cluttering the cities ($r^2 = 0.22$, $t = 2.38$, $P < 0.01$). Lebanon's active nightlife ($r^2 = 0.12$, $t = 2.12$, $P < 0.01$) and accommodation services ($r^2 = 0.16$, $t = 4.05$, $P < 0.001$) are important satisfiers that seem to significantly affect the overall satisfaction with the visits to Lebanon.

Further, the researchers used factor analysis as a data reduction tool and as a technique to establish the construct validity of the instrument. Table 2 shows fourteen items that measure five different dimensions, out of which four are consistent with the findings of previous research. The first dimension measured the travel-related behavior which consists of five items such as travel in groups, socialize with other tourists, participate in structured tours, use brochures, and receive expected levels of service. The reason the research measured the dimension via five items instead of eight as in the instrument is due to cultural differences as well as the way respondents conceive the items in English. Based on previous research, it is found that environmental factors were measured

TABLE 1. Destination Attributes and Country Resources and Services

Destination Attributes	Very Dissatisfied (1) %	Dissatisfied (2) %	Indifferent (3) %	Satisfied (4) %	Very Satisfied (5) %	Mean	Standard Deviation
Road safety standards:							
Local transportation services	23.9	22.1	21.6	27.2	3.8	2.61	1.26
Road signs	27.7	28.6	22.5	17.4	2.3	2.34	1.16
Traffic signs	25.8	36.6	22.5	12.7	0.9	2.22	1.04
Traffic	31.9	37.1	12.2	11.3	0.9	1.92	1.11
Noise	44.6	34.3	12.7	7.0	0.0	1.79	0.93
Pollution	46.5	33.8	12.2	5.2	0.9	1.76	0.94
Environmental factors:							
Abundance of public billboards, banners, etc.	13.6	16.9	20.7	35.7	10.8	3.06	1.31
Cleanliness of public properties	18.8	22.5	19.2	31.5	4.7	2.71	1.30
Overall development of coastal areas	16.4	23.9	26.3	27.2	3.8	2.71	1.21
Maintenance of coastal areas	16.0	25.8	35.7	14.6	5.2	2.59	1.16
Deforestation and fire prevention	16.0	26.8	38.5	14.1	2.3	2.53	1.07
Recycling programs	21.6	20.7	39.9	13.6	1.4	2.44	1.10
Resources and Services							
Services:							
Banking	1.9	5.2	17.8	38.5	35.7	3.98	1.03
Hotel check-in/check-out	2.8	4.7	20.2	39.4	31.9	3.90	1.05
Airport services	5.6	6.6	20.2	44.1	22.5	3.69	1.12
Service providers' mastery of foreign languages	4.7	9.9	18.0	42.3	23.0	3.65	1.16
Accommodation services	3.8	5.6	20.2	43.2	16.4	3.31	1.48
Mobile phone rentals	8.0	17.8	28.2	26.8	18.3	3.27	1.23
Price-value relationship	16.9	20.2	29.1	30.0	0.9	2.69	1.18
Availability of facilities and activities:							
Souvenir and gift shops	5.2	9.9	19.7	40.8	23.0	3.62	1.17
Healthcare services	11.7	8.0	35.7	31.0	12.2	3.20	1.20
Public phones	25.8	23.0	20.2	21.6	5.6	2.53	1.35
Handicap facilities	29.1	27.2	25.4	14.1	2.3	2.28	1.15
Public restrooms	39.4	26.8	18.8	10.3	1.9	2.00	1.13

177

TABLE 2. Factor Analysis of Tourists' Perceived Satisfaction with Visit to Lebanon

Factor	Loading	Eigenvalue	Variance Explained (%)
Factor 1: Travel-related behavior		3.342	23.874
Travel in groups	0.708		
Socialize with other tourists	0.704		
Participate in structured tours	0.703		
Use brochures or other means to identify places to visit	0.692		
Receive the service that you expected from tourist provider	0.663		
Factor 2: Environmental factors		1.897	13.546
Stocking rivers with fresh water fish for sport purposes	0.798		
Maintenance of coastal areas	0.750		
Abundance of public billboards, banners, etc.	0.526		
Factor 3: Availability of modern technology		1.648	11.768
Hotel check-in/check-out	0.858		
Electronic banking	0.848		
Factor 4: Facilities and activities		1.154	8.242
Engage in social nightlife	0.826		
Healthcare services	0.554		
Factor 5: Public services		1.063	7.593
Public restrooms	0.849		
Handicap facilities	0.801		
Total			65.024

via nine different statements. However, the researchers used three items to extract the same information using data reduction techniques. The third dimension, availability of modern technology, was measured by two items instead of four. The items are: hotel check-in/check-out and electronic banking. The fifth dimension, public services, was measured by two items: availability of public restrooms and handicap facilities.

The fourth dimension was rather interesting. It proved to be the only dimension that is inconsistent with previous research. This is because the dimension emerged out of the benefits that tourists received as well as the availability of facilities and activities in a destination. It is reasoned that this dimension measures the activities as shown by the items engage in social nightlife and healthcare services. According to previous research, the two items for this dimension belonged to benefits and activities. However, both measure activities and facilities. The activities such as active nightlife, and facilities such as availability of advanced healthcare, were used as a dependent variable measuring motives for people to visit Lebanon, which was taken as a function of the other four dimensions. Table 3 shows that two dimensions out of four are significant in explaining the variations in reasons for visiting Lebanon.

Figure 1 depicts a path analytical presentation which decomposes the relation between motives (reasons for visiting Lebanon), availability of

TABLE 3. Results of Path Analysis on Tourists' Satisfaction Factors

Factor	Coefficients	t-value	Sig.
Environment	0.262	3.763	0.000
Facilities	0.145	2.137	0.034
Travel-related behavior	0.087	1.309	0.192
Technology	0.073	1.094	0.275
Environment	0.280	4.129	0.000
Facilities	0.138	2.037	0.043
Travel-related behavior	0.096	1.449	0.149
Environment	0.295	4.394	0.000
Facilities	0.151	2.257	0.025

FIGURE 1. Path Diagram of Public Services and Environmental Factors as Affecting Motives

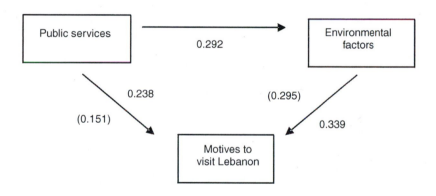

public services such as restrooms and handicap accessibility, and environmental factors into direct and indirect relations as follows. The relation between services and motives is (0.238) broken into (0.151) as direct effect, in addition to the indirect effect via environmental factors (0.086). This implies that 64 percent of the relation is direct, as seen in Table 4.

By the same token, the environmental factors affect reasons for visiting Lebanon, implying that 87 percent of the effect is direct. As shown in Figure 1, the direct effect of environmental factors plays a greater role in motivating people to visit Lebanon than the direct effect of having public services.

TABLE 4. Decomposition of Causal Effects in the Path Model

Factor	Indirect Effect	Direct Effect	Total Effect
Public services	0.086	0.151	0.238
Environmental factors	0.044	0.295	0.339

DISCUSSION

Tourism is a rather complicated activity that encompasses several different economic and social sectors. In terms of tourism impact, most researchers investigate the positive contribution of tourism and its added value (Chen, 2000; Jurowski et al., 1997; Lui et al., 1987; Perdue et al., 1990; Perdue et al., 1995). However, the authors of this study felt the need to identify the factors that negatively affect the advancement of the Lebanese tourism industry. Thus, allowing tourism planners to draft a strategy of change that converts negative forces into positive ones which brings added value and satisfaction to the overall experience in Lebanon.

Destination Attributes

Tourists appreciate the beauty of sites and monuments as much as they seek a clean and healthy environment (Allen et al., 1994). The overall aesthetic appeal of Lebanon lacks attractiveness. Poor urban planning, unclean coastal areas, and bulky billboards and banners of all kinds generate a poor and unsatisfactory "look" of the country. The inadequate government attention to environmental issues such as garbage collection and disposal, nature protection, and fumes emitted from cars and factories resulted in air and water pollution, causing health problems for Lebanese and visitors alike. Lebanon's endangered forests now cover only 7 percent of the country's surface (Unknown, 2002). Of those remaining forests, the majority are sparse and unhealthy. Lebanon's environmental groups cite a long list of problems, including those associated with quarries, pesticides, sea reclamation and industrial pollution.

As far as infrastructure is concerned, transportation is an essential element to the tourism sector where infrastructure should be improved in order to attract tourists and to ensure satisfaction. The Lebanese land transport system has reached a critical state. Despite some positive developments during the last decade such as the installation of road signs, safety rules, and development of an extensive network of roads around Lebanon, land transportation in Lebanon continues to be a complex problem. Beirut is the heart of the country's transport system and therefore is prone to suffer the most from major traffic congestion due to a poorly developed, ill-planned transport network. This translates into serious economic losses and deteriorating air quality. Greater awareness of the country's traffic problems has contributed to the formation of several civil-society projects. Road signs and traffic lights should be present everywhere and the most important is citizens' strict compliance with driving codes. Although plans to protect Lebanon's environment have been drafted, no implementation strategy has been executed to save the environment and maintain the aesthetic appeal of the country.

Country Resources and Services

One of the most frequently mentioned issues was the poor quality of services offered by the telecommunications sector as reflected in the lack of telephone booths for local and international calls, lack of reduced Internet fees, and the absence of multilingual phone operators. Lebanon's open skies policy which took effect in 2001 have increased the number of arrivals to the country. The increased number of arrivals should compel telecommunication companies to make available public phone booths, phone cards, and other communication technologies available throughout the country.

Power outages, water shortage, and poor infrastructure are all pitfalls in the service sector in Lebanon. Since Lebanon is no longer in a state of war, the Lebanese government should be actively involved in transforming the negative impact of war against the country's infrastructure.

Service within the hospitality sector was rated as satisfactory, whereas the price value relationship was found to be problematic. As for service providers' skill levels, a study prepared by Awad (2000) reported that the tourist sector needs to add 27,000 trained staff by 2010 to adequately serve the country's visitors. Schools with hospitality programs graduate about 1,400 each year, half of what the market needs. The number of tourists in Lebanon is projected to reach 1.5 million a year over the next decade (Saab, 2000). This means that the hotels must prepare their staff properly to receive the new tourists. In Lebanon, the tourism sector is expected to create 2,700 new jobs every year. Thus there is a need to develop human resources and vocational training programs in the country (IPR, 2000b).

Travel Related Behavior

Gartner (1996) stated that in order to gain a larger market share and to develop a positive tourism image, destinations need to advertise. He also added that the image formation process is critical to tourism marketing, promotion, and development. The focus should be on countries whose citizens tend to travel abroad, as well as places with large Lebanese expatriate communities. One way to overcome the country's negative public image is to professionally promote Lebanon abroad. Before the civil war, Lebanese tourism offices were found in seven cities around the world (Frankfurt, London, New York, Baghdad, Brussels, Cairo, and Jeddah). Today, except for Cairo and Paris, there are no Lebanese tourism offices anywhere in the world so information on touring Lebanon is not available (Lebanese Ministry of Tourism, 2002).

Embassies abroad must also play an active role in the dissemination of tourism-related information. Visa application procedures should be simplified or totally lifted, thus taking away one of the first obstacles a visitor may encounter while planning a trip to Lebanon. One of the impractical laws that the government has passed is barring female Russian nationals who are under the age of twenty-nine into the country. Being a family destination, Lebanon cannot afford such a law. A Russian family's travel decision and destination selection will be affected when certain family members are prevented from joining the family's vacation.

Perceived Benefits

Luchars and Hinkin (1996) stated that tourists chose affordable destinations with the most attractive benefits. To ensure customer satisfaction, destinations must provide benefits that customers consider as critical to meet expectations. If benefits are not present, customers will not be satisfied, regardless of the extras that are provided.

The economic hardships of Lebanon led the government to impose high taxes on hospitality and tourism products and services, thus negatively impacting tourists' spending and capital investment. A 1998 study which compared the cost of hospitality services among eight Middle Eastern countries found Lebanon's room rates, car rental rates, taxes, and food prices to among the highest priced in the region. According to the World Tourism Organization, Lebanon is situated in a region that is shaped by fierce competition dollars where costs of hospitality services in Lebanon are quite expensive (Younis, 1996; Fattoush, 1998; Jaber, 1998).

Although Lebanon has attracted considerable capital and investment from Arab states following the September 11 events in the United States, establishing general trust in the country is the first step towards rescuing the economy. In December 2001 alone, 100,000 tourists visited Lebanon (Lebanese Ministry of Tourism, 2002). The majority originating from Arab countries. Also, the number of visitors coming into Lebanon has increased by 25 percent in the last quarter of 2001. Overall, the number of Arab visitors coming into Lebanon post-September 11, 2001 reflected a positive spirit for the country's tourism potential.

CONCLUSION AND IMPLICATIONS

The factors that hinder tourism advancement in Lebanon are quite clear, but the question remains: what should government and tourism planners do to overcome such complexities? Government should work closely with all tourism-related stakeholders to set up rules and regulations that help both public and private sectors improve Lebanon's image and overall customer satisfaction. Measures should be taken to preserve the environment and the eco-system. Otherwise, if not protected, our tourism industry will deteriorate. Serious studies should be conducted to come up with an aggressive marketing plan for Lebanon.

The Lebanese Ministry of Tourism (2001) has identified a set of measures in order to boost tourism:

- Establish an active promotional campaign for the country.
- Speed formalities in entering the country.
- Facilitate formalities in obtaining a visa and extend its validation.
- Activate embassies abroad to promote tourism assets.
- Improve the archeological sites in Lebanon.

It is true that during the 1980s the image of Lebanon was one of war and violence; however, the war is over, and Lebanon is in the midst of its recovery journey. Data generated from this study will help Lebanon's tourism planners preserve resources, promote confidence in the country, and maximize satisfaction.

REFERENCES

Awad, F. (2000) Assessment of Human Resource Needs in Lebanon. Study prepared by Stanford Research Institute, Lebanese American University, and the United States Agency for International Development. Byblos, Lebanon.

Aboukhalil, A. (April 12, 2002) Going All Out to Promote Business and Tourism. *The Daily Star*, pp. 1-2.

Allen, L.R., Hafer, H.R., Long, P.T., & Perdue, R.R. (1994) Rural Residents' Attitudes Toward Recreation and Tourism Development. *Journal of Travel Research*, 31(4), 27-33.

Chen, J.S. (2000) An investigation of urban residents' loyalty to tourism. *Journal of Hospitality & Tourism Research*, 24(1), 5-19.

Fattoush, N. (1998) Expensive Tourism Prices are Decreasing Lebanon's Competitive Advantages. *Al-Nahar*, June 27. pp 7-8.

Gartner, William, C. (1996) *Tourism Development: Principles, Practices, and Policies*. New York: John Wiley and Sons, Inc.

Gay, L.L. (1987) *Educational Research Competencies for Analysis and Application*. Third Edition. New York: Merrill, pp. 102-107.

IPR *Strategic Business Information Database* (2000a) Lebanon: Poor Tourism Promoting Spending.

IPR *Strategic Business Information Database* (2000b) Lebanon: Tourism Statistics Outlook.

Jaber, A. (1998) Tourists are Comfortable, Yet Few are Complaining of Power Shortages, Absence of Road Signs, and High Prices. *Al-Safir*, August 6, pp 6.

Jurowski, C., Uysal, M., & Williams, D.R. (1997) A theoretical analysis of host community resident reactions to tourism. *Journal of Travel Research*, 36(2), 3-11.

Ladki, S.M., & Dah, A. (1997) Challenges Facing Post-War Tourism Development: The Case of Lebanon. *Journal of International Hospitality, Leisure & Tourism Management*, Vol. 1, No. 2, pp. 35-43.

Lebanese Ministry of Tourism (2001) *Statistical Bulletin*. Beirut, Lebanon: Author.

Lebanese Ministry of Tourism (2002) *Statistical Bulletin*. Beirut, Lebanon: Author.

Luchars, James Y. & Hinkin, Timothy R. (1996) The Service Quality Audit. *Cornell Hotel and Restaurant Administration Quarterly*, Feb., pp. 34.

Lui, J.C., Sheldon, P., & Var, T. (1987) Resident Perceptions of the Environmental Impact of Tourism. *Annals of Tourism Research*, 14, 17-37.

McCool, S.F., & Martin, S.T. (1994) Community Attachment and Attitudes Toward Tourism Development. *Journal of Travel Research*, 32(3), 29-34.

Meadows, I. (1994) Lebanon–Up from the Ashes. *Aramco World Magazine*, January-February.

Perdue, R.R., Long, P.T., & Allen, L. (1990) Resident support for tourism development. *Annals of Tourism Research*, 17(4), 586-599.

Perdue, R.R., Long, P.T., & Kang, Y.S. (1995) Resident support for gaming as a development strategy. *Journal of Travel Research*, 34(2), 3-11.

Pizam, A., & Jeong, G.H. (1996) Cross-Cultural Behavior: Perception of Korean Tour Guides. *Tourism Management*, 4(4), 277-286.

Pizam, A., & Reichel, A. (1996) The Effect of Nationality on Tourists Behavior: Israeli Tour Guides' Perceptions. *Journal of Hospitality & Leisure Marketing*, 4(1), 23-49.

Pizam, A., & Sussman, S. (1995) Does Nationality Affect Tourist Behavior? *Annals of Tourism Management*, 22(4), 901-917.

Saab, F. (2000) Speech presented at the International Chamber of Commerce. Beirut, Lebanon.

Schellen, T. (April 10, 2002) Discovering the Recipe for Success. *The Daily Star,. pp 1-2.*

Troels, A. (www.mdb.ku.dk/tarvin/diary.com)

Unknown (2002) Ahlan Wa Sahlan is the Right Kind of Language. *Lebanon Opportunities*, April, pp. 36-39.

Website: www.wto.org

Younis, M. (1996) Tourists Movement Is Less than Usual: Arrivals Complain of Expensive Prices. *Al-Safir*, Sept. 10, pp 10-11.

Index

BOOK ORDER FORM!

Order a copy of this book with this form or online at:
http://www.haworthpress.com/store/product.asp?sku=5219

Islam and Business
Cross-Cultural and Cross-National Perspectives

___ in softbound at $24.95 (ISBN: 0-7890-2517-5)
___ in hardbound at $34.95 (ISBN: 0-7890-2516-7)

COST OF BOOKS _____

POSTAGE & HANDLING _____
US: $4.00 for first book & $1.50
for each additional book
Outside US: $5.00 for first book
& $2.00 for each additional book.

SUBTOTAL _____
In Canada: add 7% GST. _____

STATE TAX _____
CA, IL, IN, MN, NY, OH & SD residents
please add appropriate local sales tax.

FINAL TOTAL _____
If paying in Canadian funds, convert
using the current exchange rate,
UNESCO coupons welcome.

❑ **BILL ME LATER:**
Bill-me option is good on US/Canada/
Mexico orders only; not good to jobbers,
wholesalers, or subscription agencies.

❑ **Signature** _____

❑ **Payment Enclosed: $** _____

❑ **PLEASE CHARGE TO MY CREDIT CARD:**
❑ Visa ❑ MasterCard ❑ AmEx ❑ Discover
❑ Diner's Club ❑ Eurocard ❑ JCB

Account # _____

Exp Date _____

Signature _____
(Prices in US dollars and subject to change without notice.)

PLEASE PRINT ALL INFORMATION OR ATTACH YOUR BUSINESS CARD		
Name		
Address		
City	State/Province	Zip/Postal Code
Country		
Tel	Fax	
E-Mail		

May we use your e-mail address for confirmations and other types of information? ❑Yes ❑No We appreciate receiving
your e-mail address. Haworth would like to e-mail special discount offers to you, as a preferred customer.
We will never share, rent, or exchange your e-mail address. We regard such actions as an invasion of your privacy.

Order From Your **Local Bookstore** or Directly From
The Haworth Press, Inc. 10 Alice Street, Binghamton, New York 13904-1580 • USA
Call Our toll-free number (1-800-429-6784) / Outside US/Canada: (607) 722-5857
Fax: 1-800-895-0582 / Outside US/Canada: (607) 771-0012
E-mail your order to us: orders@haworthpress.com

For orders outside US and Canada, you may wish to order through your local
sales representative, distributor, or bookseller.
For information, see http://haworthpress.com/distributors

(Discounts are available for individual orders in US and Canada only, not booksellers/distributors.)

Please photocopy this form for your personal use.
www.HaworthPress.com

BOF04